How it is made

Jet Engines

Text   Julian Moxon
Design   Arthur Lockwood

Contents

page	
2	What is a jet engine?
4	How a jet engine works
6	Inside a jet engine
8	Building a jet engine
10	The compressor
11	The turbine
12	How compressor and turbine discs are made
14	How compressor and turbine blades are made
16	Fuel control and the combustion chamber
18	The exhaust system
20	Assembly
24	Made by automation
26	Performance testing
28	All kinds of jet engines
30	Glossary
	Facts and Figures
31	Important dates
	Who makes jet engines?
32	Index and acknowledgements

ff

faber and faber in association with Threshold Books

What is a jet engine?

If you visit a busy airport, have a look at the engines mounted on the aircraft. You will see them hanging under the wings, or fixed to the rear of the fuselage. There may be two, three, or even four engines, depending on the type of aeroplane. A Boeing 747 jumbo jet, for example, needs four engines – which between them produce enough power to light a medium-sized town.

Once this monster has taken to the air, the jets will be running continuously for ten hours or more. On a ten-hour journey they could burn 50,000 gallons (227,305 litres) of fuel – enough to drive a car around the world sixty times!

So what exactly are jet engines? If you look in at the front of one all you will see is what seems to be a big fan. There is even less to see at the other end, because the cowling around the engine extends for quite a long way beyond the rotating parts inside. From a distance, all you can see is a hole, blackened by exhaust smoke.

The job of a jet engine is to produce a very powerful stream of air which will push the aircraft forward. Huge

A Rolls-Royce RB. 211. Four of these jet engines power a Boeing 747. You can see part of the fan sitting back in the engine cowling shell. The engineer has opened a section of the cowling to inspect the engine before take-off.

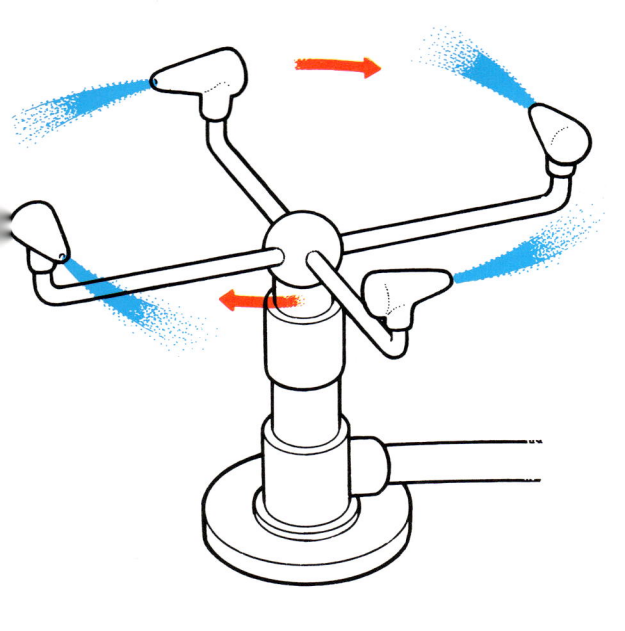

This garden sprinkler is made to spin in the direction of the arrow by the reaction of water escaping from the nozzles. The more water pressure there is, the faster the sprinkler whirls. This same principle of reaction is applied to create the thrust in a jet engine, but instead of water it uses air.

Aircraft are powered either by propeller-driven engines or by jet engines. Propellers push back a large mass of air relatively slowly, while jets force back a smaller mass, but at a much faster rate. Jets therefore work more efficiently on high speed aircraft, while propellers are better suited to slower types.

quantities of air enter at the front, pass through the rotating machinery inside, and are expelled at high speed from the exhaust at the rear. It works something like a garden sprinkler, which spins round when water is forced through the nozzles. This is known as 'jet reaction', because as the water leaves the nozzles it 'reacts' or presses against them. You can test jet reaction yourself by holding the end of a hosepipe and turning on the tap. As soon as the water comes out you will feel a force pushing the hosepipe nozzle towards you.

Instead of water, a jet engine uses air to provide the reaction. But before it can be made to do any work, the air has to be squeezed. The machinery in the engine is therefore designed to squeeze the air as much as possible before letting it escape out of the exhaust. This machinery is known as the **gas turbine**. A jet engine consists of the gas turbine, the casings that surround it, and other equipment, such as the **thrust reverser**, which helps to slow the aircraft down when it lands.

Jet engines were first used to power aircraft about forty years ago, towards the end of the Second World War. Before that, forward thrust was always provided by **propellers**, turned by a **piston engine**. When aeroplanes first took to the air at the beginning of this century, their engines were little more than copies of those used in cars. But they were soon developed, so that by the 1940s aircraft were reaching speeds of up to 400 mph (644 kmph) – which was as fast as a piston-powered aeroplane could fly. Then came the jet engine which, fortunately, was invented in time to take over from the piston engine, pushing aircraft to higher speeds than anybody had thought possible. Nowadays, jet-powered aircraft can travel way beyond 400 mph (644 kmph). Concorde, with her four jet engines each providing 28,000 pounds (12,700 kgs) of thrust, can reach 1250 mph (2011 kmph) – which is about twice the speed of sound.

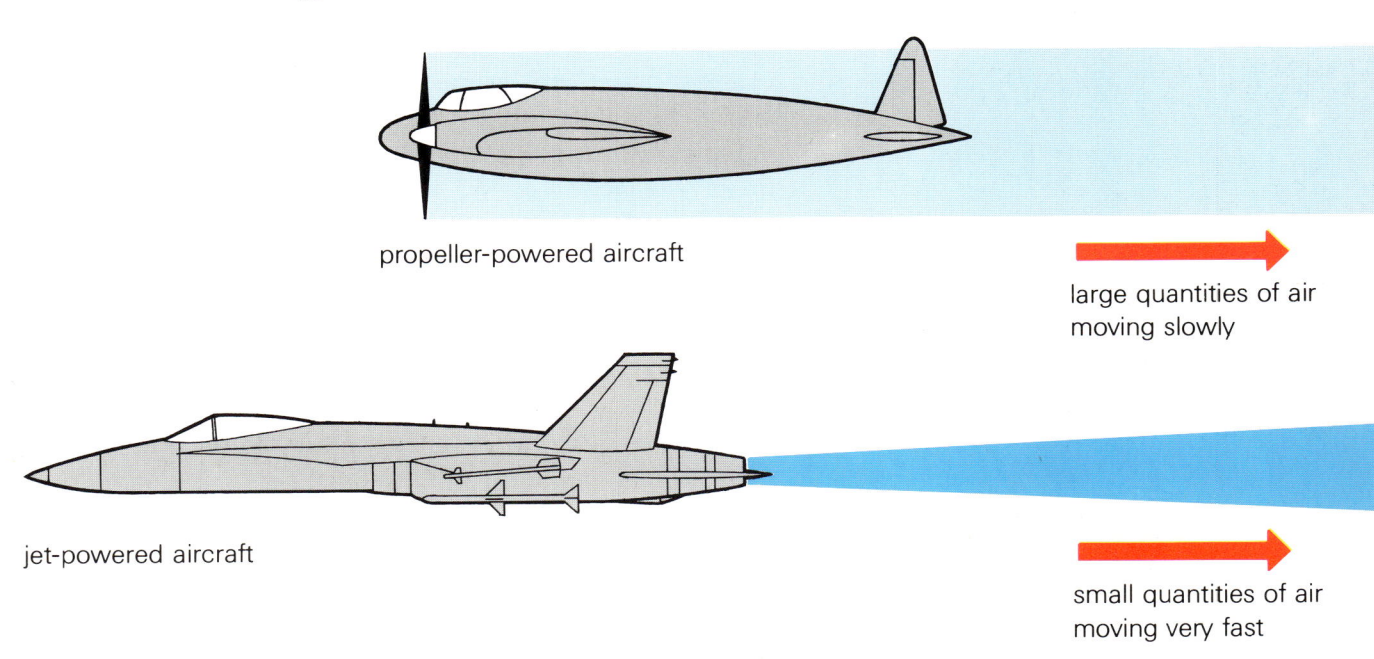

propeller-powered aircraft

large quantities of air moving slowly

jet-powered aircraft

small quantities of air moving very fast

How a jet engine works

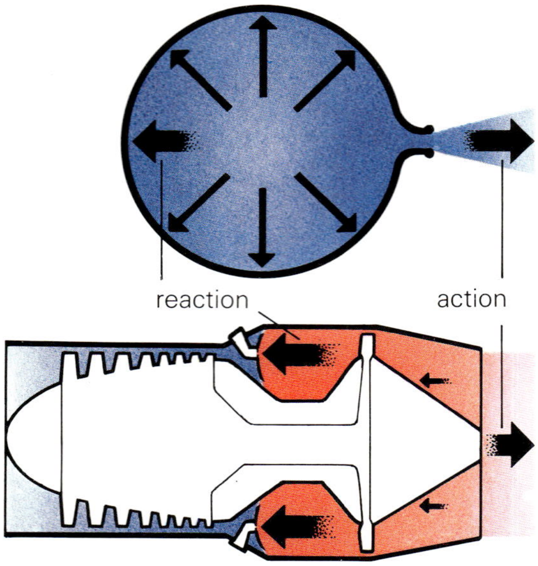

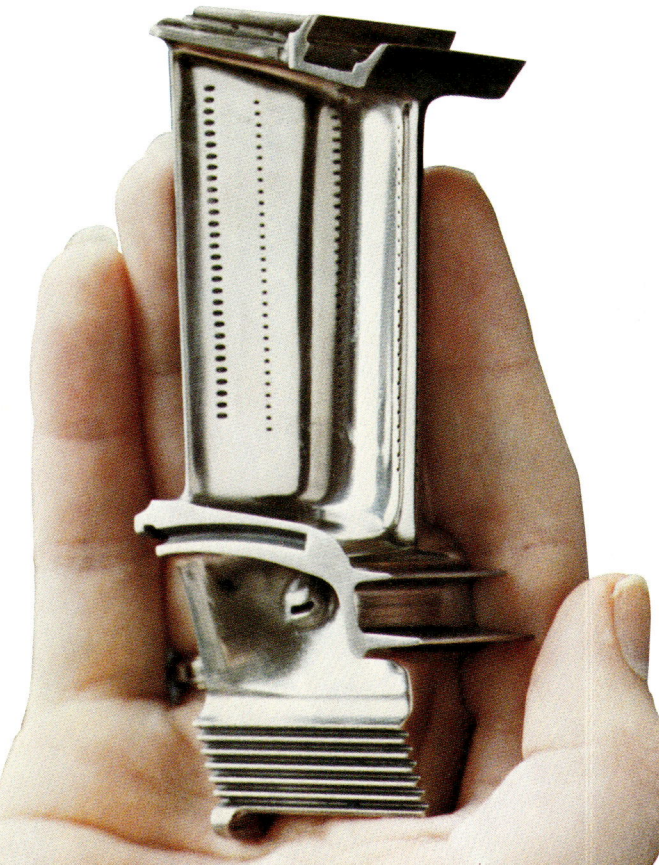

The jet engine's job is to force as much air out of its exhaust duct as possible so that it will be pushed forwards – just as a toy balloon flies across the room when the air rushes out of it.

The way in which a jet engine works is really quite simple. Think of the propeller used to power a toy aeroplane. Its blades are twisted into curves which direct the air towards the rear of the aeroplane. The faster the propeller spins, the more air there is flowing back to push the aeroplane forwards.

Inside a jet engine this pushing job is carried out by a **compressor**, which is really a series of 'propellers', one behind the other, all mounted on the same shaft. But the blades of a compressor are much shorter than those of a propeller, and there are many more of them, as you will see from the picture on page 10. Also, compressors spin round much faster than propellers, pushing enormous quantities of air back along the engine and compressing it as it goes.

Most of the air forced back by the compressor is used to push the aircraft forwards. But some of it is mixed with *fuel*. It then becomes a vapour, which is burned in a **combustion chamber** or **combustor**. This makes it expand very rapidly, and the only escape for it is through an opening in the rear of the combustion chamber. It rushes out of here with tremendous energy, and carries on through the **exhaust duct**. It then joins the air from the compressor and helps to push the aircraft forwards.

Finally there is the **turbine**, which extracts from the gas-stream the power needed to drive the compressor. It behaves just like a windmill which turns when blown by the wind. It is mounted on the same shaft as the compressor, and is blown round by the hot, high-pressure air rushing out of the combustion chamber. The turbine is one of the most difficult parts of a jet engine to make. It has to work for many hours while running in a jet of very hot gases, so it has to be immensely strong, as well as light in weight.

The power of a jet engine is measured in pounds of thrust. This may seem odd, because pounds are usually a measurement of weight, not power – but in fact it makes sense, for when we say that a jet engine produces 20,000 lbs (9072 kgs) of thrust, we mean that it is powerful enough to exert a forward force of 20,000 lbs. For example, when you push a 2 lb bag of sugar along a table you are producing a force of 2 lbs. The engines of big passenger jets can each exert up to 60,000 lbs (27,216 kgs) of thrust, which is about twenty-five times the weight of a family car.

The principle of jet propulsion is seen when an inflated balloon is released. The balloon rushes across the room, propelled by the reaction of air rushing from the nozzle. In a jet aircraft the air reacts against the machinery, pushing the engine, and the aircraft, forward.

Inside a jet engine there are hundreds of small blades, like this high-pressure turbine blade. The turbine turns the compressor, which provides the flow of air needed to drive the aircraft forward. Turbine blades sit in an extremely hot jet of gas, produced by the combustor, and have to be designed to withstand the high temperature.

Comparison of jet and piston engines
Jet and piston engines work on a similar principle. Each operates in four stages: intake, compression, combustion, and exhaust. In a jet engine, however, combustion of fuel is continuous, whereas in a piston engine, combustion occurs only once in every revolution.

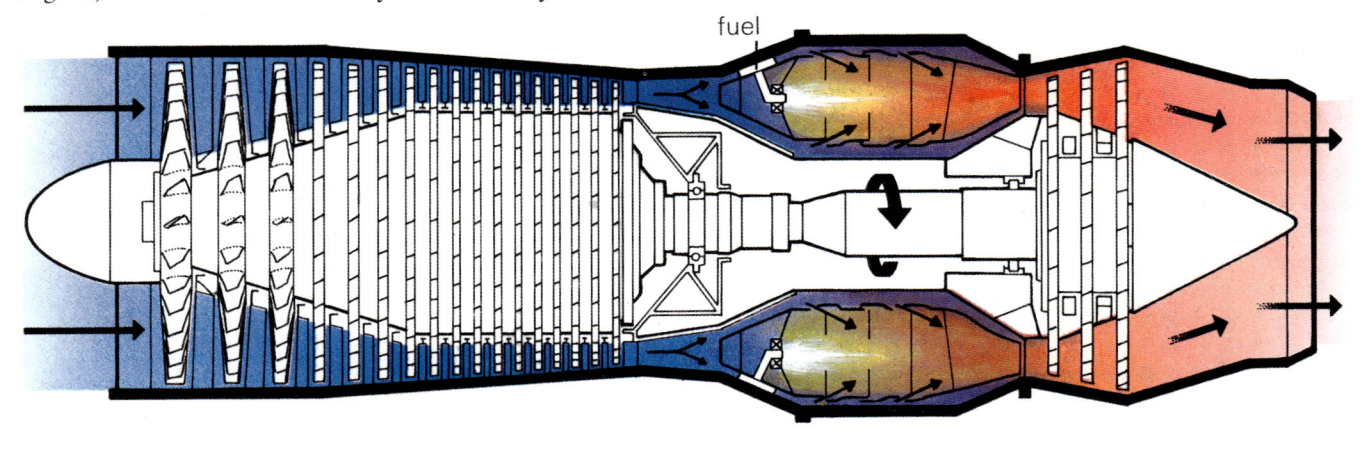

AIR INTAKE · COMPRESSION · COMBUSTION · EXHAUST

Jet Air is sucked into the intake by the compressor.

Piston As the piston travels down, a mixture of air and fuel is drawn through the inlet valve.

Jet The compressor pushes air towards the combustor, each row of blades squeezing it a little more.

Piston With both valves closed, the piston rises, compressing the air as it does so.

Jet Air is forced into the combustor, fuel is added, and a continuous torch of burning gases is formed. An igniter starts off the combustion process.

Piston With the piston at the top of its movement, a timed spark ignites the fuel/air mixture. This explodes, forcing the piston down. The piston is connected to the rear wheels via a crankshaft and gearbox.

Jet The hot combustion gases expand through the turbine and into the exhaust duct, pushing the engine forwards. The energy extracted from the exhaust by the turbine is used to drive the compressor.

Piston The piston rises, pushing waste gases out through the open exhaust valve. The gases are discharged through the exhaust pipe.

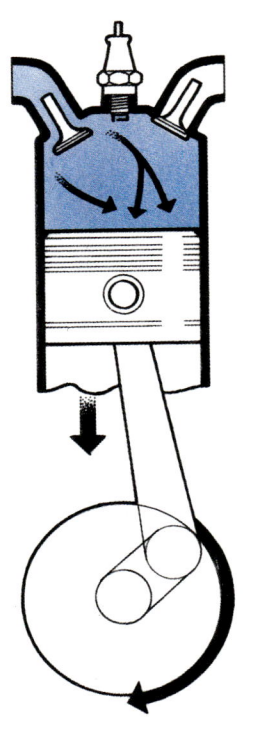

AIR/FUEL INTAKE · COMPRESSION · COMBUSTION · EXHAUST

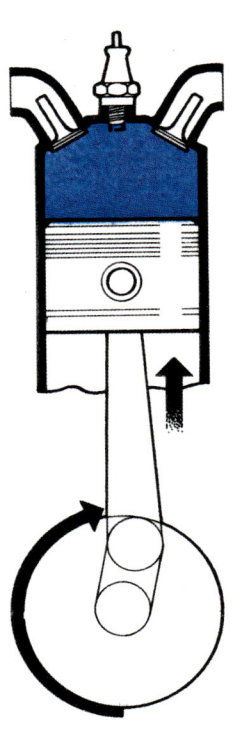

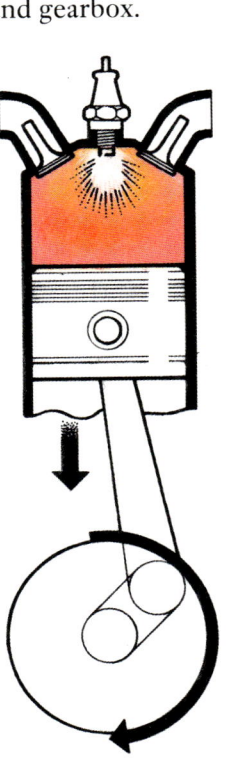

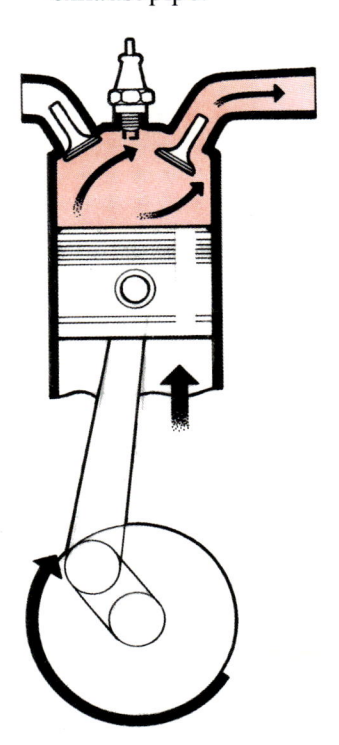

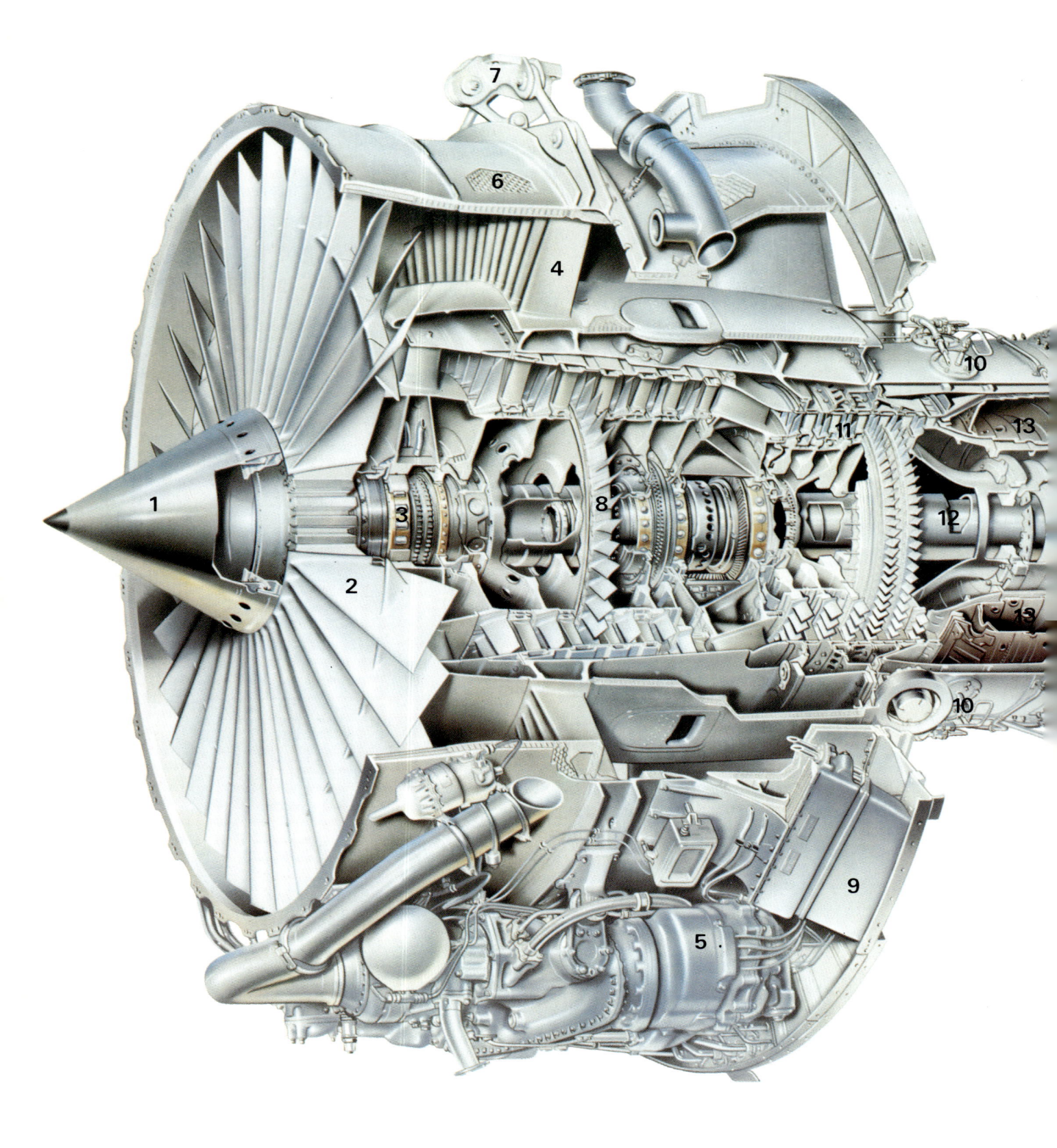

This cutaway drawing shows the Rolls-Royce RB.211-535 with its main parts identified.

1. Fan spinner
2. Fan
3. Fan support bearing
4. Fan outlet guide-vane
5. Gearbox
6. Noise suppression material
7. Front engine mounting
8. Intermediate-pressure compressor
9. Oil tank
10. Fuel manifold
11. High-pressure compressor
12. Low-pressure and intermediate-pressure engine shafts
13. Combustion chamber
14. High-pressure turbine
15. Intermediate-pressure turbine
16. Low-pressure turbine
17. Rear engine mounting
18. Discs
19. Rear support vanes
20. Exhaust cone

Inside a jet engine

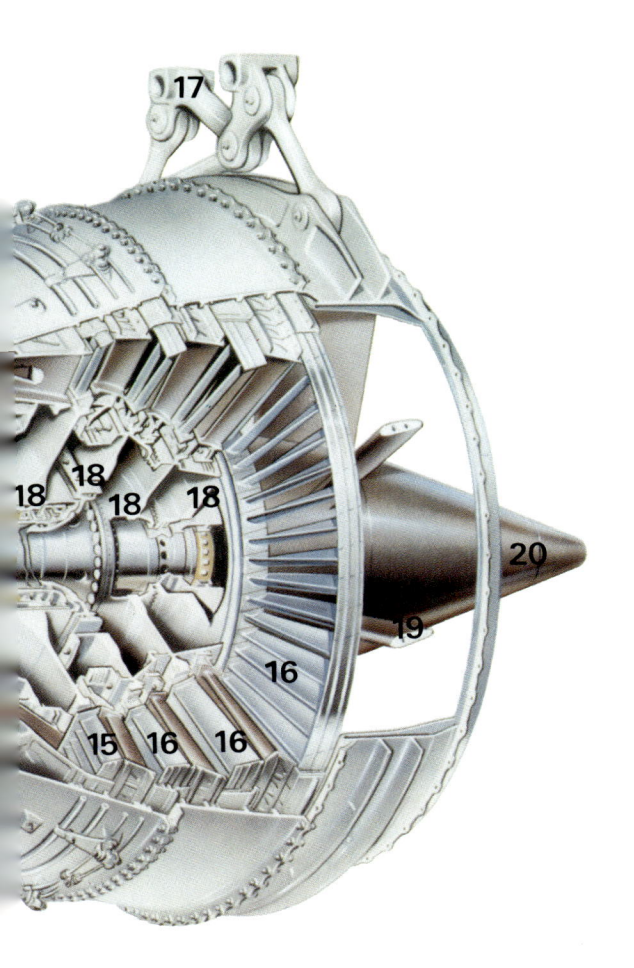

A jet engine, as you can see in the cutaway drawing, is extremely complex, consisting of around 20,000 parts. This Rolls-Royce RB.211-535 is designed in three sections, with each section mounted on a separate shaft. It is therefore called a three-shaft engine. The **low-pressure** (LP) section consists of the fan and the low-pressure turbine which drives it, while the **intermediate** section comprises the six-stage intermediate-pressure (IP) compressor and IP turbine. The air is finally squeezed in the six-stage **high-pressure** (HP) compressor, which is driven by the HP turbine. After passing through the compressors the air is burned in the combustor before expanding through the turbines and out into the exhaust duct. Three-shaft engines are built only by Rolls-Royce. Jet engines built by other manufacturers have two shafts; in these engines the fan and IP compressor form one unit, which is driven by the LP turbine.

Below is an exploded diagram showing how the engine illustrated on the opposite page is fitted inside the cowling and 'C' ducts. The complete unit is joined to the wing by the pylon (see page 21).

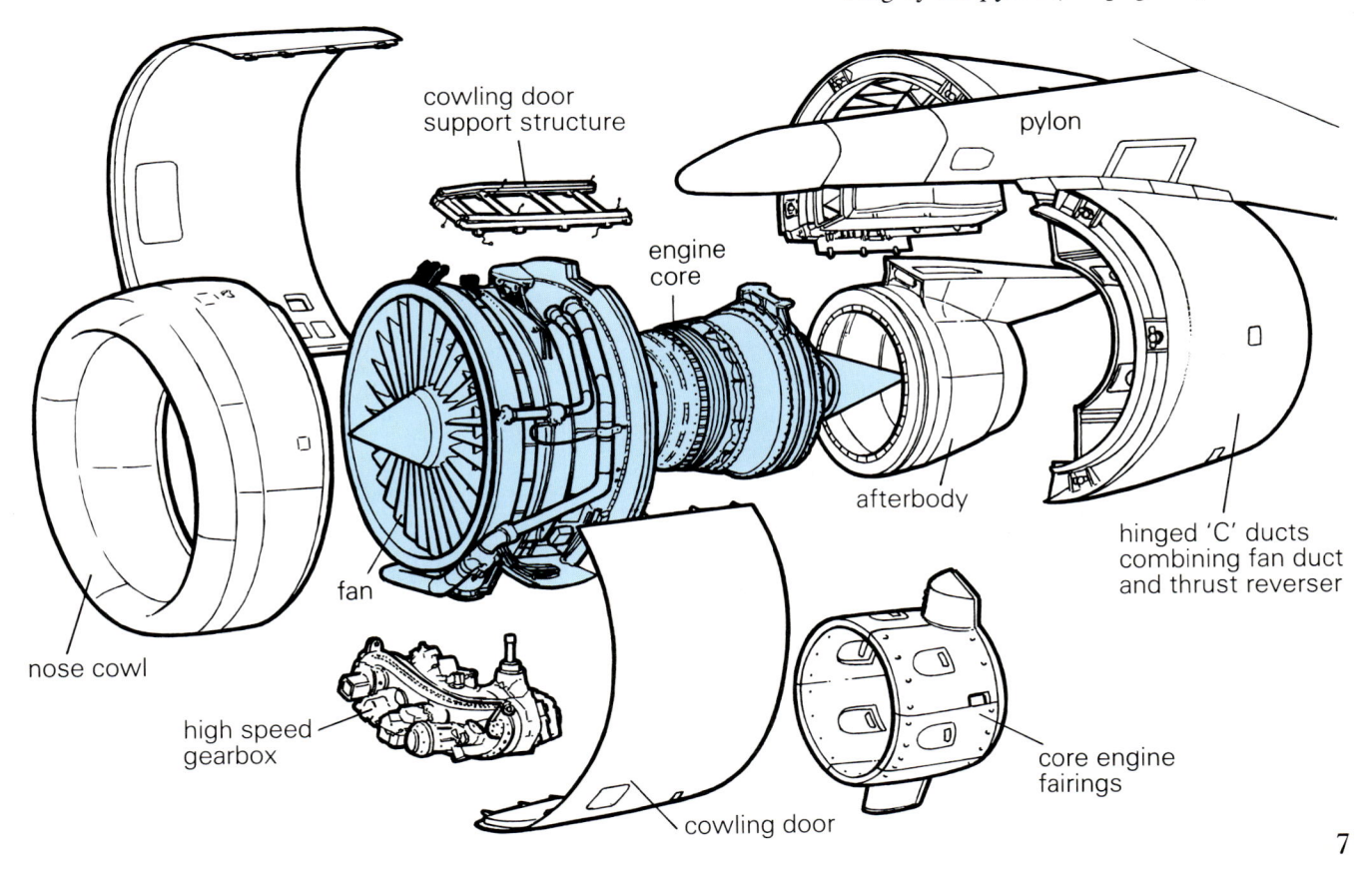

Building a jet engine

It takes about two years to build a modern jet engine – longer than it takes to build the aircraft that it will power.

A major jet engine manufacturer employs up to 40,000 people. At least half of them are engineers working on the design and looking after every stage of production and every component, from the smallest compressor blade to the finished engine.

Because a jet engine has to work so hard and because it has to be very reliable, each of its components must be made to an extremely high standard. In the type of engine which powers the Boeing 747 jumbo jets, there are almost 25,000 parts. Each part has to be designed to the highest possible standard by skilled engineers. It can take up to five years to design them all.

Making the parts and then assembling them involves a great deal of planning. Some of the parts may be produced by small engineering or electronics companies operating a long way from the main engine factory. For example, fan blades for American engines are produced by a company who specialise in the different techniques required. Turbine blades for some American engines are made in England, while castings for a British engine may be German-made.

Every single part carries its own number and individual record card. As it passes through the factory all the different processes that it goes through are recorded on the card, so that even the smallest detail of its manufacture is known. If a fault occurs during the engine's life, investigators can check back to the records and find out if the problem was anything to do with the way in which a component was made.

Computers play an increasingly important part in helping engineers to design jet engines. In this illustration the computer has produced a three-dimensional outline of a turbine blade. The operator can view the blade from any angle and ask the computer to print out details of the design, along with all the dimensions needed. Often the computer forms part of a production network which includes robots.

The traditional way of designing jet-engine components is by producing engineering drawings. Several drawings may be needed for each part, which means that for an entire jet engine many thousands have to be created. The engineers in the photograph are discussing the design of a turbine blade. Nowadays drawings are usually produced automatically by computers, working from dimensions supplied by a design engineer. They can be made in a fraction of the time that it took to draw them by hand.

The three biggest companies, Rolls-Royce, Pratt & Whitney and General Electric, have several plants in different locations. Rolls-Royce, for example, build their passenger engines at Derby in the Midlands and their military engines at Bristol in the West Country.

Some engines are produced by the manufacturers of several countries working together. Satellite links make possible the transfer of drawings and information, each manufacturer working on a separate part of the engine.

One such engine is the CFM56, a very successful 22,000 lb turbofan for medium-sized aircraft. The CFM56 fan, and the low-pressure turbine that drives it, are built by the French company Snecma, while the 'heart' of the engine, the high-pressure compressor and turbine, is the responsibility of General Electric, in America.

Complete CFM56s are assembled in both France and the USA. In each case the parts are flown across the Atlantic and carried to their final destination by road. Computers keep track of progress and the information is flashed from one country to another by satellite.

The many parts of the jet engine are tested in different ways by the most advanced equipment. This is ultrasonic testing of a fan blade, to detect flaws in the metal.

Making blades for the big fan at the front of a Rolls-Royce jet engine. Here a titanium blade skin is being removed from a hot press. The skin will be joined to its mate, forming a hollow blade. For strength, the cavity between the skins is filled with a honeycomb core of titanium.

The compressor

A big jet engine gulps down around two and a half thousand tons of air for every hour that it is working – which means that during a 6½-hour flight from London to New York it needs more than seventeen thousand tons of air. All of this air is pumped by **compressors**, which are the 'heart' of a jet engine. They work like big, powerful pumps which thoroughly squeeze the air sucked in through the engine-intake. The more they squeeze the air, the more efficiently the engine will work.

Compressors look rather like porcupines. They have many rows of blades attached to the outside of a drum, which is tapered from front to back. The long blades are at the front, the short ones at the back. Each row of blades turns in the same way as a simple electric fan, and each passes air to the row behind. As the air moves back along the compressor it has less and less space to occupy, because of the tapering (see picture), so it becomes squeezed. A modern jet-engine compressor can squeeze the air into a space about twenty times smaller than the opening at the intake. It is therefore said to have a compression ratio of 20:1.

On most modern jet engines there is an especially big set of blades at the front of the engine. They are mounted on a different shaft from that which turns the main compressor and they operate like a powerful fan, blowing air around the outside of the engine as well as through the compressor itself. The fan improves the engine's performance, particularly during low speeds at take-off and climb.

When the air passing through the compressor has been squeezed, it is burned in the combustor. It then expands very quickly, rushing out of the exhaust in a jet, and helping to push the aircraft forwards.

With so much work to do, compressors have to be very strong. Used in aircraft, they must also be light. To make something strong and light, special materials have to be used (this of course applies to all the components of a jet engine).

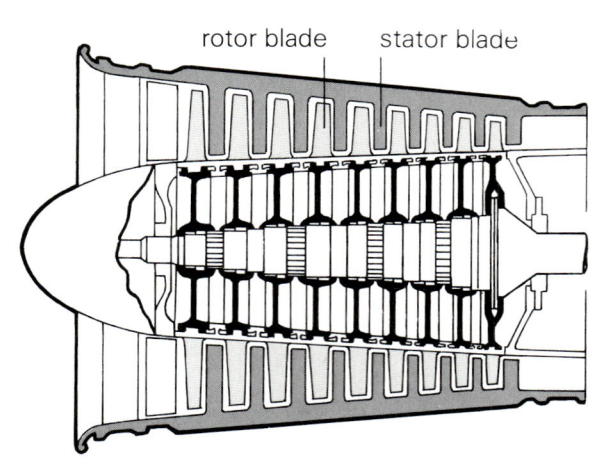

A jet engine compressor consists of a *rotor* and a *stator*. The stator blades are attached to the inside of the compressor drum and do not rotate. Air passing through the engine first meets a row of big stator blades, called guide-vanes. These direct the air at the first row of rotor blades.

This is a high-pressure compressor rotor from a modern jet engine, the Pratt & Whitney PW2037. The engine powers the 180-seat Boeing 757, and produces 37,600lbs of thrust. The compressor is made up of 12 stages, each stage consisting of a number of blades. Driven by the high-pressure turbine, it rotates up to 12,000 times a minute. Note how the blades get shorter towards the back of the compressor, where the air is squeezed as tightly as possible before it enters the combustion chamber.

The turbine

Of all the parts of the engine, turbines have the most exacting job to do. As mentioned on page 4, they work on the same principle as a windmill, though a windmill has only a few sails, while turbines needs up to one hundred blades. They are placed in a powerful jet of hot, high-pressure gas which rushes out of the combustion chamber at a temperature of up to 1200°C (2544°F) – hot enough to make the turbines glow red as they spin round. They can make as many as 20,000 revolutions per minute.

Turbines are constructed so that they take enough energy from the hot gas-jet to turn the compressor, which is fixed to the opposite end of the main engine shaft. The rest of the energy in the gas-jet passes out of the exhaust and is used to push the aircraft forwards.

The blades of a turbine are fixed to a large wheel, or **disc**, in such a way that they can be removed separately for repair. A row of blades is called a **stage**. There is nearly always more than one stage. In big jet engines up to seven turbine stages may be used. They are usually divided into two sections – the **high-pressure turbine** and the **low-pressure turbine**. The high-pressure turbine – consisting of the two stages nearest to the combustor – uses the energy which it extracts from the exhaust jet to drive the high-pressure part of the compressor. The low-pressure turbine – which is connected to a shaft passing through the centre of the engine – drives the low-pressure compressor. This compressor is the part which often has a big fan at the front of it.

The low-pressure turbine may also be used for other jobs. For example, on jet engines which power helicopters it would be joined to a shaft which turns the rotor. It can also be used for turning aircraft propellers or ships' screws.

A low-pressure turbine. This extracts enough energy from the hot gases rushing through the engine to drive the big fan at the front. There are five stages, and you can see that the blades have rings around the outside. The rings are designed to prevent the gases escaping as they pass through the turbine into the exhaust duct. The turbine blades are attached to discs, fixed to the shaft in the centre.

How compressor and turbine discs are made

If you tie a small piece of wood to the end of a length of string and whirl it round your head, you will feel the wood pulling away from you, even if you whirl it quite slowly. The same force acts on the blades of compressors and turbines spinning at some 20,000 revolutions per minute: but because they spin so fast, the pull is much bigger. In fact, the force wrenching at the blades on their mountings can at full power reach *several tons*. To stand up to this force, the blade mountings, or roots, have to be extremely strong, and very carefully made.

The disc to which the compressor and turbine blades of all large jet engines are fixed looks like a big wheel with teeth. As it has to carry the load of all the blades pulling away at once, it is a heavy, solid structure. It must never break, for if it did it would cause enormous damage to the engine.

When discs are made, they must be as perfect as possible. The smallest crack or imperfection in the metal can become the starting place for a fracture, which will grow as the disc spins. They must also be light, since they make up most of the weight of a jet engine.

The traditional method of making compressor and turbine discs is by *forging* the metal into shape. First a large block of metal is roughly cut, or *machined*, to size, then it is heated until very hot, and stamped into the right shape. Heating the metal not only makes it softer and easier to force into shape, but also helps to remove faults which could lead to cracks.

The latest method of manufacturing turbine and compressor discs ensures that the metal is almost completely free from imperfections. It is called 'powder metallurgy' and is now being used in the manufacture of some jet engines. In order to produce discs by this method, a very fine powder is made by pouring molten metal on to a fast-spinning turn-table. When the molten metal hits the surface, it breaks into millions of fine droplets which are flung from the edge of the table. The moment they leave the table, the droplets cool and solidify, forming a very fine metal powder. The cooling process happens extremely quickly, with the temperature dropping by about 1000°C (2120°F) in half a second. During this half-second the molecules within the metal powder are 'frozen' in their positions so quickly that the metal does not have time to pick up impurities.

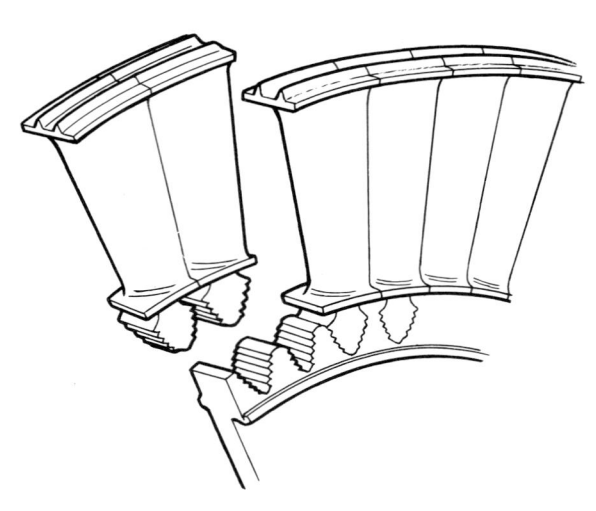

The roots of a turbine or compressor blade are shaped so that they lock into the 'teeth' of the disc which carries them. Most jet engines use the arrangement shown in the diagram above. Because of its shape this is known as a 'fir tree' root. The blades are slotted into place around the disc and secured with a bolt. They are free to rock slightly in their mountings, to help spread the enormous load which each root carries.

This is what a disc looks like before it is finally shaped. The example here is from a high-pressure turbine. It has been pressed into shape by forging. The metal is as near perfect as possible, to ensure maximum strength. After forging, the disc is mounted on to a giant cutting machine and cut automatically to exactly the correct dimensions for the engine: within a few thousandths of an inch.

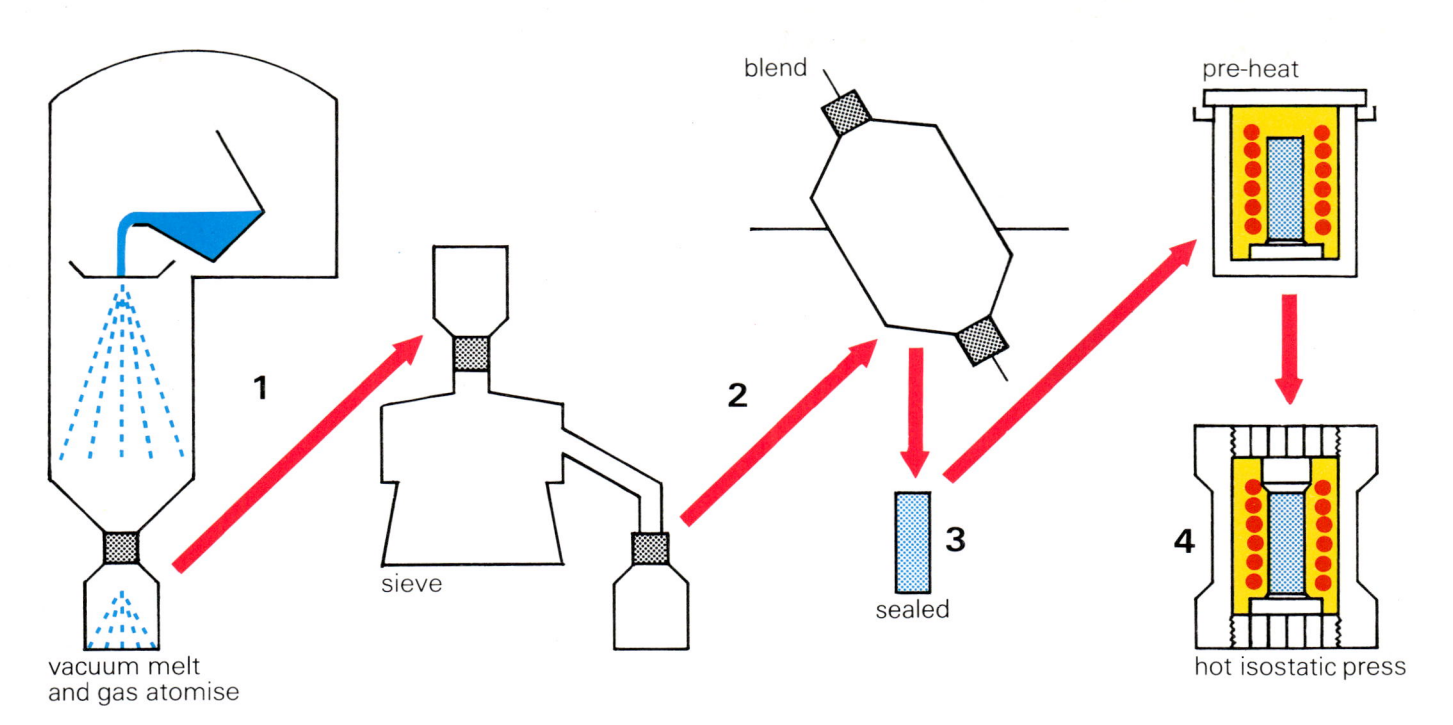

Diagram labels: 1 vacuum melt and gas atomise → sieve; 2 blend; 3 sealed; 4 pre-heat → hot isostatic press

Next, the powder is compressed, under hundreds of tons of pressure, into a shape very similar to that of the turbine or compressor disc. To make the disc ready for the engine, only a small amount of tidying up needs to be done on a large cutting machine: a process which is quick and inexpensive.

The forged disc is then machined again; the roots that will carry the blades are cut; and the finished product is despatched to be carefully inspected.

Today, much of the manufacturing work is controlled by computers. They help to design the disc, making all the calculations needed to ensure that it is as strong and as light as possible. They also control the machines which do the cutting.

Making powdered metal turbine discs. A forming case is filled with metal powder made by the process described at the end of page 12, and put into a vacuum (1). The case is vibrated, so that the powder when shaken down becomes tightly packed (2). The vacuum ensures that there are no air 'voids' within. Next the case is sealed (3) and the metal powder is subjected to extremely high pressure – about 25,000 pounds per square inch (4). It is also heated, so that the metal particles become fused together, forming the disc, which can then be removed from the forming case and machined to its final shape.

Hard-facing a high-pressure turbine disc. The disc teeth need to have a very hard surface to cope with the wear and tear of carrying turbine blades. The operator watches the spraying of a special metal on to the spinning turbine disc. Under intensive heat the hard-facing metal fuses with that of the disc.

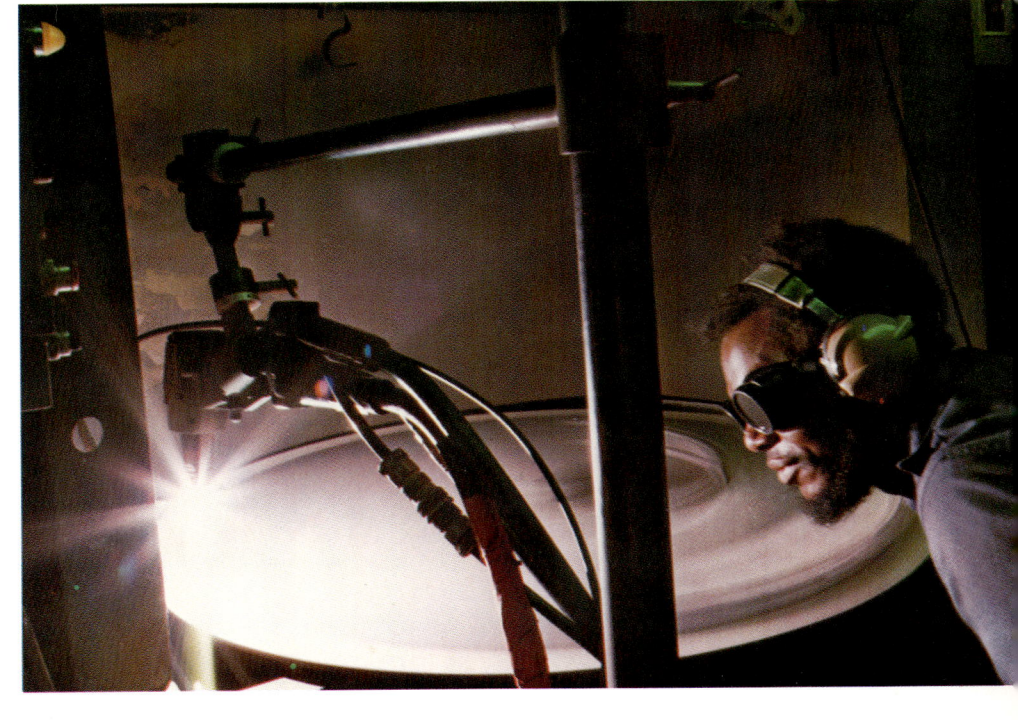

How compressor and turbine blades are made

One of the ways most frequently used for manufacturing the blades of modern compressors and turbines is by *casting*: a method first used by the Chinese about 2000 years ago for making statues. You can think of casting as being something like making a jelly in a mould. The liquid is poured into it, cools, and sets to the shape of the mould.

Before it is cast, the metal has to be heated up to a very high temperature so that it melts. It can then be poured into the *mould*, which is the shape of the compressor or turbine blades. Generally, several different types of metal are mixed together, forming what is called an *alloy*.

The moulds are made of a ceramic material, similar to that used for making cups and saucers. The molten mixture is poured into the moulds in a casting furnace, and allowed to cool. The ceramic is then broken away, revealing the freshly cast blades. These are then cut to their final shape by very accurate cutting machines. After the blades have been made, they are all carefully tested.

Compressor blades have to withstand the powerful pressure from the enormous quantities of air pumped back down the engine. They also have to withstand damage caused by objects sucked in at the intake. So they must be tough. They must also be light in weight; and they become very hot, particularly at the end nearest to the combustor, where the pressure is highest. The alloy used for these blades, therefore, is one which gives them the best combination of strength and lightness.

Turbine blades are cast in a different way from compressor blades. If you take a piece of balsa wood like that used in a model aircraft, and try to break it, you will find that it is stronger in one direction than it is in the other. This is because the wood has a 'grain'. With turbine blades, the grain in the metal is made to lie in the correct direction, which is along the blade. This is achieved while the blade cools after it has been cast. The process is called *directional solidifying*.

For turbines, special alloys have been developed so that they can cope with temperatures of up to 1300°C. They are based on nickel, and have small amounts of aluminium, titanium, and other metals designed to retain the blade's strength while it is in operation.

To reduce the enormous heat created by the gas-jets, the turbine blades are cooled by air passing through a maze of tiny holes within them. The holes, or *cooling passages*, are arranged so that the blades are cooled in exactly the right places. You can see the passages in the picture. Cooling enables the blades to operate in gas streams hotter than the melting point of the metal from which they are made.

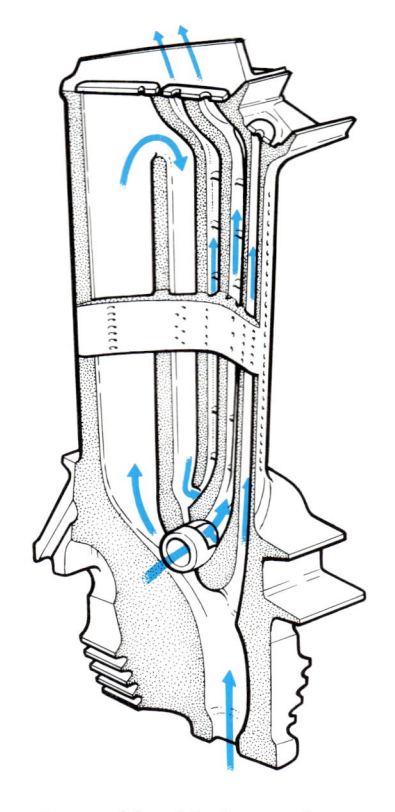

Jet engine turbine blades work at very high temperatures, sometimes becoming red hot. They usually have to be cooled by air blown via the compressor into the root of each blade. The network of cooling passages within the blade, which is very complex, ensures that the blade skin is prevented from burning. The inner passages are formed during the casting process. The hundreds of tiny holes connecting the passages to the blade surface are drilled either by a small laser beam, or by spark erosion. This is a technique that uses a carefully controlled spark to eat away the metal.

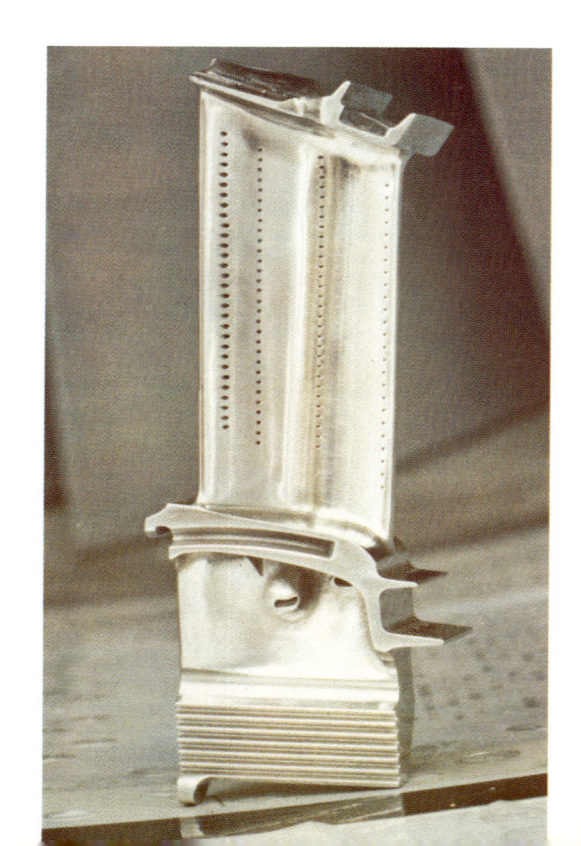

Making turbine blades using the 'lost wax' process. Wax copies of the blade are created by pouring wax into a metal mould; allowing it to set; and removing the mould. The wax blades are then mounted on a 'tree' to form a cluster. The cluster in the picture contains eight wax turbine blades, ready for dipping into a ceramic slurry.

A cluster of wax blades being removed from the ceramic slurry. The blades are dipped into the slurry several times, building up a ceramic coating about ¼-inch thick. Next, the cluster is heated to a temperature of about 1000°C, which hardens the ceramic coat and melts the wax. Molten metal is then poured into the ceramic shell and allowed to harden in special ovens. The ceramic coat is broken away, leaving the turbine blade, which is now ready to be accurately machined to its final shape.

The turbine blade is hardened under very carefully controlled conditions. This is an automatic, computer-controlled oven for making directionally solidified blades.

Fuel control and the combustion chamber

Before they can do any work, all engines need fuel. Jet engines burn a type of fuel which is very similar to paraffin. It is called Jet-A. On a long flight lasting seven or eight hours, the four engines of a jumbo jet will gulp down 30,000 gallons (136,383 litres) of it.

The Jet-A is stored in the wings of the aircraft and is fed to the engines by high-speed pumps. When it reaches the engines it passes through a **fuel control system** which accurately monitors the fuel before pumping it into the combustion chamber, where it is burned, releasing its energy to drive the turbines and to push the aircraft forwards.

Before the fuel can burn it has to be mixed with exactly the right quantity of air. This also applies to a car engine, which uses a carburettor to do the mixing. In a jet engine the mixing is carried out in the combustion chamber. If the mixture is to be completely burned, about fifteen times more air than fuel is needed. Extra air, not needed for burning fuel, passes around the combustor to prevent it from overheating.

The job of the fuel control system is to make sure that the correct amount of fuel is pumped into the combustion chamber throughout an aircraft's flight – from engine starting, through full power take-off, to cruise. In order to do this, it has to know how much air is passing through the engine, so that it can adjust the mixture correctly.

The amount of air needed by the engine changes constantly, depending on the aircraft's speed and height, and on the outside temperature. (The density of air at 30,000 feet, 9,144 metres, is much lower than it is on the ground.) So a fuel control system is very complicated. It is a kind of 'brain' which constantly looks after the fuel needs of the engine. Its **sensors** (devices which 'sense out') measure air pressure and temperature, and a number of other factors, such as engine speed.

On some very up-to-date jet engines the 'thinking' is done by a computer, which makes life easier for pilots, flight engineers and maintenance men.

When the fuel reaches the combustion chamber it is forced under great pressure through very small nozzles which break the liquid into tiny droplets. It then mixes more easily with the air which rushes through the combustion chamber.

The **combustion chamber**, as you can see from the picture, is wrapped around the middle of the engine, between the compressor and the turbines. The compressor, as described on page 10, pumps a lot of air back down the engine. Some of the air is channelled into the combustion

Right The combustion chamber, or combustor, is responsible for converting the fuel energy into power to make the turbines spin. Fuel and air are sprayed through nozzles, at very high pressure, into the chamber. The mixture is ignited, forming a continuous flame which rushes backwards. More air is introduced through holes in the side of the combustion chamber to prevent the walls from becoming too hot, and from burning. The escaping gases are directed at the turbine by the nozzle guide-vanes.

Left A partly assembled combustion chamber. The fuel spray nozzles will fit into the large holes in the rear. The holes in the walls are for cooling.

chamber, where it is thoroughly mixed with the fuel droplets before being burned.

You can think of the combustion chamber as a kind of blow torch, which when the fuel is burned produces enough heat to warm 17,000 standard-size, eight-room domestic dwellings. During the burning process the mixture of fuel and air expands very rapidly and is forced under enormous pressure out of the chamber. The gas-jet is aimed at the turbines, blowing them round so that they can turn the fan and compressors which push the aircraft forwards.

Combustion chambers have to mix the air and fuel thoroughly in a very short distance, so they are a complicated shape. And since they work for many hours at high temperatures they have to be made of very special metals. Sometimes a metal called *titanium* is used. This comes from an ore found in certain rocks. It is a very hard substance, and as it is difficult to mould into the right shapes it is only used in aircraft when there is a particularly tough job to do.

Combustion chambers are produced in several sections, which are welded together before they are mounted on the engine. The sections are made by heating up the titanium until it is soft. It is then pushed into a mould under great pressure.

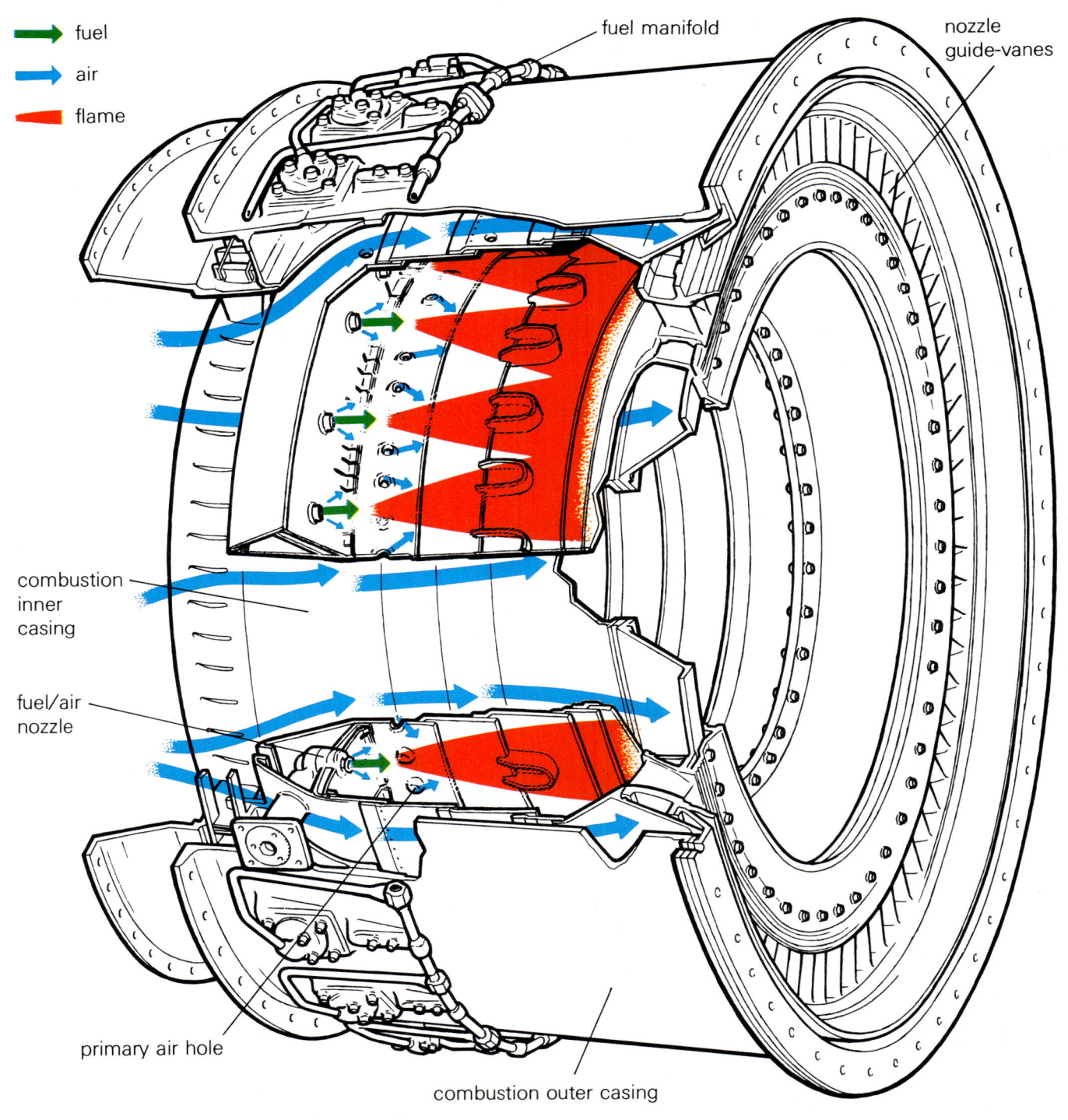

A modern fighter engine in full reheat. This is the 23,000lb-thrust Pratt & Whitney F100 which powers F-15s and F-16s. Fuel is being pumped into the exhaust system and ignited, greatly increasing the thrust of the engine. The nozzle at the rear is wide open. When reheat is reduced, or switched off, the nozzle contracts, reducing the duct area.

This is an experimental system for reducing the noise made by a civil jet-engine exhaust. The serrated ring is designed to mix the high-speed air – which is produced in the core – with the slower air pushed back by the fan. The slower the final exhaust jet, the less noise it makes. You can test this yourself by blowing through various sizes of tube.

The exhaust system

The exhaust is one of the few systems of a jet engine that you can actually see in action. Its job is to pass the gases rushing through the engine out into the atmosphere. Without it, the engine would perform very badly. By getting the shape of the exhaust duct right, the designers can improve the performance of the rest of the engine.

Aircraft flying at less than the speed of sound need exhaust systems with nozzles that are tapered towards the end. Aircraft flying beyond the speed of sound need nozzles which open out at the end, but which at slower speeds can be tapered.

When you are next at an airport, look at any passenger aircraft, and you will see that the engines are housed in **nacelles** which become narrower towards the rear end. These nacelles form the wall of the **outer exhaust duct**, which carries the air pushed back by the big fan at the front of the engine. The **inner exhaust duct**, which is narrower and extends beyond the outer duct, carries the air pumped back by the **core**, or heart, of the engine.

Between the outer and inner exhaust ducts is the **thrust reverser**, the mechanism which blocks off the air driven back by the fan, thus forcing it in the opposite direction. On landing, the reverse thrust acts as an extra brake and helps to slow the aircraft down.

When you are landing in a passenger aircraft you can hear the increase in engine noise as the wheels touch the ground. This is the moment when the pilot selects reverse thrust, opening the throttle to full power to slow the aircraft down in as short a time as possible.

Aircraft such as Concorde and jet fighters are equipped with adjustable nozzles which are automatically tapered at low speeds, and opened out when maximum power is needed for take-off and supersonic flight. The nozzles are also fitted with **afterburners**, which are used to increase the power of the engine for take-off, climb, and supersonic flight. In military aircraft, they are also switched on for combat, when the extra power is sometimes needed to outfly the enemy. If you are at an air show watching a jet fighter taking off, look carefully at the exhaust as the pilot begins his take-off run. You should see the nozzle open out at the end, and a red glow as the afterburner lights up. All modern supersonic aircraft are equipped with afterburners.

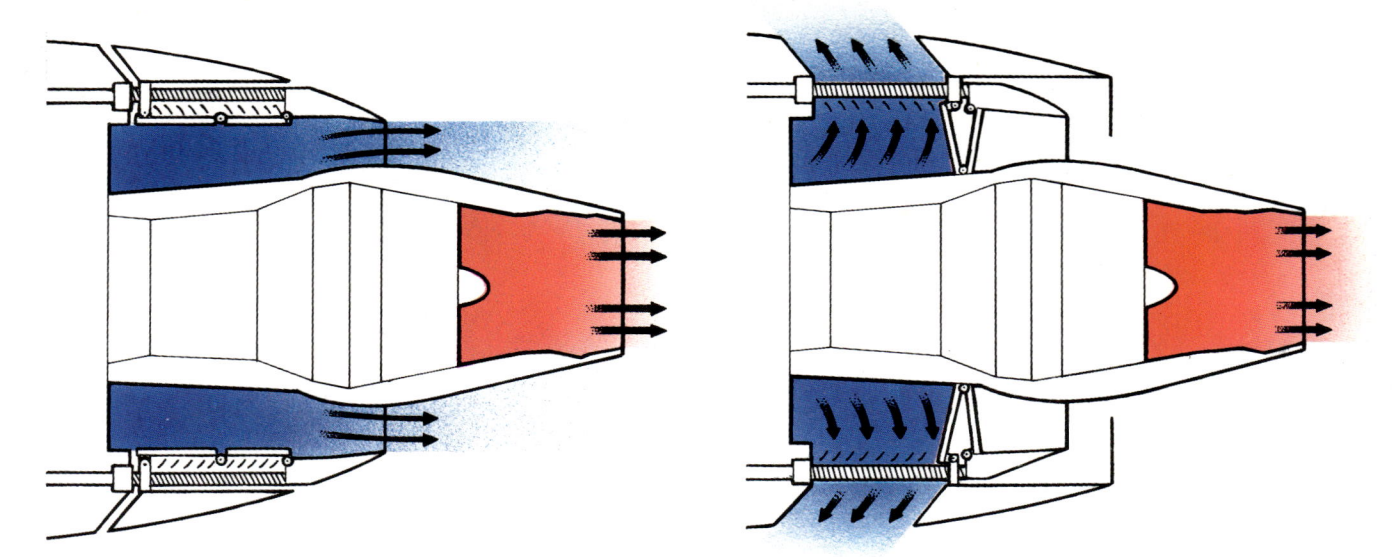

The afterburner is a simple mechanism which consists of a ring of fuel nozzles set into the exhaust duct, just behind the turbines. Air from the turbines rushes through the nozzles, is mixed with the fuel, and ignited, turning the exhaust duct into a kind of very powerful blow torch. By means of the afterburner, engine power can be doubled. It can only be used for short periods, because it gulps down a great deal of fuel, but it is a very practical way of increasing power without having to make the engine bigger. For the engines of high speed aircraft, which must be as slim as possible, this is very important.

The exhaust systems of jet engines create enormous heat, particularly if an afterburner is fitted, when the temperature at the nozzle can reach 1500°C (3180°F). This is hot enough to melt most metals, but not titanium, which is therefore often used for parts of the exhaust system which have to withstand great heat, such as the nozzle.

At present, exhaust systems on passenger aircraft are manufactured from aluminium alloy, and lined with special material designed to absorb the noise made by the engine's exhaust jet and its rotating parts.

Some of the latest engines use *composites* for the outer parts of the exhaust duct and engine nacelle. Composites consist of man-made fibres held together by resin. A very successful composite material is Fibreglass, which has many everyday uses. Even lighter and stronger than Fibreglass is Kevlar, which is now being used to build complete light aircraft. As it is so strong it is also used to surround the big fan at the front of the engine to prevent broken blades from escaping through the nacelle.

Reversing the thrust of a jet engine helps to slow the aircraft after touchdown. Only the air of the fan (shown blue) is reversed, since this provides most of the engine's thrust. Large doors block the fan duct, forcing the air to escape through a grille in the outer casing. The grille is angled so that it directs the escaping air forwards.

Sound-absorbing acoustic panels like this are used in civil jet engines to reduce fan noise. The tips of a fan blade can exceed the speed of sound, making them one of the noisiest parts of a modern turbofan. The acoustic panels are made of a special lightweight material which is wrapped around the inside of the fan duct.

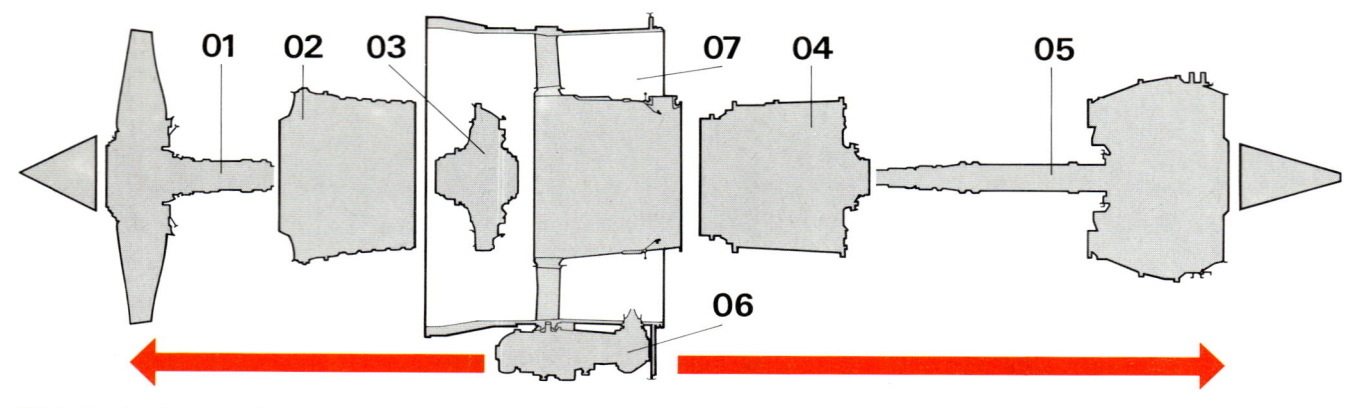

This Rolls-Royce 535 engine consists of seven modules. Each module is a pre-balanced unit, and can be replaced with a new or repaired unit without the necessity of matching it to the rest of the engine.

01 Fan
02 Intermediate-pressure compressor
03 I P module
04 High-pressure system (comprising HP compressor, combustor and HP turbine)
05 Intermediate- and low-pressure turbine
06 Gearbox
07 Fan casing

Installing the fan on a big jet engine, the Rolls-Royce RB.211. The fan is one of the 'modules' of the engine.

Assembly

When inspection of the components is complete, assembly of the engine can begin. Most engines today are built from 'modules'; you can think of them as building blocks. Rolls-Royce's biggest range of passenger engines, the RB.211 series, consists of up to eleven modules, or blocks. Smaller engines are likely to have fewer.

A module is a working section of the engine, such as a high-pressure turbine, a compressor or a combustion chamber. Each module is constructed in a different part of the factory – or by another company. When the modules are ready they are taken to the part of the factory where engines are assembled. They are then checked and slotted into place, which is a fairly simple operation. The engine is either built vertically or horizontally in a big gantry which can turn the engine over so that work can be carried out on both sides.

When all the modules have been bolted together the supporting components (known as the 'peripherals') such as oil and hydraulic pipes, generators and electrical wiring, are then added, and the engine is ready for testing.

Once it has been proved that the engine can meet all the requirements, it is transported to the aircraft manufacturer, either by air – in a big cargo plane – or by ship. Low-loading lorries then carry the engine to the aircraft factory. As it is worth at least two million dollars and weighs up to six tonnes it must be handled very carefully.

Engines are attached to the aircraft's wings by means of pylons, which are designed to carry the weight of the engines and to transfer their thrust to the airframe. Fuel passes through the pylons to the engines from tanks in the wing, while electrical and hydraulic power is transferred by wires and pipes through the pylons to the aircraft.

If you watch an aircraft as it taxies along the runway you will notice that the engines are 'nodding'. They must be allowed to swing slightly – otherwise their weight would be too heavy for the wing to bear. The pylon is designed to allow the engine to 'nod' while holding it firmly in place.

5. When the rolls have risen, Preheat the air fryer to 350°F (175°C).
6. Transfer 4 of the rolls to the air fryer basket. Air-fry for 5 minutes. Turn the rolls over and air-fry for another 4 minutes. Repeat with the remaining 4 rolls.
7. Let the rolls cool for a couple of minutes before glazing. Spread large dollops of cream cheese glaze on top of the warm cinnamon rolls, allowing some of the glaze to drip down the side of the rolls. Serve warm and enjoy!

Orange Rolls

Servings: 8
Cooking Time: 10 Minutes
Ingredients:
- parchment paper
- 3 ounces low-fat cream cheese
- 1 tablespoon low-fat sour cream or plain yogurt (not Greek yogurt)
- 2 teaspoons sugar
- ¼ teaspoon pure vanilla extract
- ¼ teaspoon orange extract
- 1 can (8 count) organic crescent roll dough
- ¼ cup chopped walnuts
- ¼ cup dried cranberries
- ¼ cup shredded, sweetened coconut
- butter-flavored cooking spray
- Orange Glaze
- ½ cup powdered sugar
- 1 tablespoon orange juice
- ¼ teaspoon orange extract
- dash of salt

Directions:
1. Cut a circular piece of parchment paper slightly smaller than the bottom of your air fryer basket. Set aside.
2. In a small bowl, combine the cream cheese, sour cream or yogurt, sugar, and vanilla and orange extracts. Stir until smooth.
3. Preheat air fryer to 300°F (150°C).
4. Separate crescent roll dough into 8 triangles and divide cream cheese mixture among them. Starting at wide end, spread cheese mixture to within 1 inch of point.
5. Sprinkle nuts and cranberries evenly over cheese mixture.
6. Starting at wide end, roll up triangles, then sprinkle with coconut, pressing in lightly to make it stick. Spray tops of rolls with butter-flavored cooking spray.
7. Place parchment paper in air fryer basket, and place 4 rolls on top, spaced evenly.
8. Cook for 10minutes, until rolls are golden brown and cooked through.
9. Repeat steps 7 and 8 to cook remaining 4 rolls. You should be able to use the same piece of parchment paper twice.
10. In a small bowl, stir together ingredients for glaze and drizzle over warm rolls.

Green Egg Quiche

Servings: 4
Cooking Time: 30 Minutes
Ingredients:
- 1 cup broccoli florets
- 2 cups baby spinach
- 2 garlic cloves, minced
- ¼ tsp ground nutmeg
- 1 tbsp olive oil
- Salt and pepper to taste
- 4 eggs
- 2 scallions, chopped
- 1 red onion, chopped
- 1 tbsp sour cream
- ½ cup grated fontina cheese

Directions:
1. Preheat air fryer to 375°F (190°C). Combine broccoli, spinach, onion, garlic, nutmeg, olive oil, and salt in a medium bowl, tossing to coat. Arrange the broccoli in a single layer in the parchment-lined frying basket and cook for 5 minutes. Remove and set to the side.
2. Use the same medium bowl to whisk eggs, salt, pepper, scallions, and sour cream. Add the roasted broccoli and ¼ cup fontina cheese until all ingredients are well combined. Pour the mixture into a greased baking dish and top with cheese. Bake in the air fryer for 15-18 minutes until the center is set. Serve and enjoy.

Shakshuka-style Pepper Cups

Servings:4
Cooking Time: 35 Minutes
Ingredients:
- 2 tbsp ricotta cheese crumbles
- 1 tbsp olive oil
- ½ yellow onion, diced
- 2 cloves garlic, minced
- ¼ tsp turmeric
- 1 can diced tomatoes
- 1 tbsp tomato paste
- ½ tsp smoked paprika
- ½ tsp salt
- ½ tsp granular sugar
- ¼ tsp ground cumin
- ¼ tsp ground coriander
- ⅛ tsp cayenne pepper
- 4 bell peppers
- 4 eggs
- 2 tbsp chopped basil

Directions:
1. Warm the olive oil in a saucepan over medium heat. Stir-fry the onion for 10 minutes or until softened. Stir in the garlic and turmeric for another 1 minute. Add diced tomatoes, tomato paste, paprika, salt, sugar, cumin, coriander, and cayenne. Remove from heat and stir.
2. Preheat air fryer to 350°F (175°C). Slice the tops off the peppers, and carefully remove the core and seeds. Put the bell peppers in the frying basket. Divide the tomato mixture among bell peppers. Crack 1 egg into tomato mixture in each pepper. Bake for 8-10 minutes. Sprinkle with ricotta cheese and cook for 1 more minute. Let rest 5 minutes. Garnish with fresh basil and serve immediately.

Mini Bacon Egg Quiches

Servings:6
Cooking Time: 30 Minutes
Ingredients:
- 3 eggs
- 2 tbsp heavy cream

- ¼ tsp Dijon mustard
- Salt and pepper to taste
- 3 oz cooked bacon, crumbled
- ¼ cup grated cheddar

Directions:
1. Preheat air fryer to 350°F. Beat the eggs with salt and pepper in a bowl until fluffy. Stir in heavy cream, mustard, cooked bacon, and cheese. Divide the mixture between 6 greased muffin cups and place them in the frying basket. Bake for 8-10 minutes. Let cool slightly before serving.

Bagels With Avocado & Tomatoes

Servings: 2
Cooking Time: 35 Minutes
Ingredients:
- 2/3 cup all-purpose flour
- ½ tsp active dry yeast
- 1/3 cup Greek yogurt
- 8 cherry tomatoes
- 1 ripe avocado
- 1 tbsp lemon juice
- 2 tbsp chopped red onions
- Black pepper to taste

Directions:
1. Preheat air fryer to 400°F (205°C). Beat the flour, dry yeast, and Greek yogurt until you get a smooth dough, adding more flour if necessary. Make 2 equal balls out of the mixture.
2. Using a rolling pin, roll each ball into a 9-inch long strip. Form a ring with each strip and press the ends together to create 2 bagels. In a bowl with hot water, soak the bagels for 1 minute. Shake excess water and let rise for 15 minutes in the fryer. Bake for 5 minutes, turn the bagels, top with tomatoes, and Bake for another 5 minutes.
3. Cut avocado in half, discard the pit and remove the flesh into a bowl. Mash with a fork and stir in lemon juice and onions. Once the bagels are ready, let cool slightly and cut them in half. Spread on each half some guacamole, top with 2 slices of Baked tomatoes, and sprinkle with pepper. Serve immediately.

Fluffy Vegetable Strata

Servings: 4
Cooking Time: 30 Minutes
Ingredients:
- ½ red onion, thickly sliced
- 8 asparagus, sliced
- 1 baby carrot, shredded
- 4 cup mushrooms, sliced
- ½ red bell pepper, chopped
- 2 bread slices, cubed
- 3 eggs
- 3 tbsp milk
- ½ cup mozzarella cheese
- 2 tsp chives, chopped

Directions:
1. Preheat air fryer to 330°F (165°C). Add the red onion, asparagus, carrots, mushrooms, red bell pepper, mushrooms, and 1 tbsp of water to a baking pan. Put it in the air fryer and Bake for 3-5 minutes, until crispy. Remove the pan, add the bread cubes, and shake to mix. Combine the eggs, milk, and chives and pour them over the veggies. Cover with mozzarella cheese. Bake for 12-15 minutes. The strata should puff up and set, while the top should be brown. Serve hot.

Parsley Egg Scramble With Cottage Cheese

Servings: 2
Cooking Time: 15 Minutes
Ingredients:
- 1 tbsp cottage cheese, crumbled
- 4 eggs
- Salt and pepper to taste
- 2 tsp heavy cream
- 1 tbsp chopped parsley

Directions:
1. Preheat air fryer to 400°F. Grease a baking pan with olive oil. Beat the eggs, salt, and pepper in a bowl. Pour it into the pan, place the pan in the frying basket, and Air Fry for 5 minutes. Using a silicone spatula, stir in heavy cream, cottage cheese, and half of parsley and Air Fry for another 2 minutes. Scatter with parsley to serve.

Flank Steak With Caramelized Onions

Servings: 2
Cooking Time: 30 Minutes
Ingredients:
- ½ lb flank steak, cubed
- 1 tbsp mustard powder
- ½ tsp garlic powder
- 2 eggs
- 1 onion, sliced thinly
- Salt and pepper to taste

Directions:
1. Preheat air fryer to 360°F (180°C). Coat the flank steak cubes with mustard and garlic powders. Place them in the frying basket along with the onion and Bake for 3 minutes. Flip the steak over and gently stir the onions and cook for another 3 minutes. Push the steak and onions over to one side of the basket, creating space for heat-safe baking dish. Crack the eggs into a ceramic dish. Place the dish in the fryer. Cook for 15 minutes at 320°F (160°C) until the egg white are set and the onion is caramelized. Season with salt and pepper. Serve warm.

Bacon, Broccoli And Swiss Cheese Bread Pudding

Servings: 2
Cooking Time: 48 Minutes
Ingredients:
- ½ pound thick cut bacon, cut into ¼-inch pieces
- 3 cups brioche bread or rolls, cut into ½-inch cubes
- 3 eggs
- 1 cup milk
- ½ teaspoon salt
- freshly ground black pepper
- 1 cup frozen broccoli florets, thawed and chopped
- 1½ cups grated Swiss cheese

Directions:
1. Preheat the air fryer to 400°F (205°C).
2. Air-fry the bacon for 6 minutes until crispy, shaking the basket a few times while it cooks to help it cook evenly. Remove the bacon and set it aside on a paper towel.

Tower Air Fryer Cookbook

3. Air-fry the brioche bread cubes for 2 minutes to dry and toast lightly. (If your brioche is a few days old and slightly stale, you can omit this step.)
4. Butter a 6- or 7-inch cake pan. Combine all the ingredients in a large bowl and toss well. Transfer the mixture to the buttered cake pan, cover with aluminum foil and refrigerate the bread pudding overnight, or for at least 8 hours.
5. Remove the casserole from the refrigerator an hour before you plan to cook, and let it sit on the countertop to come to room temperature.
6. Preheat the air fryer to 330°F (165°C). Transfer the covered cake pan, to the basket of the air fryer, lowering the dish into the basket using a sling made of aluminum foil (fold a piece of aluminum foil into a strip about 2-inches wide by 24-inches long). Fold the ends of the aluminum foil over the top of the dish before returning the basket to the air fryer. Air-fry for 20 minutes. Remove the foil and air-fry for an additional 20 minutes. If the top starts to brown a little too much before the custard has set, simply return the foil to the pan. The bread pudding has cooked through when a skewer inserted into the center comes out clean.

Cream Cheese Deviled Eggs
Servings: 4
Cooking Time: 20 Minutes
Ingredients:
- 2 cooked bacon slices, crumbled
- 4 whole eggs
- 2 tbsp mayonnaise
- 1 tsp yellow mustard
- ½ tsp dill pickle juice
- 1 tsp diced sweet pickles
- Salt and pepper to taste
- 2 tbsp cream cheese
- Parsley for sprinkling

Directions:
1. Preheat air fryer at 250°F. Place egg in the frying basket and Air Fry for 15 minutes. Then place them immediately into a bowl with ice and 1 cup of water to stop the cooking process. Let chill for 5 minutes, then carefully peel them. Cut egg in half lengthwise and spoon yolks into a bowl. Arrange the egg white halves on a plate.
2. Mash egg yolks with a fork. Stir in mayonnaise, mustard, pickle juice, diced pickles, salt, pepper and cream cheese. Pour 1 tbsp of the mixture into egg white halves, scatter with crumbled bacon and parsley and serve.

Breakfast Chicken Sausages With Apples
Servings: 6
Cooking Time: 20 Minutes
Ingredients:
- 1 lb ground chicken
- 1 cup diced apples
- 1 garlic clove, minced
- Salt and pepper to taste
- ½ tsp dried sage
- ½ tsp ginger powder
- ½ tsp ground nutmeg
- ¼ tsp cayenne pepper
- ¼ tsp fennel seed
- 1 tsp chopped onion
- ½ tsp brown sugar

Directions:
1. Preheat air fryer to 350°F (175°C). Combine all of the ingredients in a large bowl until well combined. Shape into thick patties. Transfer patties to the parchment-lined frying basket and Air Fry for 3 minutes. Flip the patties and Air Fry for another 3-4 minutes. Serve hot.

Chapter 4: Vegetable Side Dishes Recipes

Crunchy Roasted Potatoes

Servings: 5
Cooking Time: 25 Minutes
Ingredients:
- 2 pounds Small (1- to 1½-inch-diameter) red, white, or purple potatoes
- 2 tablespoons Olive oil
- 2 teaspoons Table salt
- ¾ teaspoon Garlic powder
- ½ teaspoon Ground black pepper

Directions:
1. Preheat the air fryer to 400°F (205°C).
2. Toss the potatoes, oil, salt, garlic powder, and pepper in a large bowl until the spuds are evenly and thoroughly coated.
3. When the machine is at temperature, pour the potatoes into the basket, spreading them into an even layer (although they may be stacked on top of each other). Air-fry for 25 minutes, tossing twice, until the potatoes are tender but crunchy.
4. Pour the contents of the basket into a serving bowl. Cool for 5 minutes before serving.

Simple Roasted Sweet Potatoes

Servings: 2
Cooking Time: 45 Minutes
Ingredients:
- 2 10- to 12-ounce sweet potato(es)

Directions:
1. Preheat the air fryer to 350°F (175°C).
2. Prick the sweet potato(es) in four or five different places with the tines of a flatware fork (not in a line but all around).
3. When the machine is at temperature, set the sweet potato(es) in the basket with as much air space between them as possible. Air-fry undisturbed for 45 minutes, or until soft when pricked with a fork.
4. Use kitchen tongs to transfer the sweet potato(es) to a wire rack. Cool for 5 minutes before serving.

Spicy Bean Stuffed Potatoes

Servings: 4
Cooking Time: 60 Minutes
Ingredients:
- 1 lb russet potatoes, scrubbed and perforated with a fork
- 1 can diced green chilies, including juice
- 1/3 cup grated Mexican cheese blend
- 1 green bell pepper, diced
- 1 yellow bell pepper, diced
- ¼ cup torn iceberg lettuce
- 2 tsp olive oil
- 2 tbsp sour cream
- ½ tsp chili powder
- 2-3 jalapeños, sliced
- 1 red bell pepper, chopped
- Salt and pepper to taste
- 1/3 cup canned black beans
- 4 grape tomatoes, sliced
- ¼ cup chopped parsley

Directions:
1. Preheat air fryer at 400°F. Brush olive oil over potatoes. Place them in the frying basket and Bake for 45 minutes, turning at 30 minutes mark. Let cool on a cutting board for 10 minutes until cool enough to handle. Slice each potato lengthwise and scoop out all but a ¼" layer of potato to form 4 boats.
2. Mash potato flesh, sour cream, green chilies, cheese, chili powder, jalapeños, green, yellow, and red peppers, salt, and pepper in a bowl until smooth. Fold in black beans. Divide between potato skin boats. Place potato boats in the frying basket and Bake for 2 minutes. Remove them to a serving plate. Top each boat with lettuce, tomatoes, and parsley. Sprinkle tops with salt and serve.

Chicken Salad With Sunny Citrus Dressing

Servings: 4
Cooking Time: 8 Minutes
Ingredients:
- Sunny Citrus Dressing
- 1 cup first cold-pressed extra virgin olive oil
- ⅓ cup red wine vinegar
- 2 tablespoons all natural orange marmalade
- 1 teaspoon dry mustard
- 1 teaspoon ground black pepper
- California Chicken
- 4 large chicken tenders
- 1 teaspoon olive oil
- juice of 1 small orange or clementine
- salt and pepper
- ½ teaspoon rosemary
- Salad
- 8 cups romaine or leaf lettuce, chopped or torn into bite-size pieces
- 2 clementines or small oranges, peeled and sectioned
- ½ cup dried cranberries
- 4 tablespoons sliced almonds

Directions:
1. In a 2-cup jar or container with lid, combine all dressing ingredients and shake until well blended. Refrigerate for at least 30minutes for flavors to blend.
2. Brush chicken tenders lightly with oil.
3. Drizzle orange juice over chicken.
4. Sprinkle with salt and pepper to taste.
5. Crush the rosemary and sprinkle over chicken.
6. Cook at 390°F (200°C) for 3minutes, turn over, and cook for an additional 5 minutes or until chicken is tender and juices run clear.
7. When ready to serve, toss lettuce with 2 tablespoons of dressing to coat.
8. Divide lettuce among 4 plates or bowls. Arrange chicken and clementines on top and sprinkle cranberries and almonds. Pass extra dressing at the table.

Yellow Squash

Servings: 4
Cooking Time: 10 Minutes
Ingredients:
- 1 large yellow squash (about 1½ cups)
- 2 eggs
- ¼ cup buttermilk
- 1 cup panko breadcrumbs
- ¼ cup white cornmeal
- ½ teaspoon salt

- oil for misting or cooking spray

Directions:
1. Preheat air fryer to 390°F (200°C).
2. Cut the squash into ¼-inch slices.
3. In a shallow dish, beat together eggs and buttermilk.
4. In sealable plastic bag or container with lid, combine ¼ cup panko crumbs, white cornmeal, and salt. Shake to mix well.
5. Place the remaining ¾ cup panko crumbs in a separate shallow dish.
6. Dump all the squash slices into the egg/buttermilk mixture. Stir to coat.
7. Remove squash from buttermilk mixture with a slotted spoon, letting excess drip off, and transfer to the panko/cornmeal mixture. Close bag or container and shake well to coat.
8. Remove squash from crumb mixture, letting excess fall off. Return squash to egg/buttermilk mixture, stirring gently to coat. If you need more liquid to coat all the squash, add a little more buttermilk.
9. Remove each squash slice from egg wash and dip in a dish of ¾ cup panko crumbs.
10. Mist squash slices with oil or cooking spray and place in air fryer basket. Squash should be in a single layer, but it's okay if the slices crowd together and overlap a little.
11. Cook at 390°F (200°C) for 5minutes. Shake basket to break up any that have stuck together. Mist again with oil or spray.
12. Cook 5minutes longer and check. If necessary, mist again with oil and cook an additional two minutes, until squash slices are golden brown and crisp.

Asparagus & Cherry Tomato Roast
Servings: 6
Cooking Time: 20 Minutes
Ingredients:
- 2 tbsp dill, chopped
- 2 cups cherry tomatoes
- 1 ½ lb asparagus, trimmed
- 2 tbsp olive oil
- 3 garlic cloves, minced
- ½ tsp salt

Directions:
1. Preheat air fryer to 380°F. Add all ingredients to a bowl, except for dill, and toss until the vegetables are well coated with the oil. Pour the vegetable mixture into the frying basket and Roast for 11-13 minutes, shaking once. Serve topped with fresh dill.

Curried Cauliflower With Cashews And Yogurt
Servings: 2
Cooking Time: 12 Minutes
Ingredients:
- 4 cups cauliflower florets (about half a large head)
- 1 tablespoon olive oil
- salt
- 1 teaspoon curry powder
- ½ cup toasted, chopped cashews
- Cool Yogurt Drizzle
- ¼ cup plain yogurt
- 2 tablespoons sour cream
- 1 teaspoon lemon juice
- pinch cayenne pepper
- salt
- 1 teaspoon honey
- 1 tablespoon chopped fresh cilantro, plus leaves for garnish

Directions:
1. Preheat the air fryer to 400°F (205°C).
2. Toss the cauliflower florets with the olive oil, salt and curry powder, coating evenly.
3. Transfer the cauliflower to the air fryer basket and air-fry at 400°F (205°C) for 12 minutes, shaking the basket a couple of times during the cooking process.
4. While the cauliflower is cooking, make the cool yogurt drizzle by combining all ingredients in a bowl.
5. When the cauliflower is cooked to your liking, serve it warm with the cool yogurt either underneath or drizzled over the top. Scatter the cashews and cilantro leaves around.

Home Fries
Servings: 4
Cooking Time: 20 Minutes
Ingredients:
- 3 pounds potatoes, cut into 1-inch cubes
- ½ teaspoon oil
- salt and pepper

Directions:
1. In a large bowl, mix the potatoes and oil thoroughly.
2. Cook at 390°F (200°C) for 10minutes and shake the basket to redistribute potatoes.
3. Cook for an additional 10 minutes, until brown and crisp.
4. Season with salt and pepper to taste.

Lovely Mac`n´cheese
Servings: 4
Cooking Time: 40 Minutes
Ingredients:
- 2 cups grated American cheese
- 4 cups elbow macaroni
- 3 egg, beaten
- ½ cup sour cream
- 4 tbsp butter
- ½ tsp mustard powder
- ½ tsp salt
- 1 cup milk

Directions:
1. Preheat air fryer to 350°F (175°C). Bring a pot of salted water to a boil and cook the macaroni following the packet instructions. Drain and place in a bowl.
2. Add 1 ½ cups of cheese and butter to the hot macaroni and stir to melt. Mix the beaten eggs, milk, sour cream, mustard powder, and salt in a bowl and add the mixture to the macaroni; mix gently. Spoon the macaroni mixture into a greased baking dish and transfer the dish to the air fryer. Bake for 15 minutes. Slide the dish out and sprinkle with the remaining American cheese. Cook for 5-8 more minutes until the top is bubbling and golden. Serve.

Spiced Roasted Acorn Squash

Servings: 2
Cooking Time: 45 Minutes
Ingredients:
- ½ acorn squash half
- 1 tsp butter, melted
- 2 tsp light brown sugar
- 1/8 tsp ground cinnamon
- 2 tbsp hot sauce
- ¼ cup maple syrup

Directions:
1. Preheat air fryer at 400ºF. Slice off about ¼-inch from the side of the squash half to sit flat like a bowl. In a bowl, combine all ingredients. Brush over the top of the squash and pour any remaining mixture in the middle of the squash. Place squash in the frying basket and Roast for 35 minutes. Cut it in half and divide between 2 serving plates. Serve.

Rosemary Potato Salad

Servings: 4
Cooking Time: 30 Minutes
Ingredients:
- 3 tbsp olive oil
- 2 lb red potatoes, halved
- Salt and pepper to taste
- 1 red bell pepper, chopped
- 2 green onions, chopped
- 1/3 cup lemon juice
- 3 tbsp Dijon mustard
- 1 tbsp rosemary, chopped

Directions:
1. Preheat air fryer to 350°F (175°C). Add potatoes to the frying basket and drizzle with 1 tablespoon olive oil. Season with salt and pepper. Roast the potatoes for 25 minutes, shaking twice. Potatoes will be tender and lightly golden.
2. While the potatoes are roasting, add peppers and green onions in a bowl. In a separate bowl, whisk olive oil, lemon juice, and mustard. When the potatoes are done, transfer them to a large bowl. Pour the mustard dressing over and toss to coat. Serve sprinkled with rosemary.

Crispy Noodle Salad

Servings: 3
Cooking Time: 22 Minutes
Ingredients:
- 6 ounces Fresh Chinese-style stir-fry or lo mein wheat noodles
- 1½ tablespoons Cornstarch
- ¾ cup Chopped stemmed and cored red bell pepper
- 2 Medium scallion(s), trimmed and thinly sliced
- 2 teaspoons Sambal oelek or other pulpy hot red pepper sauce (see here)
- 2 teaspoons Thai sweet chili sauce or red ketchup-like chili sauce, such as Heinz
- 2 teaspoons Regular or low-sodium soy sauce or tamari sauce
- 2 teaspoons Unseasoned rice vinegar (see here)
- 1 tablespoon White or black sesame seeds

Directions:
1. Bring a large saucepan of water to a boil over high heat. Add the noodles and boil for 2 minutes. Drain in a colander set in the sink. Rinse several times with cold water, shaking the colander to drain the noodles very well. Spread the noodles out on a large cutting board and air-dry for 10 minutes.
2. Preheat the air fryer to 400°F (205°C).
3. Toss the noodles in a bowl with the cornstarch until well coated. Spread them out across the entire basket (although they will be touching and overlapping a bit). Air-fry for 6 minutes, then turn the solid mass of noodles over as one piece. If it cracks in half or smaller pieces, just fit these back together after turning. Continue air-frying for 6 minutes, or until golden brown and crisp.
4. As the noodles cook, stir the bell pepper, scallion(s), sambal oelek, red chili sauce, soy sauce, vinegar, and sesame seeds in a serving bowl until well combined.
5. Turn the basket of noodles out onto a cutting board and cool for a minute or two. Break the mass of noodles into individual noodles and/or small chunks and add to the dressing in the serving bowl. Toss well to serve.

Buttered Brussels Sprouts

Servings: 4
Cooking Time: 30 Minutes
Ingredients:
- ¼ cup grated Parmesan
- 2 tbsp butter, melted
- 1 lb Brussels sprouts
- Salt and pepper to taste

Directions:
1. Preheat air fryer to 330°F (165°C). Trim the bottoms of the sprouts and remove any discolored leaves. Place the sprouts in a medium bowl along with butter, salt and pepper. Toss to coat, then place them in the frying basket. Roast for 20 minutes, shaking the basket twice. When done, the sprouts should be crisp with golden-brown color. Plate the sprouts in a serving dish and toss with Parmesan cheese.

Fried Eggplant Slices

Servings: 3
Cooking Time: 12 Minutes
Ingredients:
- 1½ sleeves (about 60 saltines) Saltine crackers
- ¾ cup Cornstarch
- 2 Large egg(s), well beaten
- 1 medium (about ¾ pound) Eggplant, stemmed, peeled, and cut into ¼-inch-thick rounds
- Olive oil spray

Directions:
1. Preheat the air fryer to 400°F (205°C). Also, position the rack in the center of the oven and heat the oven to 175°F (80°C).
2. Grind the saltines, in batches if necessary, in a food processor, pulsing the machine and rearranging the saltine pieces every few pulses. Or pulverize the saltines in a large, heavy zip-closed plastic bag with the bottom of a heavy saucepan. In either case, you want small bits of saltines, not just powder.
3. Set up and fill three shallow soup plates or small pie plates on your counter: one for the cornstarch, one for the beaten egg(s), and one for the pulverized saltines.
4. Set an eggplant slice in the cornstarch and turn it to coat on both sides. Use a brush to lightly remove any excess. Dip it into the beaten egg(s) and turn to coat both sides. Let any excess egg slip back into the rest, then set the slice in the

Tower Air Fryer Cookbook

saltines. Turn several times, pressing gently to coat both sides evenly but not heavily. Coat both sides of the slice with olive oil spray and set it aside. Continue dipping and coating the remaining slices.

5. Set one, two, or maybe three slices in the basket. There should be at least ½ inch between them for proper air flow. Air-fry undisturbed for 12 minutes, or until crisp and browned.

6. Use a nonstick-safe spatula to transfer the slice(s) to a large baking sheet. Slip it into the oven to keep the slices warm as you air-fry more batches, as needed, always transferring the slices to the baking sheet to stay warm.

Herby Roasted Cherry Tomatoes

Servings: 4
Cooking Time: 20 Minutes
Ingredients:
- 1 tbsp dried oregano
- 1 tbsp dried basil
- 2 tsp dried marjoram
- 1 tsp dried thyme
- 1 tsp salt
- 2 tbsp balsamic vinegar
- 20 cherry tomatoes
- 1 tbsp olive oil

Directions:
1. Preheat the air fryer to 400°F (205°C). Combine the oregano, basil, marjoram, thyme, and salt in a small bowl and mix well. Pout into a small glass jar. Poke each cherry tomato with a toothpick to prevent bursting. Put the tomatoes, balsamic vinegar and olive oil on a piece of aluminum foil and sprinkle with 1½ tsp of the herb mix; toss. Wrap the foil around the tomatoes, leaving air space in the packet, and seal loosely. Put the packet in the air fryer and Bake for 8-10 minutes or until the tomatoes are tender.

Dijon Roasted Purple Potatoes

Servings: 4
Cooking Time: 25 Minutes
Ingredients:
- 1 lb purple potatoes, scrubbed and halved
- 1 tbsp olive oil
- 1 tsp Dijon mustard
- 1 tsp lemon juice
- 2 cloves garlic, minced
- Salt and pepper to taste
- 2 tbsp butter, melted
- 1 tbsp chopped cilantro
- 1 tsp fresh rosemary

Directions:
1. Mix the olive oil, mustard, garlic, lemon juice, pepper, salt and rosemary in a bowl. Let chill covered in the fridge until ready to use.
2. Preheat air fryer at 350°F. Toss the potatoes, salt, pepper, and butter in a bowl, place the potatoes in the frying basket, and Roast for 18-20 minutes, tossing once. Transfer them into a bowl. Drizzle potatoes with the dressing and toss to coat. Garnish with cilantro to serve.

Spiced Pumpkin Wedges

Servings: 4
Cooking Time: 35 Minutes
Ingredients:
- 2 ½ cups pumpkin, cubed
- 2 tbsp olive oil
- Salt and pepper to taste
- ¼ tsp pumpkin pie spice
- 1 tbsp thyme
- ¼ cup grated Parmesan

Directions:
1. Preheat air fryer to 360°F (180°C). Put the cubed pumpkin with olive oil, salt, pumpkin pie spice, black pepper, and thyme in a bowl and stir until the pumpkin is well coated. Pour this mixture into the frying basket and Roast for 18-20 minutes, stirring once. Sprinkle the pumpkin with grated Parmesan. Serve and enjoy!

Garlicky Brussels Sprouts

Servings: 4
Cooking Time: 35 Minutes
Ingredients:
- 1 lb Brussels sprouts, halved lengthwise
- 1 tbsp olive oil
- 1 tbsp lemon juice
- ½ tsp sea salt
- ⅛ tsp garlic powder
- 4 garlic cloves, sliced
- 2 tbsp parsley, chopped
- ½ tsp red chili flakes

Directions:
1. Preheat the air fryer to 375°F (190°C). Combine the olive oil, lemon juice, salt, and garlic powder in a bowl and mix well. Add the Brussels sprouts and toss to coat. Put the Brussels sprouts in the frying basket. Air Fry for 15-20 minutes, shaking the basket once until golden and crisp. Sprinkle with garlic slices, parsley, and chili flakes. Toss and cook for 2-4 minutes more until the garlic browns a bit.

Simple Peppared Carrot Chips

Servings: 4
Cooking Time: 15 Minutes
Ingredients:
- 3 carrots, cut into coins
- 1 tbsp sesame oil
- Salt and pepper to taste

Directions:
1. Preheat air fryer at 375°F. Combine all ingredients in a bowl. Place carrots in the frying basket and Roast for 10 minutes, tossing once. Serve right away.

Mushrooms, Sautéed

Servings: 4
Cooking Time: 4 Minutes
Ingredients:
- 8 ounces sliced white mushrooms, rinsed and well drained
- ¼ teaspoon garlic powder
- 1 tablespoon Worcestershire sauce

Directions:
1. Place mushrooms in a large bowl and sprinkle with garlic powder and Worcestershire. Stir well to distribute seasonings evenly.
2. Place in air fryer basket and cook at 390°F (200°C) for 4 minutes, until tender.

Sweet Potato Curly Fries

Servings: 4
Cooking Time: 10 Minutes
Ingredients:
- 2 medium sweet potatoes, washed
- 2 tablespoons avocado oil
- ¾ teaspoon salt, divided
- 1 medium avocado
- ½ teaspoon garlic powder
- ½ teaspoon paprika
- ¼ teaspoon black pepper
- ½ juice lime
- 3 tablespoons fresh cilantro

Directions:
1. Preheat the air fryer to 400°F (205°C).
2. Using a spiralizer, create curly spirals with the sweet potatoes. Keep the pieces about 1½ inches long. Continue until all the potatoes are used.
3. In a large bowl, toss the curly sweet potatoes with the avocado oil and ½ teaspoon of the salt.
4. Place the potatoes in the air fryer basket and cook for 5 minutes; shake and cook another 5 minutes.
5. While cooking, add the avocado, garlic, paprika, pepper, the remaining ¼ teaspoon of salt, lime juice, and cilantro to a blender and process until smooth. Set aside.
6. When cooking completes, remove the fries and serve warm with the lime avocado sauce.

Simple Zucchini Ribbons

Servings: 4
Cooking Time: 15 Minutes
Ingredients:
- 2 zucchini
- 2 tsp butter, melted
- ¼ tsp garlic powder
- ¼ tsp chili flakes
- 8 cherry tomatoes, halved
- Salt and pepper to taste

Directions:
1. Preheat air fryer to 275ºF. Cut the zucchini into ribbons with a vegetable peeler. Mix them with butter, garlic, chili flakes, salt, and pepper in a bowl. Transfer to the frying basket and Air Fry for 2 minutes. Toss and add the cherry tomatoes. Cook for another 2 minutes. Serve.

Curried Fruit

Servings: 6
Cooking Time: 20 Minutes
Ingredients:
- 1 cup cubed fresh pineapple
- 1 cup cubed fresh pear (firm, not overly ripe)
- 8 ounces frozen peaches, thawed
- 1 15-ounce can dark, sweet, pitted cherries with juice
- 2 tablespoons brown sugar
- 1 teaspoon curry powder

Directions:
1. Combine all ingredients in large bowl. Stir gently to mix in the sugar and curry.
2. Pour into air fryer baking pan and cook at 360°F (180°C) for 10minutes.
3. Stir fruit and cook 10 more minutes.
4. Serve hot.

Florentine Stuffed Tomatoes

Cooking Time: 12 Minutes
Servings: 2
Ingredients:
- 1 cup frozen spinach, thawed and squeezed dry
- ¼ cup toasted pine nuts
- ¼ cup grated mozzarella cheese
- ½ cup crumbled feta cheese
- ½ cup coarse fresh breadcrumbs
- 1 tablespoon olive oil
- salt and freshly ground black pepper
- 2 to 3 beefsteak tomatoes, halved horizontally and insides scooped out

Directions:
1. Combine the spinach, pine nuts, mozzarella and feta cheeses, breadcrumbs, olive oil, salt and freshly ground black pepper in a bowl. Spoon the mixture into the tomato halves. You should have enough filling for 2 to 3 tomatoes, depending on how big they are.
2. Preheat the air fryer to 350°F (175°C).
3. Place three or four tomato halves (depending on whether you're using 2 or 3 tomatoes and how big they are) into the air fryer and air-fry for 12 minutes. The tomatoes should be soft but still manageable and the tops should be lightly browned. Repeat with second batch if necessary.
4. Let the tomatoes cool for just a minute or two before serving.

Broccoli Au Gratin

Servings: 2
Cooking Time: 25 Minutes
Ingredients:
- 2 cups broccoli florets, chopped
- 6 tbsp grated Gruyère cheese
- 1 tbsp grated Pecorino cheese
- ½ tbsp olive oil
- 1 tbsp flour
- 1/3 cup milk
- ½ tsp ground coriander
- Salt and black pepper
- 2 tbsp panko bread crumbs

Directions:
1. Whisk the olive oil, flour, milk, coriander, salt, and pepper in a bowl. Incorporate broccoli, Gruyere cheese, panko bread crumbs, and Pecorino cheese until well combined. Pour in a greased baking dish.
2. Preheat air fryer to 330°F (165°C). Put the baking dish into the frying basket. Bake until the broccoli is crisp-tender and the top is golden, or about 12-15 minutes. Serve warm.

Corn Au Gratin

Servings: 4
Cooking Time: 20 Minutes
Ingredients:
- ½ cup grated cheddar
- 3 tbsp flour
- 2 cups yellow corn
- 1 egg, beaten
- ¼ cup milk
- ½ cup heavy cream
- Salt and pepper to taste

- 2 tbsp butter, cubed

Directions:
1. Preheat air fryer to 320°F (160°C). Mix flour, corn, egg, milk, and heavy cream in a medium bowl. Stir in cheddar cheese, salt and pepper. Pour into the prepared baking pan. Top with butter. Bake for 15 minutes. Serve warm.

Roasted Brussels Sprouts With Bacon

Cooking Time: 20 Minutes
Servings: 4
Ingredients:
- 4 slices thick-cut bacon, chopped (about ¼ pound)
- 1 pound Brussels sprouts, halved (or quartered if large)
- freshly ground black pepper

Directions:
1. Preheat the air fryer to 380°F (195°C).
2. Air-fry the bacon for 5 minutes, shaking the basket once or twice during the cooking time.
3. Add the Brussels sprouts to the basket and drizzle a little bacon fat from the bottom of the air fryer drawer into the basket. Toss the sprouts to coat with the bacon fat. Air-fry for an additional 15 minutes, or until the Brussels sprouts are tender to a knifepoint.
4. Season with freshly ground black pepper.

Basic Corn On The Cob

Servings: 4
Cooking Time: 15 Minutes
Ingredients:
- 3 ears of corn, shucked and halved
- 2 tbsp butter, melted
- Salt and pepper to taste
- 1 tsp minced garlic
- 1 tsp paprika

Directions:
1. Preheat air fryer at 400ºF. Toss all ingredients in a bowl. Place corn in the frying basket and Bake for 7 minutes, turning once. Serve immediately.

Honey-roasted Parsnips

Servings: 3
Cooking Time: 23 Minutes
Ingredients:
- 1½ pounds Medium parsnips, peeled
- Olive oil spray
- 1 tablespoon Honey
- 1½ teaspoons Water
- ¼ teaspoon Table salt

Directions:
1. Preheat the air fryer to 350°F (175°C).
2. If the thick end of a parsnip is more than ½ inch in diameter, cut the parsnip just below where it swells to its large end, then slice the large section in half lengthwise. If the parsnips are larger than the basket (or basket attachment), trim off the thin end so the parsnips will fit. Generously coat the parsnips on all sides with olive oil spray.
3. When the machine is at temperature, set the parsnips in the basket with as much air space between them as possible. Air-fry undisturbed for 20 minutes.
4. Whisk the honey, water, and salt in a small bowl until smooth. Brush this mixture over the parsnips. Air-fry undisturbed for 3 minutes more, or until the glaze is lightly browned.
5. Use kitchen tongs to transfer the parsnips to a wire rack or a serving platter. Cool for a couple of minutes before serving.

Bacon-wrapped Asparagus

Servings: 4
Cooking Time: 10 Minutes
Ingredients:
- 1 tablespoon extra-virgin olive oil
- ½ teaspoon sea salt
- ¼ cup grated Parmesan cheese
- 1 pound asparagus, ends trimmed
- 8 slices bacon

Directions:
1. Preheat the air fryer to 380°F (195°C).
2. In large bowl, mix together the olive oil, sea salt, and Parmesan cheese. Toss the asparagus in the olive oil mixture.
3. Evenly divide the asparagus into 8 bundles. Wrap 1 piece of bacon around each bundle, not overlapping the bacon but spreading it across the bundle.
4. Place the asparagus bundles into the air fryer basket, not touching. Work in batches as needed.
5. Cook for 8 minutes; check for doneness, and cook another 2 minutes.

Carrots & Parsnips With Tahini Sauce

Servings: 4
Cooking Time: 20 Minutes
Ingredients:
- 2 parsnips, cut into half-moons
- 2 tsp olive oil
- ½ tsp salt
- 1 carrot, cut into sticks
- 1 tbsp tahini
- 1 tbsp lemon juice
- 1 clove garlic, minced
- 1 tbsp chopped parsley

Directions:
1. Preheat air fryer to 375ºF. Coat the parsnips and carrots with some olive oil and salt. Place them in the frying basket and Air Fry for 10 minutes, tossing once. In a bowl, whisk tahini, lemon juice, 1 tsp of water, and garlic. Pour the sauce over the cooked veggies. Scatter with parsley and serve.

Broccoli Tots

Servings: 24
Cooking Time: 10 Minutes
Ingredients:
- 2 cups broccoli florets (about ½ pound broccoli crowns)
- 1 egg, beaten
- ⅛ teaspoon onion powder
- ¼ teaspoon salt
- ⅛ teaspoon pepper
- 2 tablespoons grated Parmesan cheese
- ¼ cup panko breadcrumbs
- oil for misting

Directions:
1. Steam broccoli for 2 minutes. Rinse in cold water, drain well, and chop finely.
2. In a large bowl, mix broccoli with all other ingredients except the oil.

3. Scoop out small portions of mixture and shape into 24 tots. Lay them on a cookie sheet or wax paper as you work.
4. Spray tots with oil and place in air fryer basket in single layer.
5. Cook at 390°F (200°C) for 5minutes. Shake basket and spray with oil again. Cook 5minutes longer or until browned and crispy.

Yukon Gold Potato Purée

Servings: 4
Cooking Time: 25 Minutes
Ingredients:
- 1 lb Yukon Gold potatoes, scrubbed and cubed
- 2 tbsp butter, melted
- Salt and pepper to taste
- 1/8 cup whole milk
- ¼ cup cream cheese
- 1 tbsp butter, softened
- ¼ cup chopped dill

Directions:
1. Preheat air fryer at 350ºF. Toss the potatoes and melted butter in a bowl, place them in the frying basket, and Air Fry for 13-15 minutes, tossing once. Transfer them into a bowl. Using a fork, mash the potatoes. Stir in salt, pepper, half of the milk, cream cheese, and 1 tbsp of butter until you reach your desired consistency. Garnish with dill to serve.

Stuffed Onions

Servings: 6
Cooking Time: 27 Minutes
Ingredients:
- 6 Small 3½- to 4-ounce yellow or white onions
- Olive oil spray
- 6 ounces Bulk sweet Italian sausage meat (gluten-free, if a concern)
- 9 Cherry tomatoes, chopped
- 3 tablespoons Seasoned Italian-style dried bread crumbs (gluten-free, if a concern)
- 3 tablespoons (about ½ ounce) Finely grated Parmesan cheese

Directions:
1. Preheat the air fryer to 325°F (160°C) (or 330°F (165°C), if that's the closest setting).
2. Cut just enough off the root ends of the onions so they will stand up on a cutting board when this end is turned down. Carefully peel off just the brown, papery skin. Now cut the top quarter off each and place the onion back on the cutting board with this end facing up. Use a flatware spoon (preferably a serrated grapefruit spoon) or a melon baller to scoop out the "insides" (interior layers) of the onion, leaving enough of the bottom and side walls so that the onion does not collapse. Depending on the thickness of the layers in the onion, this may be one or two of those layers—or even three, if they're very thin.
3. Coat the insides and outsides of the onions with olive oil spray. Set the onion "shells" in the basket and air-fry for 15 minutes.
4. Meanwhile, make the filling. Set a medium skillet over medium heat for a couple of minutes, then crumble in the sausage meat. Cook, stirring often, until browned, about 4 minutes. Transfer the contents of the skillet to a medium bowl (leave the fat behind in the skillet or add it to the bowl, depending on your cross-trainer regimen). Stir in the tomatoes, bread crumbs, and cheese until well combined.
5. When the onions are ready, use a nonstick-safe spatula to gently transfer them to a cutting board. Increase the air fryer's temperature to 350°F (175°C) .
6. Pack the sausage mixture into the onion shells, gently compacting the filling and mounding it up at the top.
7. When the machine is at temperature, set the onions stuffing side up in the basket with at least ¼ inch between them. Air-fry for 12 minutes, or until lightly browned and sizzling hot.
8. Use a nonstick-safe spatula, and perhaps a flatware fork for balance, to transfer the onions to a cutting board or serving platter. Cool for 5 minutes before serving.

Teriyaki Tofu With Spicy Mayo

Servings: 2
Cooking Time: 35 Minutes + 1 Hour To Marinate
Ingredients:
- 1 scallion, chopped
- 7 oz extra-firm tofu, sliced
- 2 tbsp soy sauce
- 1 tsp toasted sesame oil
- 1 red chili, thinly sliced
- 1 tsp mirin
- 1 tsp light brown sugar
- 1 garlic clove, grated
- ½ tsp grated ginger
- 1/3 cup sesame seeds
- 1 egg
- 4 tsp mayonnaise
- 1 tbsp lime juice
- 1 tsp hot chili powder

Directions:
1. Squeeze most of the water from the tofu by lightly pressing the slices between two towels. Place the tofu in a baking dish. Use a whisk to mix soy sauce, sesame oil, red chili, mirin, brown sugar, garlic and ginger. Pour half of the marinade over the tofu. Using a spatula, carefully flip the tofu down and pour the other half of the marinade over. Refrigerate for 1 hour.
2. Preheat air fryer to 400°F (205°C). In a shallow plate, add sesame seeds. In another shallow plate, beat the egg. Remove the tofu from the refrigerator. Let any excess marinade drip off. Dip each piece in the egg mixture and then in the sesame seeds. Transfer to greased frying basket. Air Fry for 10 minutes, flipping once until toasted and crispy. Meanwhile, mix mayonnaise, lime juice, and hot chili powder and in a small bowl. Top with a dollop of hot chili mayo and some scallions. Serve and enjoy!

Balsamic Beet Chips

Servings: 4
Cooking Time: 40 Minutes
Ingredients:
- ½ tsp balsamic vinegar
- 4 beets, peeled and sliced
- 1 garlic clove, minced
- 2 tbsp chopped mint
- Salt and pepper to taste
- 3 tbsp olive oil

Directions:

1. Preheat air fryer to 380°F (195°C). Coat all ingredients in a bowl, except balsamic vinegar. Pour the beet mixture into the frying basket and Roast for 25-30 minutes, stirring once. Serve, drizzled with vinegar and enjoy!

Stuffed Avocados
Servings: 4
Cooking Time: 8 Minutes
Ingredients:
- 1 cup frozen shoepeg corn, thawed
- 1 cup cooked black beans
- ¼ cup diced onion
- ½ teaspoon cumin
- 2 teaspoons lime juice, plus extra for serving
- salt and pepper
- 2 large avocados, split in half, pit removed

Directions:
1. Mix together the corn, beans, onion, cumin, and lime juice. Season to taste with salt and pepper.
2. Scoop out some of the flesh from center of each avocado and set aside. Divide corn mixture evenly between the cavities.
3. Set avocado halves in air fryer basket and cook at 360°F (180°C) for 8 minutes, until corn mixture is hot.
4. Season the avocado flesh that you scooped out with a squirt of lime juice, salt, and pepper. Spoon it over the cooked halves.

Gorgonzola Stuffed Mushrooms
Servings: 2
Cooking Time: 15 Minutes
Ingredients:
- 12 white button mushroom caps
- 2 tbsp diced white button mushroom stems
- ¼ cup Gorgonzola cheese, crumbled
- 1 tsp olive oil
- 1 green onion, chopped
- 2 tbsp bread crumbs

Directions:
1. Preheat air fryer to 350°F. Rub around the top of each mushroom cap with olive oil. Mix the mushroom stems, green onion, and Gorgonzola cheese in a bowl.
2. Distribute and press mixture into the cups of mushrooms, then sprinkle bread crumbs on top. Place stuffed mushrooms in the frying basket and Bake for 5-7 minutes. Serve right away.

Provence French Fries
Servings: 4
Cooking Time: 25 Minutes
Ingredients:
- 2 russet potatoes
- 1 tbsp olive oil
- 1 tbsp herbs de Provence

Directions:
1. Preheat air fryer to 400°F (205°C). Slice the potatoes lengthwise into ½-inch thick strips. In a bowl, whisk the olive oil and herbs de Provence. Toss in the potatoes to coat. Arrange them in a single and Air Fry for 18-20 minutes, shaking once, until crispy. Serve warm.

Dauphinoise (potatoes Au Gratin)
Servings: 4
Cooking Time: 30 Minutes
Ingredients:
- ½ cup grated cheddar cheese
- 3 peeled potatoes, sliced
- ½ cup milk
- ½ cup heavy cream
- Salt and pepper to taste
- 1 tsp ground nutmeg

Directions:
1. Preheat air fryer to 350°F (175°C). Place the milk, heavy cream, salt, pepper, and nutmeg in a bowl and mix well. Dip in the potato slices and arrange on a baking dish. Spoon the remaining mixture over the potatoes. Scatter the grated cheddar cheese on top. Place the baking dish in the air fryer and Bake for 20 minutes. Serve warm and enjoy!

Savory Brussels Sprouts
Servings: 4
Cooking Time: 15 Minutes
Ingredients:
- 1 lb Brussels sprouts, quartered
- 2 tbsp balsamic vinegar
- 1 tbsp olive oil
- 1 tbsp honey
- Salt and pepper to taste
- 1 ½ tbsp lime juice
- Parsley for sprinkling

Directions:
1. Preheat air fryer at 350°F. Combine all ingredients in a bowl. Transfer them to the frying basket. Air Fry for 10 minutes, tossing once. Top with lime juice and parsley.

Roasted Garlic
Servings: 20
Cooking Time: 40 Minutes
Ingredients:
- 20 Peeled medium garlic cloves
- 2 tablespoons, plus more Olive oil

Directions:
1. Preheat the air fryer to 400°F (205°C).
2. Set a 10-inch sheet of aluminum foil on your work surface for a small batch, a 14-inch sheet for a medium batch, or a 16-inch sheet for a large batch. Put the garlic cloves in its center in one layer without bunching the cloves together. (Spread them out a little for even cooking.) Drizzle the small batch with 1 tablespoon oil, the medium batch with 2 tablespoons, or the large one with 3 tablespoons. Fold up the sides and seal the foil into a packet.
3. When the machine is at temperature, put the packet in the basket. Air-fry for 40 minutes, or until very fragrant. The cloves inside should be golden and soft.
4. Transfer the packet to a cutting board. Cool for 5 minutes, then open and use the cloves hot. Or cool them to room temperature, set them in a small container or jar, pour in enough olive oil to cover them, seal or cover the container, and refrigerate for up to 2 weeks.

Roasted Peppers With Balsamic Vinegar And Basil

Servings: 6
Cooking Time: 12 Minutes
Ingredients:
- 4 Small or medium red or yellow bell peppers
- 3 tablespoons Olive oil
- 1 tablespoon Balsamic vinegar
- Up to 6 Fresh basil leaves, torn up

Directions:
1. Preheat the air fryer to 400°F (205°C).
2. When the machine is at temperature, put the peppers in the basket with at least ¼ inch between them. Air-fry undisturbed for 12 minutes, until blistered, even blackened in places.
3. Use kitchen tongs to transfer the peppers to a medium bowl. Cover the bowl with plastic wrap. Set aside at room temperature for 30 minutes.
4. Uncover the bowl and use kitchen tongs to transfer the peppers to a cutting board or work surface. Peel off the filmy exterior skin. If there are blackened bits under it, these can stay on the peppers. Cut off and remove the stem ends. Split open the peppers and discard any seeds and their spongy membranes. Slice the peppers into ½-inch- to 1-inch-wide strips.
5. Put these in a clean bowl and gently toss them with the oil, vinegar, and basil. Serve at once. Or cover and store at room temperature for up to 4 hours or in the refrigerator for up to 5 days.

Roast Sweet Potatoes With Parmesan

Servings: 4
Cooking Time: 30 Minutes
Ingredients:
- 2 peeled sweet potatoes, sliced
- ¼ cup grated Parmesan
- 1 tsp olive oil
- 1 tbsp balsamic vinegar
- 1 tsp dried rosemary

Directions:
1. Preheat air fryer to 400°F (205°C). Place the sweet potatoes and some olive oil in a bowl and shake to coat. Spritz with balsamic vinegar and rosemary, then shake again. Put the potatoes in the frying basket and Roast for 18-25 minutes, shaking at least once until the potatoes are soft. Sprinkle with Parmesan cheese and serve warm.

Mashed Potato Tots

Servings: 18
Cooking Time: 10 Minutes
Ingredients:
- 1 medium potato or 1 cup cooked mashed potatoes
- 1 tablespoon real bacon bits
- 2 tablespoons chopped green onions, tops only
- ¼ teaspoon onion powder
- 1 teaspoon dried chopped chives
- salt
- 2 tablespoons flour
- 1 egg white, beaten
- ½ cup panko breadcrumbs
- oil for misting or cooking spray

Directions:
1. If using cooked mashed potatoes, jump to step 4.
2. Peel potato and cut into ½-inch cubes. (Small pieces cook more quickly.) Place in saucepan, add water to cover, and heat to boil. Lower heat slightly and continue cooking just until tender, about 10 minutes.
3. Drain potatoes and place in ice cold water. Allow to cool for a minute or two, then drain well and mash.
4. Preheat air fryer to 390°F (200°C).
5. In a large bowl, mix together the potatoes, bacon bits, onions, onion powder, chives, salt to taste, and flour. Add egg white and stir well.
6. Place panko crumbs on a sheet of wax paper.
7. For each tot, use about 2 teaspoons of potato mixture. To shape, drop the measure of potato mixture onto panko crumbs and push crumbs up and around potatoes to coat edges. Then turn tot over to coat other side with crumbs.
8. Mist tots with oil or cooking spray and place in air fryer basket, crowded but not stacked.
9. Cook at 390°F (200°C) for 10 minutes, until browned and crispy.
10. Repeat steps 8 and 9 to cook remaining tots.

Parmesan Garlic Fries

Servings: 4
Cooking Time: 20 Minutes
Ingredients:
- 2 medium Yukon gold potatoes, washed
- 1 tablespoon extra-virgin olive oil
- 1 garlic clove, minced
- 2 tablespoons finely grated parmesan cheese
- ¼ teaspoon black pepper
- ¼ teaspoon salt
- 1 tablespoon freshly chopped parsley

Directions:
1. Preheat the air fryer to 400°F (205°C).
2. Slice the potatoes into long strips about ¼-inch thick. In a large bowl, toss the potatoes with the olive oil, garlic, cheese, pepper, and salt.
3. Place the fries into the air fryer basket and cook for 4 minutes; shake the basket and cook another 4 minutes.
4. Remove and serve warm.

Okra

Servings: 4
Cooking Time: 12 Minutes
Ingredients:
- 7–8 ounces fresh okra
- 1 egg
- 1 cup milk
- 1 cup breadcrumbs
- ½ teaspoon salt
- oil for misting or cooking spray

Directions:
1. Remove stem ends from okra and cut in ½-inch slices.
2. In a medium bowl, beat together egg and milk. Add okra slices and stir to coat.
3. In a sealable plastic bag or container with lid, mix together the breadcrumbs and salt.
4. Remove okra from egg mixture, letting excess drip off, and transfer into bag with breadcrumbs.
5. Shake okra in crumbs to coat well.

6. Place all of the coated okra into the air fryer basket and mist with oil or cooking spray. Okra doesn't need to cook in a single layer, nor is it necessary to spray all sides at this point. A good spritz on top will do.
7. Cook at 390°F (200°C) for 5minutes. Shake basket to redistribute and give it another spritz as you shake.
8. Cook 5 more minutes. Shake and spray again. Cook for 2 minutes longer or until golden brown and crispy.

Smashed Fried Baby Potatoes

Servings: 3
Cooking Time: 18 Minutes
Ingredients:
- 1½ pounds baby red or baby Yukon gold potatoes
- ¼ cup butter, melted
- 1 teaspoon olive oil
- ½ teaspoon paprika
- 1 teaspoon dried parsley
- salt and freshly ground black pepper
- 2 scallions, finely chopped

Directions:
1. Bring a large pot of salted water to a boil. Add the potatoes and boil for 18 minutes or until the potatoes are fork-tender.
2. Drain the potatoes and transfer them to a cutting board to cool slightly. Spray or brush the bottom of a drinking glass with a little oil. Smash or flatten the potatoes by pressing the glass down on each potato slowly. Try not to completely flatten the potato or smash it so hard that it breaks apart.
3. Combine the melted butter, olive oil, paprika, and parsley together.
4. Preheat the air fryer to 400°F (205°C).
5. Spray the bottom of the air fryer basket with oil and transfer one layer of the smashed potatoes into the basket. Brush with some of the butter mixture and season generously with salt and freshly ground black pepper.
6. Air-fry at 400°F (205°C) for 10 minutes. Carefully flip the potatoes over and air-fry for an additional 8 minutes until crispy and lightly browned.
7. Keep the potatoes warm in a 170°F (75°C) oven or tent with aluminum foil while you cook the second batch. Sprinkle minced scallions over the potatoes and serve warm.

Southern Okra Chips

Servings: 2
Cooking Time: 20 Minutes
Ingredients:
- 2 eggs
- ¼ cup whole milk
- ¼ cup bread crumbs
- ¼ cup cornmeal
- 1 tbsp Cajun seasoning
- Salt and pepper to taste
- ⅛ tsp chili pepper
- ½ lb okra, sliced
- 1 tbsp butter, melted

Directions:
1. Preheat air fryer at 400°F. Beat the eggs and milk in a bowl. In another bowl, combine the remaining ingredients, except okra and butter. Dip okra chips in the egg mixture, then dredge them in the breadcrumbs mixture. Place okra chips in the greased frying basket and Roast for 7 minutes, shake once and brush with melted butter. Serve right away.

Smoked Avocado Wedges

Servings:4
Cooking Time: 15 Minutes
Ingredients:
- ½ tsp smoked paprika
- 2 tsp olive oil
- ½ lime, juiced
- 8 peeled avocado wedges
- 1 tsp chipotle powder
- ¼ tsp salt

Directions:
1. Preheat air fryer to 400°F. Drizzle the avocado wedges with olive oil and lime juice. In a bowl, combine chipotle powder, smoked paprika, and salt. Sprinkle over the avocado wedges. Place them in the frying basket and Air Fry for 7 minutes. Serve immediately.

Pork Tenderloin Salad

Servings: 4
Cooking Time: 25 Minutes
Ingredients:
- Pork Tenderloin
- ½ teaspoon smoked paprika
- ¼ teaspoon salt
- ¼ teaspoon garlic powder
- ½ teaspoon onion powder
- ⅛ teaspoon ginger
- 1 teaspoon extra-light olive oil
- ¾ pound pork tenderloin
- Dressing
- 3 tablespoons extra-light olive oil
- 2 tablespoons red wine vinegar
- 2 tablespoons Dijon mustard
- 1 tablespoon honey
- Salad
- ¼ sweet red bell pepper
- 1 large Granny Smith apple
- 8 cups shredded Napa cabbage

Directions:
1. Mix the tenderloin seasonings together with oil and rub all over surface of meat.
2. Place pork tenderloin in the air fryer basket and cook at 390°F (200°C) for 25minutes, until meat registers 130°F (55°C) on a meat thermometer.
3. Allow meat to rest while preparing salad and dressing.
4. In a jar, shake all dressing ingredients together until well mixed.
5. Cut the bell pepper into slivers, then core, quarter, and slice the apple crosswise.
6. In a large bowl, toss together the cabbage, bell pepper, apple, and dressing.
7. Divide salad mixture among 4 plates.
8. Slice pork tenderloin into ½-inch slices and divide among the 4 salads.
9. Serve with sweet potato or other vegetable chips.

Cinnamon Roasted Pumpkin

Servings: 2
Cooking Time: 25 Minutes
Ingredients:
- 1 lb pumpkin, halved crosswise and seeded
- 1 tsp coconut oil
- 1 tsp sugar
- ½ tsp ground nutmeg
- 1 tsp ground cinnamon

Directions:
1. Prepare the pumpkin by rubbing coconut oil on the cut sides. In a small bowl, combine sugar, nutmeg and cinnamon. Sprinkle over the pumpkin. Preheat air fryer to 325°F (160°C). Put the pumpkin in the greased frying basket, cut sides up. Bake until the squash is soft in the center, 15 minutes. Test with a knife to ensure softness. Serve.

Salt And Pepper Baked Potatoes

Cooking Time: 40 Minutes
Servings: 4
Ingredients:
- 1 to 2 tablespoons olive oil
- 4 medium russet potatoes (about 9 to 10 ounces each)
- salt and coarsely ground black pepper
- butter, sour cream, chopped fresh chives, scallions or bacon bits (optional)

Directions:
1. Preheat the air fryer to 400°F (205°C).
2. Rub the olive oil all over the potatoes and season them generously with salt and coarsely ground black pepper. Pierce all sides of the potatoes several times with the tines of a fork.
3. Air-fry for 40 minutes, turning the potatoes over halfway through the cooking time.
4. Serve the potatoes, split open with butter, sour cream, fresh chives, scallions or bacon bits.

Turkish Mutabal (eggplant Dip)

Servings: 2
Cooking Time: 40 Minutes
Ingredients:
- 1 medium eggplant
- 2 tbsp tahini
- 2 tbsp lemon juice
- 1 tsp garlic powder
- ¼ tsp sumac
- 1 tsp chopped parsley

Directions:
1. Preheat air fryer to 400°F (205°C). Place the eggplant in a pan and Roast for 30 minutes, turning once. Let cool for 5-10 minutes. Scoop out the flesh and place it in a bowl. Squeeze any excess water; discard the water. Mix the flesh, tahini, lemon juice, garlic, and sumac until well combined. Scatter with parsley and serve.

Roman Artichokes

Servings: 4
Cooking Time: 12 Minutes
Ingredients:
- 2 9-ounce box(es) frozen artichoke heart quarters, thawed
- 1½ tablespoons Olive oil
- 2 teaspoons Minced garlic
- 1 teaspoon Table salt
- Up to ½ teaspoon Red pepper flakes

Directions:
1. Preheat the air fryer to 400°F (205°C).
2. Gently toss the artichoke heart quarters, oil, garlic, salt, and red pepper flakes in a bowl until the quarters are well coated.
3. When the machine is at temperature, scrape the contents of the bowl into the basket. Spread the artichoke heart quarters out into as close to one layer as possible. Air-fry undisturbed for 8 minutes. Gently toss and rearrange the quarters so that any covered or touching parts are now exposed to the air currents, then air-fry undisturbed for 4 minutes more, until very crisp.
4. Gently pour the contents of the basket onto a wire rack. Cool for a few minutes before serving.

Tower Air Fryer Cookbook

Chapter 5: Vegetarians Recipes

Spring Veggie Empanadas

Servings: 4
Cooking Time: 75 Minutes

Ingredients:
- 10 empanada pastry discs
- 1 tbsp olive oil
- 1 shallot, minced
- 1 garlic clove, minced
- ½ cup whole milk
- 1 cup chopped broccoli
- ½ cup chopped cauliflower
- ½ cup diced carrots
- ¼ cup diced celery
- ⅛ tsp ground nutmeg
- 1 tsp cumin powder
- 1 tsp minced ginger
- 1 egg

Directions:
1. Melt the olive oil in a pot over medium heat. Stir in shallot and garlic and cook through for 1 minute. Next, add 1 tablespoon of flour and continue stirring. Whisk in milk, then lower the heat. After that, add broccoli, cauliflower, carrots, celery, cumin powder, pepper, ginger, and nutmeg. Cook for 2 minutes then remove from the heat. Allow to cool for 5 minutes.
2. Preheat air fryer to 350°F (175°C). Lightly flour a flat work surface and turn out the pastry discs. Scoop ¼ of the vegetables in the center of each circle. Whisk the egg and 1 teaspoon of water in a small bowl and brush the entire edge of the circle with the egg wash and fold the dough over the filling into a half-moon shape. Crimp the edge with a fork to seal. Arrange the patties in a single layer in the frying basket and bake for 12 minutes. Flip the patties and bake for another 10 to 12 minutes until the outside crust is golden. Serve immediately and enjoy.

Sesame Orange Tofu With Snow Peas

Servings: 4
Cooking Time: 40 Minutes

Ingredients:
- 14 oz tofu, cubed
- 1 tbsp tamari
- 1 tsp olive oil
- 1 tsp sesame oil
- 1 ½ tbsp cornstarch, divided
- ½ tsp salt
- ¼ tsp garlic powder
- 1 cup snow peas
- ½ cup orange juice
- ¼ cup vegetable broth
- 1 orange, zested
- 1 garlic clove, minced
- ¼ tsp ground ginger
- 2 scallions, chopped
- 1 tbsp sesame seeds
- 2 cups cooked jasmine rice
- 2 tbsp chopped parsley

Directions:
1. Preheat air fryer to 400°F (205°C). Combine tofu, tamari, olive oil, and sesame oil in a large bowl until tofu is coated. Add in 1 tablespoon cornstarch, salt, and garlic powder and toss. Arrange the tofu on the frying basket. Air Fry for 5 minutes, then shake the basket. Add snow peas and Air Fry for 5 minutes. Place tofu mixture in a bowl.
2. Bring the orange juice, vegetable broth, orange zest, garlic, and ginger to a boil over medium heat in a small saucepan. Whisk the rest of the cornstarch and 1 tablespoon water in a small bowl to make a slurry. Pour the slurry into the saucepan and constantly stir for 2 minutes until the sauce has thickened. Let off the heat for 2 minutes. Pour the orange sauce, scallions, and sesame seeds in the bowl with the tofu and stir to coat. Serve with jasmine rice sprinkled with parsley. Enjoy!

Lentil Burritos With Cilantro Chutney

Servings: 4
Cooking Time: 30 Minutes

Ingredients:
- 1 cup cilantro chutney
- 1 lb cooked potatoes, mashed
- 2 tsp sunflower oil
- 3 garlic cloves, minced
- 1 ½ tbsp fresh lime juice
- 1 ½ tsp cumin powder
- 1 tsp onion powder
- 1 tsp coriander powder
- Salt to taste
- ½ tsp turmeric
- ¼ tsp cayenne powder
- 4 large flour tortillas
- 1 cup cooked lentils
- ½ cup shredded cabbage
- ¼ cup minced red onions

Directions:
1. Preheat air fryer to 390°F (200°C). Place the mashed potatoes, sunflower oil, garlic, lime, cumin, onion powder, coriander, salt, turmeric, and cayenne in a large bowl. Stir well until combined. Lay the tortillas out flat on the counter. In the middle of each, distribute the potato filling. Add some of the lentils, cabbage, and red onions on top of the potatoes. Close the wraps by folding the bottom of the tortillas up and over the filling, then folding the sides in, then roll the bottom up to form a burrito. Place the wraps in the greased frying basket, seam side down. Air Fry for 6-8 minutes, flipping once until golden and crispy. Serve topped with cilantro chutney.

Spinach & Brie Frittata

Servings: 4
Cooking Time: 25 Minutes

Ingredients:
- 5 eggs
- Salt and pepper to taste
- ½ cup baby spinach
- 1 shallot, diced
- 4 oz brie cheese, cubed
- 1 tomato, sliced

Directions:
1. Preheat air fryer to 320ºF. Whisk all ingredients, except for the tomato slices, in a bowl. Transfer to a baking pan greased with olive oil and top with tomato slices. Place the pan in the frying basket and Bake for 14 minutes. Let cool for 5 minutes before slicing. Serve and enjoy!

Balsamic Caprese Hasselback

Servings: 4
Cooking Time: 15 Minutes
Ingredients:
- 4 tomatoes
- 12 fresh basil leaves
- 1 ball fresh mozzarella
- Salt and pepper to taste
- 1 tbsp olive oil
- 2 tsp balsamic vinegar
- 1 tbsp basil, torn

Directions:
1. Preheat air fryer to 325°F. Remove the bottoms from the tomatoes to create a flat surface. Make 4 even slices on each tomato, 3/4 of the way down. Slice the mozzarella and the cut into 12 pieces. Stuff 1 basil leaf and a piece of mozzarella into each slice. Sprinkle with salt and pepper. Place the stuffed tomatoes in the frying basket and Air Fry for 3 minutes. Transfer to a large serving plate. Drizzle with olive oil and balsamic vinegar and scatter the basil over. Serve and enjoy!

Cheddar Bean Taquitos

Servings: 4
Cooking Time: 25 Minutes
Ingredients:
- 1 cup refried beans
- 2 cups cheddar shreds
- ½ jalapeño pepper, minced
- ¼ chopped white onion
- 1 tsp oregano
- 15 soft corn tortillas

Directions:
1. Preheat air fryer at 350°F. Spread refried beans, jalapeño pepper, white onion, oregano and cheddar shreds down the center of each corn tortilla. Roll each tortilla tightly. Place tacos, seam side down, in the frying basket, and Air Fry for 4 minutes. Serve immediately.

Rice & Bean Burritos

Servings: 4
Cooking Time: 20 Minutes
Ingredients:
- 1 bell pepper, sliced
- ½ red onion, thinly sliced
- 2 garlic cloves, peeled
- 1 tbsp olive oil
- 1 cup cooked brown rice
- 1 can pinto beans
- ½ tsp salt
- ¼ tsp chili powder
- ¼ tsp ground cumin
- ¼ tsp smoked paprika
- 1 tbsp lime juice
- 4 tortillas
- 2 tsp grated Parmesan cheese
- 1 avocado, diced
- 4 tbsp salsa
- 2 tbsp chopped cilantro

Directions:
1. Preheat air fryer to 400°F (205°C). Combine bell pepper, onion, garlic, and olive oil. Place in the frying basket and Roast for 5 minutes. Shake and roast for another 5 minutes.
2. Remove the garlic from the basket and mince finely. Add to a large bowl along with brown rice, pinto beans, salt, chili powder, cumin, paprika, and lime juice. Divide the roasted vegetable mixture between the tortillas. Top with rice mixture, Parmesan, avocado, cilantro, and salsa. Fold in the sides, then roll the tortillas over the filling. Serve.

Black Bean Stuffed Potato Boats

Servings: 4
Cooking Time: 55 Minutes
Ingredients:
- 4 russets potatoes
- 1 cup chipotle mayonnaise
- 1 cup canned black beans
- 2 tomatoes, chopped
- 1 scallion, chopped
- 1/3 cup chopped cilantro
- 1 poblano chile, minced
- 1 avocado, diced

Directions:
1. Preheat air fryer to 390°F (200°C). Clean the potatoes, poke with a fork, and spray with oil. Put in the air fryer and Bake for 30 minutes or until softened.
2. Heat the beans in a pan over medium heat. Put the potatoes on a plate and cut them across the top. Open them with a fork so you can stuff them. Top each potato with chipotle mayonnaise, beans, tomatoes, scallions, cilantro, poblano chile, and avocado. Serve immediately.

Crispy Apple Fries With Caramel Sauce

Servings: 4
Cooking Time: 15 Minutes
Ingredients:
- 4 medium apples, cored
- ¼ tsp cinnamon
- ¼ tsp nutmeg
- 1 cup caramel sauce

Directions:
1. Preheat air fryer to 350°F (175°C). Slice the apples to a 1/3-inch thickness for a crunchy chip. Place in a large bowl and sprinkle with cinnamon and nutmeg. Place the slices in the air fryer basket. Bake for 6 minutes. Shake the basket, then cook for another 4 minutes or until crunchy. Serve drizzled with caramel sauce and enjoy!

Vegan Buddha Bowls(2)

Servings: 4
Cooking Time: 20 Minutes
Ingredients:
- 1 carrot, peeled and julienned
- ½ onion, sliced into half-moons
- ¼ cup apple cider vinegar
- ½ tsp ground ginger
- ⅛ tsp cayenne pepper
- 1 parsnip, diced
- 1 tsp avocado oil
- 4 oz extra-firm tofu, cubed
- ½ tsp five-spice powder

- ½ tsp chili powder
- 2 tsp fresh lime zest
- 1 cup fresh arugula
- ½ cup cooked quinoa
- 2 tbsp canned kidney beans
- 2 tbsp canned sweetcorn
- 1 avocado, diced
- 2 tbsp pine nuts

Directions:
1. Preheat air fryer to 350°F. Combine carrot, vinegar, ginger, and cayenne in a bowl. In another bowl, combine onion, parsnip, and avocado oil. In a third bowl, mix the tofu, five-spice powder, and chili powder.
2. Place the onion mixture in the greased basket. Air Fry for 6 minutes. Stir in tofu mixture and cook for 8 more minutes. Mix in lime zest. Divide arugula, cooked quinoa, kidney beans, sweetcorn, drained carrots, avocado, pine nuts, and tofu mixture between 2 bowls. Serve.

Tomato & Squash Stuffed Mushrooms

Servings: 2
Cooking Time: 15 Minutes
Ingredients:
- 12 whole white button mushrooms
- 3 tsp olive oil
- 2 tbsp diced zucchini
- 1 tsp soy sauce
- ¼ tsp salt
- 2 tbsp tomato paste
- 1 tbsp chopped parsley

Directions:
1. Preheat air fryer to 350°F. Remove the stems from the mushrooms. Chop the stems finely and set in a bowl. Brush 1 tsp of olive oil around the top ridge of mushroom caps. To the bowl of the stem, add all ingredients, except for parsley, and mix. Divide and press mixture into tops of mushroom caps. Place the mushrooms in the frying basket and Air Fry for 5 minutes. Top with parsley. Serve.

Pinto Taquitos

Servings: 4
Cooking Time: 8 Minutes
Ingredients:
- 12 corn tortillas (6- to 7-inch size)
- Filling
- ½ cup refried pinto beans
- ½ cup grated sharp Cheddar or Pepper Jack cheese
- ¼ cup corn kernels (if frozen, measure after thawing and draining)
- 2 tablespoons chopped green onion
- 2 tablespoons chopped jalapeño pepper (seeds and ribs removed before chopping)
- ½ teaspoon lime juice
- ½ teaspoon chile powder, plus extra for dusting
- ½ teaspoon cumin
- ½ teaspoon garlic powder
- oil for misting or cooking spray
- salsa, sour cream, or guacamole for dipping

Directions:
1. Mix together all filling Ingredients.
2. Warm refrigerated tortillas for easier rolling. (Wrap in damp paper towels and microwave for 30 to 60 seconds.)
3. Working with one at a time, place 1 tablespoon of filling on tortilla and roll up. Spray with oil or cooking spray and dust outside with chile powder to taste.
4. Place 6 taquitos in air fryer basket (4 on bottom layer, 2 stacked crosswise on top). Cook at 390°F (200°C) for 8 minutes, until crispy and brown.
5. Repeat step 4 to cook remaining taquitos.
6. Serve plain or with salsa, sour cream, or guacamole for dipping.

Pizza Portobello Mushrooms

Servings: 2
Cooking Time: 18 Minutes
Ingredients:
- 2 portobello mushroom caps, gills removed (see Figure 13-1)
- 1 teaspoon extra-virgin olive oil
- ¼ cup diced onion
- 1 teaspoon minced garlic
- 1 medium zucchini, shredded
- 1 teaspoon dried oregano
- ½ teaspoon black pepper
- ¼ teaspoon salt
- ⅓ cup marinara sauce
- ¼ cup shredded part-skim mozzarella cheese
- ¼ teaspoon red pepper flakes
- 2 tablespoons Parmesan cheese
- 2 tablespoons chopped basil

Directions:
1. Preheat the air fryer to 370°F (185°C).
2. Lightly spray the mushrooms with an olive oil mist and place into the air fryer to cook for 10 minutes, cap side up.
3. Add the olive oil to a pan and sauté the onion and garlic together for about 2 to 4 minutes. Stir in the zucchini, oregano, pepper, and salt, and continue to cook. When the zucchini has cooked down (usually about 4 to 6 minutes), add in the marinara sauce. Remove from the heat and stir in the mozzarella cheese.
4. Remove the mushrooms from the air fryer basket when cooking completes. Reset the temperature to 350°F (175°C).
5. Using a spoon, carefully stuff the mushrooms with the zucchini marinara mixture.
6. Return the stuffed mushrooms to the air fryer basket and cook for 5 to 8 minutes, or until the cheese is lightly browned. You should be able to easily insert a fork into the mushrooms when they're cooked.
7. Remove the mushrooms and sprinkle the red pepper flakes, Parmesan cheese, and fresh basil over the top.
8. Serve warm.

Broccoli Cheddar Stuffed Potatoes

Servings: 2
Cooking Time: 42 Minutes
Ingredients:
- 2 large russet potatoes, scrubbed
- 1 tablespoon olive oil
- salt and freshly ground black pepper
- 2 tablespoons butter
- ¼ cup sour cream
- 3 tablespoons half-and-half (or milk)

- 1¼ cups grated Cheddar cheese, divided
- ¾ teaspoon salt
- freshly ground black pepper
- 1 cup frozen baby broccoli florets, thawed and drained

Directions:
1. Preheat the air fryer to 400°F (205°C).
2. Rub the potatoes all over with olive oil and season generously with salt and freshly ground black pepper. Transfer the potatoes into the air fryer basket and air-fry for 30 minutes, turning the potatoes over halfway through the cooking process.
3. Remove the potatoes from the air fryer and let them rest for 5 minutes. Cut a large oval out of the top of both potatoes. Leaving half an inch of potato flesh around the edge of the potato, scoop the inside of the potato out and into a large bowl to prepare the potato filling. Mash the scooped potato filling with a fork and add the butter, sour cream, half-and-half, 1 cup of the grated Cheddar cheese, salt and pepper to taste. Mix well and then fold in the broccoli florets.
4. Stuff the hollowed out potato shells with the potato and broccoli mixture. Mound the filling high in the potatoes – you will have more filling than room in the potato shells.
5. Transfer the stuffed potatoes back to the air fryer basket and air-fry at 360°F (1805°C) for 10 minutes. Sprinkle the remaining Cheddar cheese on top of each stuffed potato, lower the heat to 330°F (165°C) and air-fry for an additional minute or two to melt cheese.

Italian-style Fried Cauliflower

Servings: 4
Cooking Time: 35 Minutes
Ingredients:
- 2 eggs
- 1/3 cup all-purpose flour
- ½ tsp Italian seasoning
- ½ cup bread crumbs
- 1 tsp garlic powder
- 3 tsp grated Parmesan cheese
- Salt and pepper to taste
- 1 head cauliflower, cut into florets
- ½ tsp ground coriander

Directions:
1. Preheat air fryer to 370°F (185°C). Set out 3 small bowls. In the first, mix the flour with Italian seasoning. In the second, beat the eggs. In the third bowl, combine the crumbs, garlic, Parmesan, ground coriander, salt, and pepper.
2. Dip the cauliflower in the flour, then dredge in egg, and finally in the bread crumb mixture. Place a batch of cauliflower in the greased frying basket and spray with cooking oil. Bake for 10-12 minutes, shaking once until golden. Serve warm and enjoy!

Spicy Sesame Tempeh Slaw With Peanut Dressing

Servings: 2
Cooking Time: 8 Minutes
Ingredients:
- 2 cups hot water
- 1 teaspoon salt
- 8 ounces tempeh, sliced into 1-inch-long pieces
- 2 tablespoons low-sodium soy sauce
- 2 tablespoons rice vinegar
- 1 tablespoon filtered water
- 2 teaspoons sesame oil
- ½ teaspoon fresh ginger
- 1 clove garlic, minced
- ¼ teaspoon black pepper
- ½ jalapeño, sliced
- 4 cups cabbage slaw
- 4 tablespoons Peanut Dressing (see the following recipe)
- 2 tablespoons fresh chopped cilantro
- 2 tablespoons chopped peanuts

Directions:
1. Mix the hot water with the salt and pour over the tempeh in a glass bowl. Stir and cover with a towel for 10 minutes.
2. Discard the water and leave the tempeh in the bowl.
3. In a medium bowl, mix the soy sauce, rice vinegar, filtered water, sesame oil, ginger, garlic, pepper, and jalapeño. Pour over the tempeh and cover with a towel. Place in the refrigerator to marinate for at least 2 hours.
4. Preheat the air fryer to 370°F (185°C). Remove the tempeh from the bowl and discard the remaining marinade.
5. Liberally spray the metal trivet that goes into the air fryer basket and place the tempeh on top of the trivet.
6. Cook for 4 minutes, flip, and cook another 4 minutes.
7. In a large bowl, mix the cabbage slaw with the Peanut Dressing and toss in the cilantro and chopped peanuts.
8. Portion onto 4 plates and place the cooked tempeh on top when cooking completes. Serve immediately.

Mexican Twice Air-fried Sweet Potatoes

Servings: 2
Cooking Time: 42 Minutes
Ingredients:
- 2 large sweet potatoes
- olive oil
- salt and freshly ground black pepper
- ⅓ cup diced red onion
- ⅓ cup diced red bell pepper
- ½ cup canned black beans, drained and rinsed
- ½ cup corn kernels, fresh or frozen
- ½ teaspoon chili powder
- 1½ cups grated pepper jack cheese, divided
- Jalapeño peppers, sliced

Directions:
1. Preheat the air fryer to 400°F (205°C).
2. Rub the outside of the sweet potatoes with olive oil and season with salt and freshly ground black pepper. Transfer the potatoes into the air fryer basket and air-fry at 400°F (205°C) for 30 minutes, rotating the potatoes a few times during the cooking process.
3. While the potatoes are air-frying, start the potato filling. Preheat a large sauté pan over medium heat on the stovetop. Add the onion and pepper and sauté for a few minutes, until the vegetables start to soften. Add the black beans, corn, and chili powder and sauté for another 3 minutes. Set the mixture aside.
4. Remove the sweet potatoes from the air fryer and let them rest for 5 minutes. Slice off one inch of the flattest side of both potatoes. Scrape the potato flesh out of the potatoes, leaving half an inch of potato flesh around the edge of the potato. Place all the potato flesh into a large bowl and mash

it with a fork. Add the black bean mixture and 1 cup of the pepper jack cheese to the mashed sweet potatoes. Season with salt and freshly ground black pepper and mix well. Stuff the hollowed out potato shells with the black bean and sweet potato mixture, mounding the filling high in the potatoes.

5. Transfer the stuffed potatoes back into the air fryer basket and air-fry at 370°F (185°C) for 10 minutes. Sprinkle the remaining cheese on top of each stuffed potato, lower the heat to 340°F (170°C) and air-fry for an additional 2 minutes to melt the cheese. Top with a couple slices of Jalapeño pepper and serve warm with a green salad.

Veggie-stuffed Bell Peppers

Servings: 4
Cooking Time: 40 Minutes
Ingredients:
- ½ cup canned fire-roasted diced tomatoes, including juice
- 2 red bell peppers
- 4 tsp olive oil
- ½ yellow onion, diced
- 1 zucchini, diced
- ¾ cup chopped mushrooms
- ¼ cup tomato sauce
- 2 tsp Italian seasoning
- ¼ tsp smoked paprika
- Salt and pepper to taste

Directions:
1. Cut bell peppers in half from top to bottom and discard the seeds. Brush inside and tops of the bell peppers with some olive oil. Set aside. Warm the remaining olive oil in a skillet over medium heat. Stir-fry the onion, zucchini, and mushrooms for 5 minutes until the onions are tender. Combine tomatoes and their juice, tomato sauce, Italian seasoning, paprika, salt, and pepper in a bowl.
2. Preheat air fryer to 350°F. Divide both mixtures between bell pepper halves. Place bell pepper halves in the frying basket and Air Fry for 8 minutes. Serve immediately.

Quinoa Green Pizza

Servings: 2
Cooking Time: 25 Minutes
Ingredients:
- ¾ cup quinoa flour
- ½ tsp dried basil
- ½ tsp dried oregano
- 1 tbsp apple cider vinegar
- 1/3 cup ricotta cheese
- 2/3 cup chopped broccoli
- ½ tsp garlic powder

Directions:
1. Preheat air fryer to 350°F (175°C). Whisk quinoa flour, basil, oregano, apple cider vinegar, and ½ cup of water until smooth. Set aside. Cut 2 pieces of parchment paper. Place the quinoa mixture on one paper, top with another piece, and flatten to create a crust. Discard the top piece of paper. Bake for 5 minutes, turn and discard the other piece of paper. Spread the ricotta cheese over the crust, scatter with broccoli, and sprinkle with garlic. Grill at 400°F for 5 minutes until golden brown. Serve warm.

Healthy Living Mushroom Enchiladas

Servings: 4
Cooking Time: 40 Minutes
Ingredients:
- 2 cups sliced mushrooms
- ½ onion, thinly sliced
- 2 garlic cloves, minced
- 1 tbsp olive oil
- 10 oz spinach, chopped
- ½ tsp ground cumin
- 1 tbsp dried oregano
- 1 tsp chili powder
- ¼ cup grated feta cheese
- ¼ tsp red pepper flakes
- 1 cup grated mozzarella cheese
- 1 cup sour cream
- 2 tbsp mayonnaise
- Juice of 1 lime
- Salt and pepper to taste
- 8 corn tortillas
- 1 jalapeño pepper, diced
- ¼ cup chopped cilantro

Directions:
1. Preheat air fryer to 400°F (205°C). Combine mushrooms, onion, oregano, garlic, chili powder, olive oil, and salt in a small bowl until well coated. Transfer to the greased frying basket. Cook for 5 minutes, then shake the basket. Cook for another 3 to 4 minutes, then transfer to a medium bowl. Wipe out the frying basket. Take the garlic cloves from the mushroom mixture and finely mince them. Return half of the garlic to the bowl with the mushrooms. Stir in spinach, cumin, red pepper flakes, and ½ cup of mozzarella. Place the other half of the minced garlic in a small bowl along with sour cream, mayonnaise, feta, the rest of the mozzarella, lime juice, and black pepper.
2. To prepare the enchiladas, spoon 2 tablespoons of mushroom mixture in the center of each tortilla. Roll the tortilla and place it seam-side down in the baking dish. Repeat for the rest of the tortillas. Top with sour cream mixture and garnish with jalapenos. Place the dish in the frying basket and bake for 20 minutes until heated through and just brown on top. Top with cilantro. Serve.

Charred Cauliflower Tacos

Servings: 4
Cooking Time: 10 Minutes
Ingredients:
- 1 head cauliflower, washed and cut into florets
- 2 tablespoons avocado oil
- 2 teaspoons taco seasoning
- 1 medium avocado
- ½ teaspoon garlic powder
- ¼ teaspoon black pepper
- ¼ teaspoon salt
- 2 tablespoons chopped red onion
- 2 teaspoons fresh squeezed lime juice
- ¼ cup chopped cilantro
- Eight 6-inch corn tortillas
- ½ cup cooked corn
- ½ cup shredded purple cabbage

Directions:

1. Preheat the air fryer to 390°F (200°C).
2. In a large bowl, toss the cauliflower with the avocado oil and taco seasoning. Set the metal trivet inside the air fryer basket and liberally spray with olive oil.
3. Place the cauliflower onto the trivet and cook for 10 minutes, shaking every 3 minutes to allow for an even char.
4. While the cauliflower is cooking, prepare the avocado sauce. In a medium bowl, mash the avocado; then mix in the garlic powder, pepper, salt, and onion. Stir in the lime juice and cilantro; set aside.
5. Remove the cauliflower from the air fryer basket.
6. Place 1 tablespoon of avocado sauce in the middle of a tortilla, and top with corn, cabbage, and charred cauliflower. Repeat with the remaining tortillas. Serve immediately.

Pizza Eggplant Rounds

Servings: 4
Cooking Time: 25 Minutes
Ingredients:
- 3 tsp olive oil
- ¼ cup diced onion
- ½ tsp garlic powder
- ½ tsp dried oregano
- ½ cup diced mushrooms
- ½ cup marinara sauce
- 1 eggplant, sliced
- 1 tsp salt
- 1 cup shredded mozzarella
- 2 tbsp Parmesan cheese
- ¼ cup chopped basil

Directions:
1. Warm 2 tsp of olive oil in a skillet over medium heat. Add in onion and mushrooms and cook for 5 minutes until the onions are translucent. Stir in marinara sauce, then add oregano and garlic powder. Turn the heat off.
2. Preheat air fryer at 375°F. Rub the remaining olive oil over both sides of the eggplant circles. Lay circles on a large plate and sprinkle with salt and black pepper. Top each circle with the marinara sauce mixture and shredded mozzarella and Parmesan cheese. Place eggplant circles in the frying basket and Bake for 5 minutes. Scatter with the basil and serve.

Fried Potatoes With Bell Peppers

Servings: 4
Cooking Time: 30 Minutes
Ingredients:
- 3 russet potatoes, cubed
- 1 tbsp canola oil
- 1 tbsp olive oil
- 1 tsp paprika
- Salt and pepper to taste
- 1 chopped shallot
- ½ chopped red bell peppers
- ½ diced yellow bell peppers

Directions:
1. Preheat air fryer to 370°F (185°C). Whisk the canola oil, olive oil, paprika, salt, and pepper in a bowl. Toss in the potatoes to coat. Place the potatoes in the air fryer and Bake for 20 minutes, shaking the basket periodically. Top the potatoes with shallot and bell peppers and cook for an additional 3-4 minutes or until the potatoes are cooked through and the peppers are soft. Serve warm.

Spinach And Cheese Calzone

Servings: 2
Cooking Time: 10 Minutes
Ingredients:
- ⅔ cup frozen chopped spinach, thawed
- 1 cup grated mozzarella cheese
- 1 cup ricotta cheese
- ½ teaspoon Italian seasoning
- ½ teaspoon salt
- freshly ground black pepper
- 1 store-bought or homemade pizza dough* (about 12 to 16 ounces)
- 2 tablespoons olive oil
- pizza or marinara sauce (optional)

Directions:
1. Drain and squeeze all the water out of the thawed spinach and set it aside. Mix the mozzarella cheese, ricotta cheese, Italian seasoning, salt and freshly ground black pepper together in a bowl. Stir in the chopped spinach.
2. Divide the dough in half. With floured hands or on a floured surface, stretch or roll one half of the dough into a 10-inch circle. Spread half of the cheese and spinach mixture on half of the dough, leaving about one inch of dough empty around the edge.
3. Fold the other half of the dough over the cheese mixture, almost to the edge of the bottom dough to form a half moon. Fold the bottom edge of dough up over the top edge and crimp the dough around the edges in order to make the crust and seal the calzone. Brush the dough with olive oil. Repeat with the second half of dough to make the second calzone.
4. Preheat the air fryer to 360°F (180°C).
5. Brush or spray the air fryer basket with olive oil. Air-fry the calzones one at a time for 10 minutes, flipping the calzone over half way through. Serve with warm pizza or marinara sauce if desired.

Meatless Kimchi Bowls

Servings: 4
Cooking Time: 20 Minutes
Ingredients:
- 2 cups canned chickpeas
- 1 carrot, julienned
- 6 scallions, sliced
- 1 zucchini, diced
- 2 tbsp coconut aminos
- 2 tsp sesame oil
- 1 tsp rice vinegar
- 2 tsp granulated sugar
- 1 tbsp gochujang
- ¼ tsp salt
- ½ cup kimchi
- 2 tsp roasted sesame seeds

Directions:
1. Preheat air fryer to 350°F. Combine all ingredients, except for the kimchi, 2 scallions, and sesame seeds, in a baking pan. Place the pan in the frying basket and Air Fry for 6 minutes. Toss in kimchi and cook for 2 more minutes. Divide between 2 bowls and garnish with the remaining scallions and sesame seeds. Serve immediately.

Thai Peanut Veggie Burgers

Servings: 6
Cooking Time: 14 Minutes
Ingredients:
- One 15.5-ounce can cannellini beans
- 1 teaspoon minced garlic
- ¼ cup chopped onion
- 1 Thai chili pepper, sliced
- 2 tablespoons natural peanut butter
- ½ teaspoon black pepper
- ½ teaspoon salt
- ⅓ cup all-purpose flour (optional)
- ½ cup cooked quinoa
- 1 large carrot, grated
- 1 cup shredded red cabbage
- ¼ cup peanut dressing
- ¼ cup chopped cilantro
- 6 Hawaiian rolls
- 6 butterleaf lettuce leaves

Directions:
1. Preheat the air fryer to 350°F (175°C).
2. To a blender or food processor fitted with a metal blade, add the beans, garlic, onion, chili pepper, peanut butter, pepper, and salt. Pulse for 5 to 10 seconds. Do not over process. The mixture should be coarse, not smooth.
3. Remove from the blender or food processor and spoon into a large bowl. Mix in the cooked quinoa and carrots. At this point, the mixture should begin to hold together to form small patties. If the dough appears to be too sticky (meaning you likely processed a little too long), add the flour to hold the patties together.
4. Using a large spoon, form 8 equal patties out of the batter.
5. Liberally spray a metal trivet with olive oil spray and set in the air fryer basket. Place the patties into the basket, leaving enough space to be able to turn them with a spatula.
6. Cook for 7 minutes, flip, and cook another 7 minutes.
7. Remove from the heat and repeat with additional patties.
8. To serve, place the red cabbage in a bowl and toss with peanut dressing and cilantro. Place the veggie burger on a bun, and top with a slice of lettuce and cabbage slaw.

Spicy Vegetable And Tofu Shake Fry

Servings: 4
Cooking Time: 17 Minutes
Ingredients:
- 4 teaspoons canola oil, divided
- 2 tablespoons rice wine vinegar
- 1 tablespoon sriracha chili sauce
- ¼ cup soy sauce*
- ½ teaspoon toasted sesame oil
- 1 teaspoon minced garlic
- 1 tablespoon minced fresh ginger
- 8 ounces extra firm tofu
- ½ cup vegetable stock or water
- 1 tablespoon honey
- 1 tablespoon cornstarch
- ½ red onion, chopped
- 1 red or yellow bell pepper, chopped
- 1 cup green beans, cut into 2-inch lengths
- 4 ounces mushrooms, sliced
- 2 scallions, sliced
- 2 tablespoons fresh cilantro leaves
- 2 teaspoons toasted sesame seeds

Directions:
1. Combine 1 tablespoon of the oil, vinegar, sriracha sauce, soy sauce, sesame oil, garlic and ginger in a small bowl. Cut the tofu into bite-sized cubes and toss the tofu in with the marinade while you prepare the other vegetables. When you are ready to start cooking, remove the tofu from the marinade and set it aside. Add the water, honey and cornstarch to the marinade and bring to a simmer on the stovetop, just until the sauce thickens. Set the sauce aside.
2. Preheat the air fryer to 400°F (205°C).
3. Toss the onion, pepper, green beans and mushrooms in a bowl with a little canola oil and season with salt. Air-fry at 400°F (205°C) for 11 minutes, shaking the basket and tossing the vegetables every few minutes. When the vegetables are cooked to your preferred doneness, remove them from the air fryer and set aside.
4. Add the tofu to the air fryer basket and air-fry at 400°F (205°C) for 6 minutes, shaking the basket a few times during the cooking process. Add the vegetables back to the basket and air-fry for another minute. Transfer the vegetables and tofu to a large bowl, add the scallions and cilantro leaves and toss with the sauce. Serve over rice with sesame seeds sprinkled on top.

Italian Stuffed Bell Peppers

Servings: 4
Cooking Time: 75 Minutes
Ingredients:
- 4 green and red bell peppers, tops and insides discarded
- 2 russet potatoes, scrubbed and perforated with a fork
- 2 tsp olive oil
- 2 Italian sausages, cubed
- 2 tbsp milk
- 2 tbsp yogurt
- 1 tsp olive oil
- 1 tbsp Italian seasoning
- Salt and pepper to taste
- ¼ cup canned corn kernels
- ½ cup mozzarella shreds
- 2 tsp chopped parsley
- 1 cup bechamel sauce

Directions:
1. Preheat air fryer at 400ºF. Rub olive oil over both potatoes and sprinkle with salt and pepper. Place them in the frying basket and Bake for 45 minutes, flipping at 30 minutes mark. Let cool onto a cutting board for 5 minutes until cool enough to handle. Scoop out cooled potato into a bowl. Discard skins.
2. Place Italian sausages in the frying basket and Air Fry for 2 minutes. Using the back of a fork, mash cooked potatoes, yogurt, milk, olive oil, Italian seasoning, salt, and pepper until smooth. Toss in cooked sausages, corn, and mozzarella cheese. Stuff bell peppers with the potato mixture. Place bell peppers in the frying basket and Bake for 10 minutes. Serve immediately sprinkled with parsley and bechamel sauce on side.

Fake Shepherd's Pie

Servings: 6
Cooking Time: 40 Minutes
Ingredients:
- ½ head cauliflower, cut into florets
- 1 sweet potato, diced
- 1 tbsp olive oil
- ¼ cup cheddar shreds
- 2 tbsp milk
- Salt and pepper to taste
- 2 tsp avocado oil
- 1 cup beefless grounds
- ½ onion, diced
- 2 cloves garlic, minced
- 1 carrot, diced
- ½ cup green peas
- 1 stalk celery, diced
- 2/3 cup tomato sauce
- 1 tsp chopped rosemary
- 1 tsp thyme leaves

Directions:
1. Place cauliflower and sweet potato in a pot of salted boiling water over medium heat and simmer for 7 minutes until fork tender. Strain and transfer to a bowl. Put in avocado oil, cheddar, milk, salt and pepper. Mash until smooth.
2. Warm olive oil in a skillet over medium-high heat and stir in beefless grounds and vegetables and stir-fry for 4 minutes until veggies are tender. Stir in tomato sauce, rosemary, thyme, salt, and black pepper. Set aside.
3. Preheat air fryer to 350ºF. Spoon filling into a round cake pan lightly greased with olive oil and cover with the topping. Using the tines of a fork, run shallow lines in the top of cauliflower for a decorative touch. Place cake pan in the frying basket and Air Fry for 12 minutes. Let sit for 10 minutes before serving.

Vegetable Couscous

Servings: 4
Cooking Time: 10 Minutes
Ingredients:
- 4 ounces white mushrooms, sliced
- ½ medium green bell pepper, julienned
- 1 cup cubed zucchini
- ¼ small onion, slivered
- 1 stalk celery, thinly sliced
- ¼ teaspoon ground coriander
- ¼ teaspoon ground cumin
- salt and pepper
- 1 tablespoon olive oil
- Couscous
- ¾ cup uncooked couscous
- 1 cup vegetable broth or water
- ½ teaspoon salt (omit if using salted broth)

Directions:
1. Combine all vegetables in large bowl. Sprinkle with coriander, cumin, and salt and pepper to taste. Stir well, add olive oil, and stir again to coat vegetables evenly.
2. Place vegetables in air fryer basket and cook at 390ºF (200ºC) for 5minutes. Stir and cook for 5 more minutes, until tender.
3. While vegetables are cooking, prepare the couscous: Place broth or water and salt in large saucepan. Heat to boiling, stir in couscous, cover, and remove from heat.
4. Let couscous sit for 5minutes, stir in cooked vegetables, and serve hot.

Caprese-style Sandwiches

Servings: 2
Cooking Time: 20 Minutes
Ingredients:
- 2 tbsp balsamic vinegar
- 4 sandwich bread slices
- 2 oz mozzarella shreds
- 3 tbsp pesto sauce
- 2 tomatoes, sliced
- 8 basil leaves
- 8 baby spinach leaves
- 2 tbsp olive oil

Directions:
1. Preheat air fryer at 350ºF. Drizzle balsamic vinegar on the bottom of bread slices and smear with pesto sauce. Then, layer mozzarella cheese, tomatoes, baby spinach leaves and basil leaves on top. Add top bread slices. Rub the outside top and bottom of each sandwich with olive oil. Place them in the frying basket and Bake for 5 minutes, flipping once. Serve right away.

Mushroom Lasagna

Servings: 4
Cooking Time: 40 Minutes
Ingredients:
- 2 tbsp olive oil
- 1 zucchini, diced
- ½ cup diced mushrooms
- ¼ cup diced onion
- 1 cup marinara sauce
- 1 cup ricotta cheese
- 1/3 cup grated Parmesan
- 1 egg
- 2 tsp Italian seasoning
- 2 tbsp fresh basil, chopped
- ½ tsp thyme
- 1 tbsp red pepper flakes
- ½ tsp salt
- 5 lasagna noodle sheets
- 1 cup grated mozzarella

Directions:
1. Heat the oil in a skillet over medium heat. Add zucchini, mushrooms, 1 tbsp of basil, thyme, red pepper flakes and onion and cook for 4 minutes until the veggies are tender. Toss in marinara sauce, and bring it to a bowl. Then, low the heat and simmer for 3 minutes.
2. Preheat air fryer at 375ºF. Combine ricotta cheese, Parmesan cheese, egg, Italian seasoning, and salt in a bowl. Spoon ¼ of the veggie mixture into a cake pan. Add a layer of lasagna noodles on top, breaking apart noodles first to fit pan. Then, top with 1/3 of ricotta mixture and ¼ of mozzarella cheese. Repeat the layer 2 more times, finishing with mozzarella cheese on top. Cover cake pan with aluminum foil.
3. Place cake pan in the frying basket and Bake for 12 minutes. Remove the foil and cook for 3 more minutes. Let rest for 10 minutes before slicing. Serve immediately sprinkled with the remaining fresh basil.

Pinto Bean Casserole

Servings: 2
Cooking Time: 15 Minutes
Ingredients:
- 1 can pinto beans
- ¼ cup tomato sauce
- 2 tbsp cornstarch
- 2 garlic cloves, minced
- ½ tsp dried oregano
- ½ tsp cumin
- 1 tsp smoked paprika
- Salt and pepper to taste

Directions:
1. Preheat air fryer to 390°F (200°C). Stir the beans, tomato sauce, cornstarch, garlic, oregano, cumin, smoked paprika, salt, and pepper in a bowl until combined. Pour the bean mix into a greased baking pan. Bake in the fryer for 4 minutes. Remove, stir, and Bake for 4 minutes or until the mix is thick and heated through. Serve hot.

Vegan French Toast

Servings: 4
Cooking Time: 15 Minutes
Ingredients:
- 1 ripe banana, mashed
- ¼ cup protein powder
- ½ cup milk
- 2 tbsp ground flaxseed
- 4 bread slices
- 2 tbsp agave syrup

Directions:
1. Preheat air fryer to 370°F (185°C). Combine the banana, protein powder, milk, and flaxseed in a shallow bowl and mix well Dip bread slices into the mixture. Place the slices on a lightly greased pan in a single layer and pour any of the remaining mixture evenly over the bread. Air Fry for 10 minutes, or until golden brown and crispy, flipping once. Serve warm topped with agave syrup.

Honey Pear Chips

Servings: 4
Cooking Time: 30 Minutes
Ingredients:
- 2 firm pears, thinly sliced
- 1 tbsp lemon juice
- ½ tsp ground cinnamon
- 1 tsp honey

Directions:
1. Preheat air fryer to 380°F (195°C). Arrange the pear slices on the parchment-lined cooking basket. Drizzle with lemon juice and honey and sprinkle with cinnamon. Air Fry for 6-8 minutes, shaking the basket once, until golden. Leave to cool. Serve immediately or save for later in an airtight container. Good for 2 days.

Effortless Mac 'n' Cheese

Servings: 4
Cooking Time: 15 Minutes
Ingredients:
- 1 cup heavy cream
- 1 cup milk
- ½ cup mozzarella cheese
- 2 tsp grated Parmesan cheese
- 16 oz cooked elbow macaroni

Directions:
1. Preheat air fryer to 400°F (205°C). Whisk the heavy cream, milk, mozzarella cheese, and Parmesan cheese until smooth in a bowl. Stir in the macaroni and pour into a baking dish. Cover with foil and Bake in the air fryer for 6 minutes. Remove foil and Bake until cooked through and bubbly, 3-5 minutes. Serve warm.

Veggie Burgers

Servings: 4
Cooking Time: 15 Minutes
Ingredients:
- 2 cans black beans, rinsed and drained
- ½ cup cooked quinoa
- ½ cup shredded raw sweet potato
- ¼ cup diced red onion
- 2 teaspoons ground cumin
- 1 teaspoon coriander powder
- ½ teaspoon salt
- oil for misting or cooking spray
- 8 slices bread
- suggested toppings: lettuce, tomato, red onion, Pepper Jack cheese, guacamole

Directions:
1. In a medium bowl, mash the beans with a fork.
2. Add the quinoa, sweet potato, onion, cumin, coriander, and salt and mix well with the fork.
3. Shape into 4 patties, each ¾-inch thick.
4. Mist both sides with oil or cooking spray and also mist the basket.
5. Cook at 390°F (200°C) for 15minutes.
6. Follow the recipe for Toast, Plain & Simple.
7. Pop the veggie burgers back in the air fryer for a minute or two to reheat if necessary.
8. Serve on the toast with your favorite burger toppings.

Pine Nut Eggplant Dip

Servings: 4
Cooking Time: 35 Minutes
Ingredients:
- 2 ½ tsp olive oil
- 1 eggplant, halved lengthwise
- 1/2 cup Parmesan cheese
- 2 tsp pine nuts
- 1 tbsp chopped walnuts
- ¼ cup tahini
- 1 tbsp lemon juice
- 2 cloves garlic, minced
- 1/8 tsp ground cumin
- 1 tsp smoked paprika
- Salt and pepper to taste
- 1 tbsp chopped parsley

Directions:
1. Preheat air fryer at 375ºF. Rub olive oil over eggplant and pierce the eggplant flesh 3 times with a fork. Place eggplant, flat side down, in the frying basket and Bake for 25 minutes. Let cool onto a cutting board for 5 minutes until cool enough to handle. Scoop out eggplant flesh. Add pine nuts and walnuts to the basket and Air Fry for 2 minutes,

shaking every 30 seconds to ensure they don´t burn. Set aside in a bowl.
2. In a food processor, blend eggplant flesh, tahini, lemon juice, garlic, smoked paprika, cumin, salt, and pepper until smooth. Transfer to a bowl. Scatter with the roasted pine nuts, Parmesan cheese, and parsley. Drizzle the dip with the remaining olive oil. Serve and enjoy!

Sicilian-style Vegetarian Pizza
Servings: 2
Cooking Time: 20 Minutes
Ingredients:
- 1 pizza pie crust
- ¼ cup ricotta cheese
- ½ tbsp tomato paste
- ½ white onion, sliced
- ½ tsp dried oregano
- ¼ cup Sicilian olives, sliced
- ¼ cup grated mozzarella

Directions:
1. Preheat air fryer to 350°F (175°C). Lay the pizza dough on a parchment paper sheet. Spread the tomato paste evenly over the pie crust, allowing at least ½ inch border. Sprinkle with oregano and scatter the ricotta cheese on top. Cover with onion and Sicilian olive slices and finish with a layer of mozzarella cheese. Bake for 10 minutes until the cheese has melted and lightly crisped, and the crust is golden brown. Serve sliced and enjoy!

Chicano Rice Bowls
Servings: 4
Cooking Time: 10 Minutes
Ingredients:
- 1 cup sour cream
- 2 tbsp milk
- 1 tsp ground cumin
- 1 tsp chili powder
- 1/8 tsp cayenne pepper
- 1 tbsp tomato paste
- 1 white onion, chopped
- 1 clove garlic, minced
- ½ tsp ground turmeric
- ½ tsp salt
- 1 cup canned black beans
- 1 cup canned corn kernels
- 1 tsp olive oil
- 4 cups cooked brown rice
- 3 tomatoes, diced
- 1 avocado, diced

Directions:
1. Whisk the sour cream, milk, cumin, ground turmeric, chili powder, cayenne pepper, and salt in a bowl. Let chill covered in the fridge until ready to use.
2. Preheat air fryer at 350°F. Combine beans, white onion, tomato paste, garlic, corn, and olive oil in a bowl. Transfer it into the frying basket and Air Fry for 5 minutes. Divide cooked rice into 4 serving bowls. Top each with bean mixture, tomatoes, and avocado and drizzle with sour cream mixture over. Serve immediately.

Crispy Avocados With Pico De Gallo
Servings: 2
Cooking Time: 15 Minutes
Ingredients:
- 1 cup diced tomatoes
- 1 tbsp lime juice
- 1 tsp lime zest
- 2 tbsp chopped cilantro
- 1 serrano chiles, minced
- 2 cloves garlic, minced
- 1 tbsp diced white onions
- ½ tsp salt
- 2 avocados, halved and pitted
- 4 tbsp cheddar shreds

Directions:
1. Preheat air fryer to 350°F. Combine all ingredients, except for avocados and cheddar cheese, in a bowl and let chill covered in the fridge. Place avocado halves, cut sides-up, in the frying basket, scatter cheese shreds over top of avocado halves, and Air Fry for 4 minutes. Top with pico de gallo and serve.

Spicy Bean Patties
Servings: 4
Cooking Time: 20 Minutes
Ingredients:
- 1 cup canned black beans
- 1 bread slice, torn
- 2 tbsp spicy brown mustard
- 1 tbsp chili powder
- 1 egg white
- 2 tbsp grated carrots
- ¼ diced green bell pepper
- 1-2 jalapeño peppers, diced
- ¼ tsp ground cumin
- ¼ tsp smoked paprika
- 2 tbsp cream cheese
- 1 tbsp olive oil

Directions:
1. Preheat air fryer at 350°F. Using a fork, mash beans until smooth. Stir in the remaining ingredients, except olive oil. Form mixture into 4 patties. Place bean patties in the greased frying basket and Air Fry for 6 minutes, turning once, and brush with olive oil. Serve immediately.

Curried Cauliflower
Servings: 2
Cooking Time: 30 Minutes
Ingredients:
- 1 cup canned diced tomatoes
- 2 cups milk
- 2 tbsp lime juice
- 1 tbsp allspice
- 1 tbsp curry powder
- 1 tsp ground ginger
- ½ tsp ground cumin
- 12 oz frozen cauliflower
- 16 oz cheddar cheese, cubed
- ¼ cup chopped cilantro

Directions:
1. Preheat air fryer to 375°F (190°C). Combine the tomatoes and their juices, milk, lime juice, allspice, curry powder, ginger, and cumin in a baking pan. Toss in cauliflower and cheddar cheese until coated. Roast for 15 minutes, stir and Roast for another 10 minutes until bubbly. Scatter with cilantro before serving.

Golden Fried Tofu

Servings: 4
Cooking Time: 20 Minutes
Ingredients:
- ¼ cup flour
- ¼ cup cornstarch
- 1 tsp garlic powder
- ¼ tsp onion powder
- Salt and pepper to taste
- 1 firm tofu, cubed
- 2 tbsp cilantro, chopped

Directions:
1. Preheat air fryer to 390°F (200°C). Combine the flour, cornstarch, salt, garlic, onion powder, and black pepper in a bowl. Stir well. Place the tofu cubes in the flour mix. Toss to coat. Spray the tofu with oil and place them in a single layer in the greased frying basket. Air Fry for 14-16 minutes, flipping the pieces once until golden and crunchy. Top with freshly chopped cilantro and serve immediately.

Tacos

Servings: 24
Cooking Time: 8 Minutes Per Batch

Ingredients:
- 1 24-count package 4-inch corn tortillas
- 1½ cups refried beans (about ¾ of a 15-ounce can)
- 4 ounces sharp Cheddar cheese, grated
- ½ cup salsa
- oil for misting or cooking spray

Directions:
1. Preheat air fryer to 390°F (200°C).
2. Wrap refrigerated tortillas in damp paper towels and microwave for 30 to 60 seconds to warm. If necessary, rewarm tortillas as you go to keep them soft enough to fold without breaking.
3. Working with one tortilla at a time, top with 1 tablespoon of beans, 1 tablespoon of grated cheese, and 1 teaspoon of salsa. Fold over and press down very gently on the center. Press edges firmly all around to seal. Spray both sides with oil or cooking spray.
4. Cooking in two batches, place half the tacos in the air fryer basket. To cook 12 at a time, you may need to stand them upright and lean some against the sides of basket. It's okay if they're crowded as long as you leave a little room for air to circulate around them.
5. Cook for 8 minutes or until golden brown and crispy.
6. Repeat steps 4 and 5 to cook remaining tacos.

Chapter 6: Poultry Recipes

Glazed Chicken Thighs

Servings: 4
Cooking Time: 25 Minutes
Ingredients:
- 1 lb boneless, skinless chicken thighs
- ¼ cup balsamic vinegar
- 3 tbsp honey
- 2 tbsp brown sugar
- 1 tsp whole-grain mustard
- ¼ cup soy sauce
- 3 garlic cloves, minced
- Salt and pepper to taste
- ½ tsp smoked paprika
- 2 tbsp chopped shallots

Directions:
1. Preheat air fryer to 375°F (190°C). Whisk vinegar, honey, sugar, soy sauce, mustard, garlic, salt, pepper, and paprika in a small bowl. Arrange the chicken in the frying basket and brush the top of each with some of the vinegar mixture. Air Fry for 7 minutes, then flip the chicken. Brush the tops with the rest of the vinegar mixture and Air Fry for another 5 to 8 minutes. Allow resting for 5 minutes before slicing. Serve warm sprinkled with shallots.

Chicken Flautas

Servings: 6
Cooking Time: 8 Minutes
Ingredients:
- 6 tablespoons whipped cream cheese
- 1 cup shredded cooked chicken
- 6 tablespoons mild pico de gallo salsa
- ⅓ cup shredded Mexican cheese
- ½ teaspoon taco seasoning
- Six 8-inch flour tortillas
- 2 cups shredded lettuce
- ½ cup guacamole

Directions:
1. Preheat the air fryer to 370°F (185°C).
2. In a large bowl, mix the cream cheese, chicken, salsa, shredded cheese, and taco seasoning until well combined.
3. Lay the tortillas on a flat surface. Divide the cheese-and-chicken mixture into 6 equal portions; then place the mixture in the center of the tortillas, spreading evenly, leaving about 1 inch from the edge of the tortilla.
4. Spray the air fryer basket with olive oil spray. Roll up the flautas and place them edge side down into the basket. Lightly mist the top of the flautas with olive oil spray.
5. Repeat until the air fryer basket is full. You may need to cook these in batches, depending on the size of your air fryer.
6. Cook for 7 minutes, or until the outer edges are browned.
7. Remove from the air fryer basket and serve warm over a bed of shredded lettuce with guacamole on top.

Quick Chicken For Filling

Servings: 2
Cooking Time: 8 Minutes
Ingredients:
- 1 pound chicken tenders, skinless and boneless
- ½ teaspoon ground cumin
- ½ teaspoon garlic powder
- cooking spray

Directions:
1. Sprinkle raw chicken tenders with seasonings.
2. Spray air fryer basket lightly with cooking spray to prevent sticking.
3. Place chicken in air fryer basket in single layer.
4. Cook at 390°F (200°C) for 4minutes, turn chicken strips over, and cook for an additional 4minutes.
5. Test for doneness. Thick tenders may require an additional minute or two.

Tortilla Crusted Chicken Breast

Servings: 2
Cooking Time: 12 Minutes
Ingredients:
- ⅓ cup flour
- 1 teaspoon salt
- 1½ teaspoons chili powder
- 1 teaspoon ground cumin
- freshly ground black pepper
- 1 egg, beaten
- ¾ cup coarsely crushed yellow corn tortilla chips
- 2 (3- to 4-ounce) boneless chicken breasts
- vegetable oil
- ½ cup salsa
- ½ cup crumbled queso fresco
- fresh cilantro leaves
- sour cream or guacamole (optional)

Directions:
1. Set up a dredging station with three shallow dishes. Combine the flour, salt, chili powder, cumin and black pepper in the first shallow dish. Beat the egg in the second shallow dish. Place the crushed tortilla chips in the third shallow dish.
2. Dredge the chicken in the spiced flour, covering all sides of the breast. Then dip the chicken into the egg, coating the chicken completely. Finally, place the chicken into the tortilla chips and press the chips onto the chicken to make sure they adhere to all sides of the breast. Spray the coated chicken breasts on both sides with vegetable oil.
3. Preheat the air fryer to 380°F (195°C).
4. Air-fry the chicken for 6 minutes. Then turn the chicken breasts over and air-fry for another 6 minutes. (Increase the cooking time if you are using chicken breasts larger than 3 to 4 ounces.)
5. When the chicken has finished cooking, serve each breast with a little salsa, the crumbled queso fresco and cilantro as the finishing touch. Serve some sour cream and/or guacamole at the table, if desired.

Italian Roasted Chicken Thighs

Servings: 6
Cooking Time: 14 Minutes
Ingredients:
- 6 boneless chicken thighs
- ½ teaspoon dried oregano
- ½ teaspoon garlic powder
- ½ teaspoon sea salt
- ½ teaspoon black pepper
- ¼ teaspoon crushed red pepper flakes

Directions:
1. Pat the chicken thighs with paper towel.

Tower Air Fryer Cookbook

2. In a small bowl, mix the oregano, garlic powder, salt, pepper, and crushed red pepper flakes. Rub the spice mixture onto the chicken thighs.
3. Preheat the air fryer to 400°F (205°C).
4. Place the chicken thighs in the air fryer basket and spray with cooking spray. Cook for 10 minutes, turn over, and cook another 4 minutes. When cooking completes, the internal temperature should read 165°F (75°C).

Chicken Adobo

Servings: 6
Cooking Time: 12 Minutes
Ingredients:
- 6 boneless chicken thighs
- ¼ cup soy sauce or tamari
- ½ cup rice wine vinegar
- 4 cloves garlic, minced
- ⅛ teaspoon crushed red pepper flakes
- ½ teaspoon black pepper

Directions:
1. Place the chicken thighs into a resealable plastic bag with the soy sauce or tamari, the rice wine vinegar, the garlic, and the crushed red pepper flakes. Seal the bag and let the chicken marinate at least 1 hour in the refrigerator.
2. Preheat the air fryer to 400°F (205°C).
3. Drain the chicken and pat dry with a paper towel. Season the chicken with black pepper and liberally spray with cooking spray.
4. Place the chicken in the air fryer basket and cook for 9 minutes, turn over at 9 minutes and check for an internal temperature of 165°F (75°C), and cook another 3 minutes.

Harissa Chicken Wings

Servings: 4
Cooking Time: 25 Minutes
Ingredients:
- 8 whole chicken wings
- 1 tsp garlic powder
- ¼ tsp dried oregano
- 1 tbsp harissa seasoning

Directions:
1. Preheat air fryer to 400°F (205°C). Season the wings with garlic, harissa seasoning, and oregano. Place them in the greased frying basket and spray with cooking oil spray. Air Fry for 10 minutes, shake the basket, and cook for another 5-7 minutes until golden and crispy. Serve warm.

Cantonese Chicken Drumsticks

Servings: 4
Cooking Time: 30 Minutes
Ingredients:
- 3 tbsp lime juice
- 3 tbsp oyster sauce
- 6 chicken drumsticks
- 1 tbsp peanut oil
- 3 tbsp honey
- 3 tbsp brown sugar
- 2 tbsp ketchup
- ¼ cup pineapple juice

Directions:
1. Preheat air fryer to 350°F (175°C). Drizzle some lime juice and oyster sauce on the drumsticks. Transfer to the frying basket and drizzle with peanut oil. Shake the basket to coat. Bake for 18 minutes until the drumsticks are almost done.
2. Meanwhile, combine the rest of the lime juice and the oyster sauce along with the honey, sugar, ketchup and pineapple juice in a 6-inch metal bowl. When the chicken is done, transfer to the bowl and coat the chicken with the sauce. Put the metal bowl in the basket and cook for 5-7 minutes, turning halfway, until golden and cooked through. Serve and enjoy!

Super-simple Herby Turkey

Servings: 4
Cooking Time: 35 Minutes
Ingredients:
- 2 turkey tenderloins
- 2 tbsp olive oil
- Salt and pepper to taste
- 2 tbsp minced rosemary
- 1 tbsp minced thyme
- 1 tbsp minced sage

Directions:
1. Preheat the air fryer to 350°F (175°C). Brush the tenderloins with olive oil and sprinkle with salt and pepper. Mix rosemary, thyme, and sage, then rub the seasoning onto the meat. Put the tenderloins in the frying basket and Bake for 22-27 minutes, flipping once until cooked through. Lay the turkey on a serving plate, cover with foil, and let stand for 5 minutes. Slice before serving.

Creole Chicken Drumettes

Servings: 4
Cooking Time: 50 Minutes
Ingredients:
- 1 lb chicken drumettes
- ½ cup flour
- ½ cup heavy cream
- ½ cup sour cream
- ½ cup bread crumbs
- 1 tbsp Creole seasoning
- 2 tbsp melted butter

Directions:
1. Preheat air fryer to 370ºF. Combine chicken drumettes and flour in a bowl. Shake away excess flour and set aside. Mix the heavy cream and sour cream in a bowl. In another bowl, combine bread crumbs and Creole seasoning. Dip floured drumettes in cream mixture, then dredge them in crumbs. Place the chicken drumettes in the greased frying basket and Air Fry for 20 minutes, tossing once and brushing with melted butter. Let rest for a few minutes on a plate and serve.

Mushroom & Turkey Bread Pizza

Servings: 4
Cooking Time: 35 Minutes
Ingredients:
- 10 cooked turkey sausages, sliced
- 1 cup shredded mozzarella cheese
- 1 cup shredded Cheddar cheese
- 1 French loaf bread
- 2 tbsp butter, softened
- 1 tsp garlic powder

- 1 1/3 cups marinara sauce
- 1 tsp Italian seasoning
- 2 scallions, chopped
- 1 cup mushrooms, sliced

Directions:
1. Preheat the air fryer to 370°F (185°C). Cut the bread in half crosswise, then split each half horizontally. Combine butter and garlic powder, then spread on the cut sides of the bread. Bake the halves in the fryer for 3-5 minutes or until the leaves start to brown. Set the toasted bread on a work surface and spread marinara sauce over the top. Sprinkle the Italian seasoning, then top with sausages, scallions, mushrooms, and cheeses. Set the pizzas in the air fryer and Bake for 8-12 minutes or until the cheese is melted and starting to brown. Serve hot.

Goat Cheese Stuffed Turkey Roulade

Servings: 4
Cooking Time: 55 Minutes
Ingredients:
- 1 boneless turkey breast, skinless
- Salt and pepper to taste
- 4 oz goat cheese
- 1 tbsp marjoram
- 1 tbsp sage
- 2 garlic cloves, minced
- 2 tbsp olive oil
- 2 tbsp chopped cilantro

Directions:
1. Preheat air fryer to 380°F (195°C). Butterfly the turkey breast with a sharp knife and season with salt and pepper. Mix together the goat cheese, marjoram, sage, and garlic in a bowl. Spread the cheese mixture over the turkey breast, then roll it up tightly, tucking the ends underneath.
2. Put the turkey breast roulade onto a piece of aluminum foil, wrap it up, and place it into the air fryer. Bake for 30 minutes. Turn the turkey breast, brush the top with oil, and then continue to cook for another 10-15 minutes. Slice and serve sprinkled with cilantro.

Chicken Tikka

Servings: 4
Cooking Time: 15 Minutes
Ingredients:
- ¼ cup plain Greek yogurt
- 1 clove garlic, minced
- 1 tablespoon ketchup
- 1 tablespoon extra-virgin olive oil
- 1 tablespoon lemon juice
- ½ teaspoon salt
- ½ teaspoon ground cumin
- ½ teaspoon paprika
- ¼ teaspoon ground cinnamon
- ½ teaspoon ground black pepper
- ½ teaspoon cayenne pepper
- 1 pound boneless, skinless chicken thighs

Directions:
1. In a large bowl, stir together the yogurt, garlic, ketchup, olive oil, lemon juice, salt, cumin, paprika, cinnamon, black pepper, and cayenne pepper until combined.
2. Add the chicken thighs to the bow and fold the yogurt-spice mixture over the chicken thighs until they're covered with the marinade. Cover with plastic wrap and place in the refrigerator for 30 minutes.
3. When ready to cook the chicken, remove from the refrigerator and preheat the air fryer to 370°F (175°C).
4. Liberally spray the air fryer basket with olive oil mist. Place the chicken thighs into the air fryer basket, leaving space between the thighs to turn.
5. Cook for 10 minutes, turn the chicken thighs, and cook another 5 minutes (or until the internal temperature reaches 165°F (7°C)).
6. Remove the chicken from the air fryer and serve warm with desired sides.

Chicken Pasta Pie

Servings: 4
Cooking Time: 40 Minutes
Ingredients:
- 1/3 cup green bell peppers, diced
- ¼ cup yellow bell peppers, diced
- ½ cup mozzarella cheese, grated
- 3/4 cup grated Parmesan cheese
- 2/3 cup ricotta cheese
- 2 tbsp butter, melted
- 1 egg
- ¼ tsp salt
- 6 oz cooked spaghetti
- 2 tsp olive oil
- 1/3 cup diced onions
- 2 cloves minced garlic
- ¼ lb ground chicken
- 1 cup marinara sauce
- ½ tsp dried oregano

Directions:
1. Combine the ricotta cheese, 1 tbsp of Parmesan cheese, minced garlic, and salt in a bowl. Whisk the melted butter and egg in another bowl. Add the remaining Parmesan cheese and cooked spaghetti and mix well. Set aside. Warm the olive oil in a skillet over medium heat. Add in onions, green bell peppers, yellow bell peppers and cook for 3 minutes until the onions tender. Stir in ground chicken and cook for 5 minutes until no longer pink.
2. Preheat air fryer at 350ºF. Press spaghetti mixture into a greased baking pan, then spread ricotta mixture on top, and finally top with the topping mixture, followed by the marinara sauce. Place baking pan in the frying basket and Bake for 10 minutes. Scatter with mozzarella cheese on top and cook for 4 more minutes. Let rest for 20 minutes before releasing the sides of the baking pan. Cut into slices and serve sprinkled with oregano.

Easy Turkey Meatballs

Servings: 4
Cooking Time: 20 Minutes
Ingredients:
- 1 lb ground turkey
- ½ celery stalk, chopped
- 1 egg
- ¼ tsp red pepper flakes
- ¼ cup bread crumbs
- Salt and pepper to taste
- ½ tsp garlic powder
- ½ tsp onion powder

- ½ tsp cayenne pepper

Directions:
1. Preheat air fryer to 360°F (180°C). Add all of the ingredients to a bowl and mix well. Shape the mixture into 12 balls and arrange them on the greased frying basket. Air Fry for 10-12 minutes or until the meatballs are cooked through and browned. Serve and enjoy!

Chicken Schnitzel Dogs

Servings: 4
Cooking Time: 10 Minutes
Ingredients:
- ½ cup flour
- ½ teaspoon salt
- 1 teaspoon marjoram
- 1 teaspoon dried parsley flakes
- ½ teaspoon thyme
- 1 egg
- 1 teaspoon lemon juice
- 1 teaspoon water
- 1 cup breadcrumbs
- 4 chicken tenders, pounded thin
- oil for misting or cooking spray
- 4 whole-grain hotdog buns
- 4 slices Gouda cheese
- 1 small Granny Smith apple, thinly sliced
- ½ cup shredded Napa cabbage
- coleslaw dressing

Directions:
1. In a shallow dish, mix together the flour, salt, marjoram, parsley, and thyme.
2. In another shallow dish, beat together egg, lemon juice, and water.
3. Place breadcrumbs in a third shallow dish.
4. Cut each of the flattened chicken tenders in half lengthwise.
5. Dip flattened chicken strips in flour mixture, then egg wash. Let excess egg drip off and roll in breadcrumbs. Spray both sides with oil or cooking spray.
6. Cook at 390°F (200°C) for 5minutes. Spray with oil, turn over, and spray other side.
7. Cook for 3 to 5minutes more, until well done and crispy brown.
8. To serve, place 2 schnitzel strips on bottom of each hot dog bun. Top with cheese, sliced apple, and cabbage. Drizzle with coleslaw dressing and top with other half of bun.

Italian Herb Stuffed Chicken

Servings: 4
Cooking Time: 30 Minutes
Ingredients:
- 2 tbsp olive oil
- 3 tbsp balsamic vinegar
- 3 garlic cloves, minced
- 1 tomato, diced
- 2 tbsp Italian seasoning
- 1 tbsp chopped fresh basil
- 1 tsp thyme, chopped
- 4 chicken breasts

Directions:
1. Preheat air fryer to 370°F (185°C). Combine the olive oil, balsamic vinegar, garlic, thyme, tomato, half of the Italian seasoning, and basil in a medium bowl. Set aside.
2. Cut 4-5 slits into the chicken breasts ¾ of the way through. Season with the rest of the Italian seasoning and place the chicken with the slits facing up, in the greased frying basket. Bake for 7 minutes. Spoon the bruschetta mixture into the slits of the chicken. Cook for another 3 minutes. Allow chicken to sit and cool for a few minutes. Serve and enjoy!

Southern-style Chicken Legs

Servings: 6
Cooking Time: 20 Minutes
Ingredients:
- 2 cups buttermilk
- 1 tablespoon hot sauce
- 12 chicken legs
- ½ teaspoon salt
- ½ teaspoon pepper
- 1 teaspoon paprika
- ½ teaspoon onion powder
- 1 teaspoon garlic powder
- 1 cup all-purpose flour

Directions:
1. In an airtight container, place the buttermilk, hot sauce, and chicken legs and refrigerate for 4 to 8 hours.
2. In a medium bowl, whisk together the salt, pepper, paprika, onion powder, garlic powder, and flour. Drain the chicken legs from the buttermilk and dip the chicken legs into the flour mixture, stirring to coat well.
3. Preheat the air fryer to 390°F (200°C).
4. Place the chicken legs in the air fryer basket and spray with cooking spray. Cook for 10 minutes, turn the chicken legs over, and cook for another 8 to 10 minutes. Check for an internal temperature of 165°F (75°C).

Hazelnut Chicken Salad With Strawberries

Servings:4
Cooking Time: 30 Minutes
Ingredients:
- 2 chicken breasts, cubed
- Salt and pepper to taste
- ¾ cup mayonnaise
- 1 tbsp lime juice
- ½ cup chopped hazelnuts
- ½ cup chopped celery
- ½ cup diced strawberries

Directions:
1. Preheat air fryer to 350ºF. Sprinkle chicken cubes with salt and pepper. Place them in the frying basket and Air Fry for 9 minutes, shaking once. Remove to a bowl and leave it to cool. Add the mayonnaise, lime juice, hazelnuts, celery, and strawberries. Serve.

Cajun Chicken Kebabs

Servings: 4
Cooking Time: 30 Minutes
Ingredients:
- 3 tbsp lemon juice
- 2 tsp olive oil

- 2 tbsp chopped parsley
- ½ tsp dried oregano
- ½ Cajun seasoning
- 1 lb chicken breasts, cubed
- 1 cup cherry tomatoes
- 1 zucchini, cubed

Directions:
1. Preheat air fryer to 400°F (205°C). Combine the lemon juice, olive oil, parsley, oregano, and Cajun seasoning in a bowl. Toss in the chicken and stir, making sure all pieces are coated. Allow to marinate for 10 minutes. Take 8 bamboo skewers and poke the chicken, tomatoes, and zucchini, alternating the pieces. Use a brush to put more marinade on them, then lay them in the air fryer. Air Fry the kebabs for 15 minutes, turning once, or until the chicken is cooked through, with no pink showing. Get rid of the leftover marinade. Serve and enjoy!

Crispy Fried Onion Chicken Breasts

Servings: 2
Cooking Time: 13 Minutes
Ingredients:
- ¼ cup all-purpose flour*
- salt and freshly ground black pepper
- 1 egg
- 2 tablespoons Dijon mustard
- 1½ cups crispy fried onions (like French's®)
- ½ teaspoon paprika
- 2 (5-ounce) boneless, skinless chicken breasts
- vegetable or olive oil, in a spray bottle

Directions:
1. Preheat the air fryer to 380°F (195°C).
2. Set up a dredging station with three shallow dishes. Place the flour in the first shallow dish and season well with salt and freshly ground black pepper. Combine the egg and Dijon mustard in a second shallow dish and whisk until smooth. Place the fried onions in a sealed bag and using a rolling pin, crush them into coarse crumbs. Combine these crumbs with the paprika in the third shallow dish.
3. Dredge the chicken breasts in the flour. Shake off any excess flour and dip them into the egg mixture. Let any excess egg drip off. Then coat both sides of the chicken breasts with the crispy onions. Press the crumbs onto the chicken breasts with your hands to make sure they are well adhered.
4. Spray or brush the bottom of the air fryer basket with oil. Transfer the chicken breasts to the air fryer basket and air-fry at 380°F (195°C) for 13 minutes, turning the chicken over halfway through the cooking time.
5. Serve immediately.

Bacon & Chicken Flatbread

Servings: 2
Cooking Time: 35 Minutes
Ingredients:
- 1 flatbread dough
- 1 chicken breast, cubed
- 1 cup breadcrumbs
- 2 eggs, beaten
- Salt and pepper to taste
- 2 tsp dry rosemary
- 1 tsp fajita seasoning
- 1 tsp onion powder
- 3 bacon strips
- ½ tbsp ranch sauce

Directions:
1. Preheat air fryer to 360°F (180°C). Place the breadcrumbs, onion powder, rosemary, salt, and pepper in a mixing bowl. Coat the chicken with the mixture, dip into the beaten eggs, then roll again into the dry ingredients. Arrange the coated chicken pieces on one side of the greased frying basket. On the other side of the basket, lay the bacon strips. Air Fry for 6 minutes. Turn the bacon pieces over and flip the chicken and cook for another 6 minutes.
2. Roll the flatbread out and spread the ranch sauce all over the surface. Top with the bacon and chicken and sprinkle with fajita seasoning. Close the bread to contain the filling and place it in the air fryer. Cook for 10 minutes, flipping the flatbread once until golden brown. Let it cool for a few minutes. Then slice and serve.

Chicken Cutlets With Broccoli Rabe And Roasted Peppers

Servings: 2
Cooking Time: 10 Minutes
Ingredients:
- ½ bunch broccoli rabe
- olive oil, in a spray bottle
- salt and freshly ground black pepper
- ⅔ cup roasted red pepper strips
- 2 (4-ounce) boneless, skinless chicken breasts
- 2 tablespoons all-purpose flour*
- 1 egg, beaten
- ⅓ cup seasoned breadcrumbs*
- 2 slices aged provolone cheese

Directions:
1. Bring a medium saucepot of salted water to a boil on the stovetop. Blanch the broccoli rabe for 3 minutes in the boiling water and then drain. When it has cooled a little, squeeze out as much water as possible, drizzle a little olive oil on top, season with salt and black pepper and set aside. Dry the roasted red peppers with a clean kitchen towel and set them aside as well.
2. Place each chicken breast between 2 pieces of plastic wrap. Use a meat pounder to flatten the chicken breasts to about ½-inch thick. Season the chicken on both sides with salt and pepper.
3. Preheat the air fryer to 400°F (205°C).
4. Set up a dredging station with three shallow dishes. Place the flour in one dish, the egg in a second dish and the breadcrumbs in a third dish. Coat the chicken on all sides with the flour. Shake off any excess flour and dip the chicken into the egg. Let the excess egg drip off and coat both sides of the chicken in the breadcrumbs. Spray the chicken with olive oil on both sides and transfer to the air fryer basket.
5. Air-fry the chicken at 400°F (205°C) for 5 minutes. Turn the chicken over and air-fry for another minute. Then, top the chicken breast with the broccoli rabe and roasted peppers. Place a slice of the provolone cheese on top and secure it with a toothpick or two.
6. Air-fry at 360° (180°C) for 3 to 4 minutes to melt the cheese and warm everything together.

Chicken Wellington

Servings: 2
Cooking Time: 31 Minutes
Ingredients:
- 2 (5-ounce) boneless, skinless chicken breasts
- ½ cup White Worcestershire sauce
- 3 tablespoons butter
- ½ cup finely diced onion (about ½ onion)
- 8 ounces button mushrooms, finely chopped
- ¼ cup chicken stock
- 2 tablespoons White Worcestershire sauce (or white wine)
- salt and freshly ground black pepper
- 1 tablespoon chopped fresh tarragon
- 2 sheets puff pastry, thawed
- 1 egg, beaten
- vegetable oil

Directions:
1. Place the chicken breasts in a shallow dish. Pour the White Worcestershire sauce over the chicken coating both sides and marinate for 30 minutes.
2. While the chicken is marinating, melt the butter in a large skillet over medium-high heat on the stovetop. Add the onion and sauté for a few minutes, until it starts to soften. Add the mushrooms and sauté for 5 minutes until the vegetables are brown and soft. Deglaze the skillet with the chicken stock, scraping up any bits from the bottom of the pan. Add the White Worcestershire sauce and simmer for 3 minutes until the mixture reduces and starts to thicken. Season with salt and freshly ground black pepper. Remove the mushroom mixture from the heat and stir in the fresh tarragon. Let the mushroom mixture cool.
3. Preheat the air fryer to 360°F (180°C).
4. Remove the chicken from the marinade and transfer it to the air fryer basket. Tuck the small end of the chicken breast under the thicker part to shape it into a circle rather than an oval. Pour the marinade over the chicken and air-fry for 10 minutes.
5. Roll out the puff pastry and cut out two 6-inch squares. Brush the perimeter of each square with the egg wash. Place half of the mushroom mixture in the center of each puff pastry square. Place the chicken breasts, top side down on the mushroom mixture. Starting with one corner of puff pastry and working in one direction, pull the pastry up over the chicken to enclose it and press the ends of the pastry together in the middle. Brush the pastry with the egg wash to seal the edges. Turn the Wellingtons over and set aside.
6. To make a decorative design with the remaining puff pastry, cut out four 10-inch strips. For each Wellington, twist two of the strips together, place them over the chicken breast wrapped in puff pastry, and tuck the ends underneath to seal it. Brush the entire top and sides of the Wellingtons with the egg wash.
7. Preheat the air fryer to 350°F (175°C).
8. Spray or brush the air fryer basket with vegetable oil. Air-fry the chicken Wellingtons for 13 minutes. Carefully turn the Wellingtons over. Air-fry for another 8 minutes. Transfer to serving plates, light a candle and enjoy!

Buttery Chicken Legs

Servings: 4
Cooking Time: 50 Minutes
Ingredients:
- 1 tsp baking powder
- 1 tsp dried mustard
- 1 tsp smoked paprika
- 1 tsp garlic powder
- 1 tsp dried thyme
- Salt and pepper to taste
- 1 ½ lb chicken legs
- 3 tbsp butter, melted

Directions:
1. Preheat air fryer to 370°F. Combine all ingredients, except for butter, in a bowl until coated. Place the chicken legs in the greased frying basket. Air Fry for 18 minutes, flipping once and brushing with melted butter on both sides. Let chill onto a serving plate for 5 minutes before serving.

Indian Chicken Tandoori

Servings: 2
Cooking Time: 35 Minutes
Ingredients:
- 2 chicken breasts, cubed
- ½ cup hung curd
- 1 tsp turmeric powder
- 1 tsp red chili powder
- 1 tsp chaat masala powder
- Pinch of salt

Directions:
1. Preheat air fryer to 350°F (175°C). Mix the hung curd, turmeric, red chili powder, chaat masala powder, and salt in a mixing bowl. Stir until the mixture is free of lumps. Coat the chicken with the mixture, cover, and refrigerate for 30 minutes to marinate. Place the marinated chicken chunks in a baking pan and drizzle with the remaining marinade. Bake for 25 minutes until the chicken is juicy and spiced. Serve warm.

Asian Sweet Chili Chicken

Servings: 4
Cooking Time: 30 Minutes
Ingredients:
- 2 chicken breasts, cut into 1-inch pieces
- 1 cup cornstarch
- 1 tsp chicken seasoning
- Salt and pepper to taste
- 2 eggs
- 1 ½ cups sweet chili sauce

Directions:
1. Preheat air fryer to 360°F (180°C). Mix cornstarch, chicken seasoning, salt and pepper in a large bowl. In another bowl, beat the eggs. Dip the chicken in the cornstarch mixture to coat. Next, dip the chicken into the egg, then return to the cornstarch. Transfer chicken to the air fryer.
2. Lightly spray all of the chicken with cooking oil. Air Fry for 15-16 minutes, shaking the basket once or until golden. Transfer chicken to a serving dish and drizzle with sweet-and-sour sauce. Serve immediately.

Chicken Fried Steak With Gravy

Servings: 4
Cooking Time: 10 Minutes Per Batch
Ingredients:
- ½ cup flour
- 2 teaspoons salt, divided
- freshly ground black pepper
- ¼ teaspoon garlic powder
- 1 cup buttermilk
- 1 cup fine breadcrumbs
- 4 tenderized top round steaks (about 6 to 8 ounces each; ½-inch thick)
- vegetable or canola oil
- For the Gravy:
- 2 tablespoons butter or bacon drippings
- ¼ onion, minced (about ¼ cup)
- 1 clove garlic, smashed
- ¼ teaspoon dried thyme
- 3 tablespoons flour
- 1 cup milk
- salt and lots of freshly ground black pepper
- a few dashes of Worcestershire sauce

Directions:
1. Set up a dredging station. Combine the flour, 1 teaspoon of salt, black pepper and garlic powder in a shallow bowl. Pour the buttermilk into a second shallow bowl. Finally, put the breadcrumbs and 1 teaspoon of salt in a third shallow bowl.
2. Dip the tenderized steaks into the flour, then the buttermilk, and then the breadcrumb mixture, pressing the crumbs onto the steak. Place them on a baking sheet and spray both sides generously with vegetable or canola oil.
3. Preheat the air fryer to 400°F (205°C).
4. Transfer the steaks to the air fryer basket, two at a time, and air-fry for 10 minutes, flipping the steaks over halfway through the cooking time. This will cook your steaks to medium. If you want the steaks cooked a little more or less, add or subtract a minute or two. Hold the first batch of steaks warm in a 170°F (75°C) oven while you cook the second batch.
5. While the steaks are cooking, make the gravy. Melt the butter in a small saucepan over medium heat on the stovetop. Add the onion, garlic and thyme and cook for five minutes, until the onion is soft and just starting to brown. Stir in the flour and cook for another five minutes, stirring regularly, until the mixture starts to brown. Whisk in the milk and bring the mixture to a boil to thicken. Season to taste with salt, lots of freshly ground black pepper and a few dashes of Worcestershire sauce.
6. Plate the chicken fried steaks with mashed potatoes and vegetables and serve the gravy at the table to pour over the top.

Cal-mex Turkey Patties

Servings: 4
Cooking Time: 30 Minutes
Ingredients:
- 1/3 cup crushed corn tortilla chips
- 1/3 cup grated American cheese
- 1 egg, beaten
- ¼ cup salsa
- Salt and pepper to taste
- 1 lb ground turkey
- 1 tbsp olive oil
- 1 tsp chili powder

Directions:
1. Preheat air fryer to 330°F (165°C). Mix together egg, tortilla chips, salsa, cheese, salt, and pepper in a bowl. Using your hands, add the ground turkey and mix gently until just combined. Divide the meat into 4 equal portions and shape into patties about ½ inch thick. Brush the patties with olive oil and sprinkle with chili powder. Air Fry the patties for 14-16 minutes, flipping once until cooked through and golden. Serve and enjoy!

Intense Buffalo Chicken Wings

Servings: 2
Cooking Time: 40 Minutes
Ingredients:
- 8 chicken wings
- ½ cup melted butter
- 2 tbsp Tabasco sauce
- ½ tbsp lemon juice
- 1 tbsp Worcestershire sauce
- 2 tsp cayenne pepper
- 1 tsp garlic powder
- 1 tsp lemon zest
- Salt and pepper to taste

Directions:
1. Preheat air fryer to 350°F (175°C). Place the melted butter, Tabasco, lemon juice, Worcestershire sauce, cayenne, garlic powder, lemon zest, salt, and pepper in a bowl and stir to combine. Dip the chicken wings into the mixture, coating thoroughly. Lay the coated chicken wings on the foil-lined frying basket in an even layer. Air Fry for 16-18 minutes. Shake the basket several times during cooking until the chicken wings are crispy brown. Serve.

Yummy Maple-mustard Chicken Kabobs

Servings: 4
Cooking Time: 35 Minutes+ Chilling Time
Ingredients:
- 1 lb boneless, skinless chicken thighs, cubed
- 1 green bell pepper, chopped
- ½ cup honey mustard
- ½ yellow onion, chopped
- 8 cherry tomatoes
- 2 tbsp chopped scallions

Directions:
1. Toss chicken cubes and honey mustard in a bowl and let chill covered in the fridge for 30 minutes. Preheat air fryer to 350ºF. Thread chicken cubes, onion, cherry tomatoes, and bell peppers, alternating, onto 8 skewers. Place them on a kebab rack. Place rack in the frying basket and Air Fry for 12 minutes. Top with scallions to serve.

Teriyaki Chicken Legs

Servings: 2
Cooking Time: 20 Minutes
Ingredients:
- 4 tablespoons teriyaki sauce
- 1 tablespoon orange juice

- 1 teaspoon smoked paprika
- 4 chicken legs
- cooking spray

Directions:
1. Mix together the teriyaki sauce, orange juice, and smoked paprika. Brush on all sides of chicken legs.
2. Spray air fryer basket with nonstick cooking spray and place chicken in basket.
3. Cook at 360°F (180°C) for 6 minutes. Turn and baste with sauce. Cook for 6 more minutes, turn and baste. Cook for 8 minutes more, until juices run clear when chicken is pierced with a fork.

Chicken Strips

Servings: 4
Cooking Time: 8 Minutes
Ingredients:
- 1 pound chicken tenders
- Marinade
- ¼ cup olive oil
- 2 tablespoons water
- 2 tablespoons honey
- 2 tablespoons white vinegar
- ½ teaspoon salt
- ½ teaspoon crushed red pepper
- 1 teaspoon garlic powder
- 1 teaspoon onion powder
- ½ teaspoon paprika

Directions:
1. Combine all marinade ingredients and mix well.
2. Add chicken and stir to coat. Cover tightly and let marinate in refrigerator for 30 minutes.
3. Remove tenders from marinade and place them in a single layer in the air fryer basket.
4. Cook at 390°F (200°C) for 3 minutes. Turn tenders over and cook for 5 minutes longer or until chicken is done and juices run clear.
5. Repeat step 4 to cook remaining tenders.

Irresistible Cheesy Chicken Sticks

Servings: 2
Cooking Time: 30 Minutes
Ingredients:
- 6 mozzarella sticks
- 1 cup flour
- 2 eggs, beaten
- 1 lb ground chicken
- 1 ½ cups breadcrumbs
- ¼ tsp crushed chilis
- ¼ tsp cayenne pepper
- ½ tsp garlic powder
- ¼ tsp shallot powder
- ½ tsp oregano

Directions:
1. Preheat air fryer to 390°F (200°C). Combine crushed chilis, cayenne pepper, garlic powder, shallot powder, and oregano in a bowl. Add the ground chicken and mix well with your hands until evenly combined. In another mixing bowl, beat the eggs until fluffy and until the yolks and whites are fully combined, and set aside.
2. Pour the beaten eggs, flour, and bread crumbs into 3 separate bowls. Roll the mozzarella sticks in the flour, then dip them in the beaten eggs. With hands, wrap the stick in a thin layer of the chicken mixture. Finally, coat the sticks in the crumbs. Place the sticks in the greased frying basket fryer and Air Fry for 18-20 minutes, turning once until crispy. Serve hot.

Chicken Parmigiana

Servings: 2
Cooking Time: 35 Minutes
Ingredients:
- 2 chicken breasts
- 1 cup breadcrumbs
- 2 eggs, beaten
- Salt and pepper to taste
- 1 tbsp dried basil
- 1 cup passata
- 2 provolone cheese slices
- 1 tbsp Parmesan cheese

Directions:
1. Preheat air fryer to 350°F (175°C). Mix the breadcrumbs, basil, salt, and pepper in a mixing bowl. Coat the chicken breasts with the crumb mixture, then dip in the beaten eggs. Finally, coat again with the dry ingredients. Arrange the coated chicken breasts on the greased frying basket and Air Fry for 20 minutes. At the 10-minutes mark, turn the breasts over and cook for the remaining 10 minutes.
2. Pour half of the passata into a baking pan. When the chicken is ready, remove it to the passata-covered pan. Pour the remaining passata over the fried chicken and arrange the provolone cheese slices on top and sprinkle with Parmesan cheese. Bake for 5 minutes until the chicken is crisped and the cheese melted and lightly toasted. Serve.

Spring Chicken Salad

Servings: 4
Cooking Time: 25 Minutes
Ingredients:
- 3 chicken breasts, cubed
- 1 small red onion, sliced
- 1 red bell pepper, sliced
- 1 cup green beans, sliced
- 2 tbsp ranch salad dressing
- 2 tbsp lemon juice
- ½ tsp dried basil
- 10 oz spring mix

Directions:
1. Preheat air fryer to 400°F (205°C). Put the chicken, red onion, red bell pepper, and green beans in the frying basket and Roast for 10-13 minutes until the chicken is cooked through. Shake the basket at least once while cooking. As the chicken is cooking, combine the ranch dressing, lemon juice, and basil. When the chicken is done, remove it and along with the veggies to a bowl and pour the dressing over. Stir to coat. Serve with spring mix.

Mexican Turkey Meatloaves

Servings: 4
Cooking Time: 30 Minutes
Ingredients:
- ¼ cup jarred chunky mild salsa
- 1 lb ground turkey
- 1/3 cup bread crumbs

- 1/3 cup canned black beans
- 1/3 cup frozen corn
- ¼ cup minced onion
- ¼ cup chopped scallions
- 2 tbsp chopped cilantro
- 1 egg, beaten
- 1 tbsp tomato puree
- 1 tsp salt
- ½ tsp ground cumin
- 1 tsp Mulato chile powder
- ½ tsp ground aniseed
- ¼ tsp ground cloves
- 2 tbsp ketchup
- 2 tbsp jarred mild salsa

Directions:
1. In a bowl, use your hands to mix the turkey, bread crumbs, beans, corn, salsa, onion, scallions, cilantro, egg, tomato puree, salt, chile powder, aniseed, cloves, and cumin. Shape into 4 patties about 1-inch in thickness.
2. Preheat air fryer to 350°F (175°C). Put the meatloaves in the greased frying basket and Bake for about 18-20 minutes, flipping once until cooked through. Stir together the ketchup and salsa in a small bowl. When all loaves are cooked, brush them with the glaze and return to the fryer to heat up for 2 minutes. Serve immediately.

Spinach And Feta Stuffed Chicken Breasts

Servings: 4
Cooking Time: 27 Minutes
Ingredients:
- 1 (10-ounce) package frozen spinach, thawed and drained well
- 1 cup feta cheese, crumbled
- ½ teaspoon freshly ground black pepper
- 4 boneless chicken breasts
- salt and freshly ground black pepper
- 1 tablespoon olive oil

Directions:
1. Prepare the filling. Squeeze out as much liquid as possible from the thawed spinach. Rough chop the spinach and transfer it to a mixing bowl with the feta cheese and the freshly ground black pepper.
2. Prepare the chicken breast. Place the chicken breast on a cutting board and press down on the chicken breast with one hand to keep it stabilized. Make an incision about 1-inch long in the fattest side of the breast. Move the knife up and down inside the chicken breast, without poking through either the top or the bottom, or the other side of the breast. The inside pocket should be about 3-inches long, but the opening should only be about 1-inch wide. If this is too difficult, you can make the incision longer, but you will have to be more careful when cooking the chicken breast since this will expose more of the stuffing.
3. Once you have prepared the chicken breasts, use your fingers to stuff the filling into each pocket, spreading the mixture down as far as you can.
4. Preheat the air fryer to 380°F (195°C).
5. Lightly brush or spray the air fryer basket and the chicken breasts with olive oil. Transfer two of the stuffed chicken breasts to the air fryer. Air-fry for 12 minutes, turning the chicken breasts over halfway through the cooking time. Remove the chicken to a resting plate and air-fry the second two breasts for 12 minutes. Return the first batch of chicken to the air fryer with the second batch and air-fry for 3 more minutes. When the chicken is cooked, an instant read thermometer should register 165°F (75°C) in the thickest part of the chicken, as well as in the stuffing.
6. Remove the chicken breasts and let them rest on a cutting board for 2 to 3 minutes. Slice the chicken on the bias and serve with the slices fanned out.

Fancy Chicken Piccata

Servings: 4
Cooking Time: 30 Minutes
Ingredients:
- 1 lb chicken breasts, cut into cutlets
- Salt and pepper to taste
- 2 egg whites
- 2/3 cup bread crumbs
- 1 tsp Italian seasoning
- 1 tbsp whipped butter
- ½ cup chicken broth
- ½ onion powder
- ¼ cup fino sherry
- Juice of 1 lemon
- 1 tbsp capers, drained
- 1 lemon, sliced
- 2 tbsp chopped parsley

Directions:
1. Preheat air fryer to 370°F (185°C). Place the cutlets between two sheets of parchment paper. Pound to a ¼-inch thickness and season with salt and pepper. Beat egg whites with 1 tsp of water in a bowl. Put the bread crumbs, Parmesan cheese, onion powder, and Italian seasoning in a second bowl. Dip the cutlet in the egg bowl, and then in the crumb mix. Put the cutlets in the greased frying basket. Air Fry for 6 minutes, flipping once until crispy and golden.
2. Melt butter in a skillet. Stir in broth, sherry, lemon juice, lemon halves, and black pepper. Bring to a boil over high heat until the sauce is reduced by half, 4 minutes. Remove from heat. Pick out the lemon rinds and discard them. Stir in capers. Plate a cutlet, spoon some sauce over and garnish with lemon sleeves and parsley to serve.

Maewoon Chicken Legs

Servings: 4
Cooking Time: 30 Minutes + Chilling Time
Ingredients:
- 4 scallions, sliced, whites and greens separated
- ¼ cup tamari
- 2 tbsp sesame oil
- 1 tsp sesame seeds
- ¼ cup honey
- 2 tbsp gochujang
- 2 tbsp ketchup
- 4 cloves garlic, minced
- ½ tsp ground ginger
- Salt and pepper to taste
- 1 tbsp parsley
- 1 ½ lb chicken legs

Directions:

Tower Air Fryer Cookbook

1. Whisk all ingredients, except chicken and scallion greens, in a bowl. Reserve ¼ cup of marinade. Toss chicken legs in the remaining marinade and chill for 30 minutes.
2. Preheat air fryer at 400°F. Place chicken legs in the greased frying basket and Air Fry for 10 minutes. Turn chicken. Cook for 8 more minutes. Let sit in a serving dish for 5 minutes. Coat the cooked chicken with the reserved marinade and scatter with scallion greens, sesame seeds and parsley to serve.

Chicken Cordon Bleu Patties

Servings: 4
Cooking Time: 30 Minutes
Ingredients:
- 1/3 cup grated Fontina cheese
- 3 tbsp milk
- 1/3 cup bread crumbs
- 1 egg, beaten
- ½ tsp dried parsley
- Salt and pepper to taste
- 1 ¼ lb ground chicken
- ¼ cup finely chopped ham

Directions:
1. Preheat air fryer to 350°F (175°C). Mix milk, breadcrumbs, egg, parsley, salt and pepper in a bowl. Using your hands, add the chicken and gently mix until just combined. Divide into 8 portions and shape into thin patties. Place on waxed paper. On 4 of the patties, top with ham and Fontina cheese, then place another patty on top of that. Gently pinch the edges together so that none of the ham or cheese is peeking out. Arrange the burgers in the greased frying basket and Air Fry until cooked through, for 14-16 minutes. Serve and enjoy!

Turkey Scotch Eggs

Servings: 4
Cooking Time: 30 Minutes
Ingredients:
- 1 ½ lb ground turkey
- 1 tbsp ground cumin
- 1 tsp ground coriander
- 2 garlic cloves, minced
- 3 raw eggs
- 1 ½ cups bread crumbs
- 6 hard-cooked eggs, peeled
- ½ cup flour

Directions:
1. Preheat air fryer to 370°F (175°C). Place the ground turkey, cumin, coriander, garlic, one egg, and ½ cup of bread crumbs in a large bowl and mix until well incorporated.
2. Divide into 6 equal portions, then flatten each into long ovals. Set aside. In a shallow bowl, beat the remaining raw eggs. In another shallow bowl, add flour. Do the same with another plate for bread crumbs. Roll each cooked egg in flour, then wrap with one oval of chicken sausage until completely covered.
3. Roll again in flour, then coat in the beaten egg before rolling in bread crumbs. Arrange the eggs in the greased frying basket. Air Fry for 12-14 minutes, flipping once until the sausage is cooked and the eggs are brown. Serve.

Chicken Burgers With Blue Cheese Sauce

Servings: 4
Cooking Time: 40 Minutes
Ingredients:
- ¼ cup crumbled blue cheese
- ¼ cup sour cream
- 2 tbsp mayonnaise
- 1 tbsp red hot sauce
- Salt to taste
- 3 tbsp buffalo wing sauce
- 1 lb ground chicken
- 2 tbsp grated carrot
- 2 tbsp diced celery
- 1 egg white

Directions:
1. Whisk the blue cheese, sour cream, mayonnaise, red hot sauce, salt, and 1 tbsp of buffalo sauce in a bowl. Let sit covered in the fridge until ready to use.
2. Preheat air fryer at 350°F. In another bowl, combine the remaining ingredients. Form mixture into 4 patties, making a slight indentation in the middle of each. Place patties in the greased frying basket and Air Fry for 13 minutes until you reach your desired doneness, flipping once. Serve with the blue cheese sauce.

Chicken Parmesan

Servings: 4
Cooking Time: 11 Minutes
Ingredients:
- 4 chicken tenders
- Italian seasoning
- salt
- ¼ cup cornstarch
- ½ cup Italian salad dressing
- ¼ cup panko breadcrumbs
- ¼ cup grated Parmesan cheese, plus more for serving
- oil for misting or cooking spray
- 8 ounces spaghetti, cooked
- 1 24-ounce jar marinara sauce

Directions:
1. Pound chicken tenders with meat mallet or rolling pin until about ¼-inch thick.
2. Sprinkle both sides with Italian seasoning and salt to taste.
3. Place cornstarch and salad dressing in 2 separate shallow dishes.
4. In a third shallow dish, mix together the panko crumbs and Parmesan cheese.
5. Dip flattened chicken in cornstarch, then salad dressing. Dip in the panko mixture, pressing into the chicken so the coating sticks well.
6. Spray both sides with oil or cooking spray. Place in air fryer basket in single layer.
7. Cook at 390°F (200°C) for 5minutes. Spray with oil again, turning chicken to coat both sides. See tip about turning.
8. Cook for an additional 6 minutes or until chicken juices run clear and outside is browned.
9. While chicken is cooking, heat marinara sauce and stir into cooked spaghetti.
10. To serve, divide spaghetti with sauce among 4 dinner plates, and top each with a fried chicken tender. Pass additional Parmesan at the table for those who want extra cheese.

Spicy Honey Mustard Chicken

Servings: 4
Cooking Time: 30 Minutes
Ingredients:
- 1/3 cup tomato sauce
- 2 tbsp yellow mustard
- 2 tbsp apple cider vinegar
- 1 tbsp honey
- 2 garlic cloves, minced
- 1 Fresno pepper, minced
- 1 tsp onion powder
- 4 chicken breasts

Directions:
1. Preheat air fryer to 370°F (185°C). Mix the tomato sauce, mustard, apple cider vinegar, honey, garlic, Fresno pepper, and onion powder in a bowl, then use a brush to rub the mix over the chicken breasts. Put the chicken in the air fryer and Grill for 10 minutes. Remove it, turn it, and rub with more sauce. Cook further for about 5 minutes. Remove the basket and flip the chicken. Add more sauce, return to the fryer, and cook for 3-5 more minutes or until the chicken is cooked through. Serve warm.

Buttered Chicken Thighs

Servings: 4
Cooking Time: 30 Minutes
Ingredients:
- 4 bone-in chicken thighs, skinless
- 2 tbsp butter, melted
- 1 tsp garlic powder
- 1 tsp lemon zest
- Salt and pepper to taste
- 1 lemon, sliced

Directions:
1. Preheat air fryer to 380°F (195°C). Stir the chicken thighs in the butter, lemon zest, garlic powder, and salt. Divide the chicken thighs between 4 pieces of foil and sprinkle with black pepper, and then top with slices of lemon. Bake in the air fryer for 20-22 minutes until golden. Serve.

Basic Chicken Breasts(2)

Servings: 4
Cooking Time: 15 Minutes
Ingredients:
- 2 tsp olive oil
- 2 chicken breasts
- Salt and pepper to taste
- ½ tsp garlic powder
- ½ tsp rosemary

Directions:
1. Preheat air fryer to 350°F. Rub the chicken breasts with olive oil over tops and bottom and sprinkle with garlic powder, rosemary, salt, and pepper. Place the chicken in the frying basket and Air Fry for 9 minutes, flipping once. Let rest onto a serving plate for 5 minutes before cutting into cubes. Serve and enjoy!

Peachy Chicken Chunks With Cherries

Servings: 4
Cooking Time: 16 Minutes
Ingredients:
- ⅓ cup peach preserves
- 1 teaspoon ground rosemary
- ½ teaspoon black pepper
- ½ teaspoon salt
- ½ teaspoon marjoram
- 1 teaspoon light olive oil
- 1 pound boneless chicken breasts, cut in 1½-inch chunks
- oil for misting or cooking spray
- 10-ounce package frozen unsweetened dark cherries, thawed and drained

Directions:
1. In a medium bowl, mix together peach preserves, rosemary, pepper, salt, marjoram, and olive oil.
2. Stir in chicken chunks and toss to coat well with the preserve mixture.
3. Spray air fryer basket with oil or cooking spray and lay chicken chunks in basket.
4. Cook at 390°F (200°C) for 7 minutes. Stir. Cook for 8 more minutes or until chicken juices run clear.
5. When chicken has cooked through, scatter the cherries over and cook for additional minute to heat cherries.

Crunchy Chicken Strips

Servings: 4
Cooking Time: 40 Minutes
Ingredients:
- 1 chicken breast, sliced into strips
- 1 tbsp grated Parmesan cheese
- 1 cup breadcrumbs
- 1 tbsp chicken seasoning
- 2 eggs, beaten
- Salt and pepper to taste

Directions:
1. Preheat air fryer to 350°F (175°C). Mix the breadcrumbs, Parmesan cheese, chicken seasoning, salt, and pepper in a mixing bowl. Coat the chicken with the crumb mixture, then dip in the beaten eggs. Finally, coat again with the dry ingredients. Arrange the coated chicken pieces on the greased frying basket and Air Fry for 15 minutes. Turn over halfway through cooking and cook for another 15 minutes. Serve immediately.

Chicken & Rice Sautée

Servings: 4
Cooking Time: 25 Minutes
Ingredients:
- 1 can pineapple chunks, drained, ¼ cup juice reserved
- 1 cup cooked long-grain rice
- 1 lb chicken breasts, cubed
- 1 red onion, chopped
- 1 tbsp peanut oil
- 1 peeled peach, cubed
- 1 tbsp cornstarch
- ½ tsp ground ginger
- ¼ tsp chicken seasoning

Directions:
1. Preheat air fryer to 400°F (205°C). Combine the chicken, red onion, pineapple, and peanut oil in a metal bowl, then put the bowl in the fryer. Air Fry for 9 minutes, remove and stir. Toss the peach in and put the bowl back into the fryer for 3 minutes. Slide out and stir again. Mix the reserved pineapple juice, corn starch, ginger, and chicken seasoning in a bowl, then pour over the chicken mixture and stir well. Put the bowl back into the fryer and cook for 3 more minutes or until the chicken is cooked through and the sauce is thick. Serve over cooked rice.

Tower Air Fryer Cookbook

Chapter 7: Fish And Seafood Recipes

Tuna Nuggets In Hoisin Sauce

Servings: 4
Cooking Time: 7 Minutes
Ingredients:
- ½ cup hoisin sauce
- 2 tablespoons rice wine vinegar
- 2 teaspoons sesame oil
- 1 teaspoon garlic powder
- 2 teaspoons dried lemongrass
- ¼ teaspoon red pepper flakes
- ½ small onion, quartered and thinly sliced
- 8 ounces fresh tuna, cut into 1-inch cubes
- cooking spray
- 3 cups cooked jasmine rice

Directions:
1. Mix the hoisin sauce, vinegar, sesame oil, and seasonings together.
2. Stir in the onions and tuna nuggets.
3. Spray air fryer baking pan with nonstick spray and pour in tuna mixture.
4. Cook at 390°F (200°C) for 3minutes. Stir gently.
5. Cook 2minutes and stir again, checking for doneness. Tuna should be barely cooked through, just beginning to flake and still very moist. If necessary, continue cooking and stirring in 1-minute intervals until done.
6. Serve warm over hot jasmine rice.

Dijon Shrimp Cakes

Servings: 4
Cooking Time: 30 Minutes
Ingredients:
- 1 cup cooked shrimp, minced
- ¾ cup saltine cracker crumbs
- 1 cup lump crabmeat
- 3 green onions, chopped
- 1 egg, beaten
- ¼ cup mayonnaise
- 2 tbsp Dijon mustard
- 1 tbsp lemon juice

Directions:
1. Preheat the air fryer to 375°F (190°C). Combine the crabmeat, shrimp, green onions, egg, mayonnaise, mustard, ¼ cup of cracker crumbs, and the lemon juice in a bowl and mix gently. Make 4 patties, sprinkle with the rest of the cracker crumbs on both sides, and spray with cooking oil. Line the frying basket with a round parchment paper with holes poked in it. Coat the paper with cooking spray and lay the patties on it. Bake for 10-14 minutes or until the patties are golden brown. Serve warm.

Cajun-seasoned Shrimp

Servings: 2
Cooking Time: 15 Minutes
Ingredients:
- 1 lb shelled tail on shrimp, deveined
- 2 tsp grated Parmesan cheese
- 2 tbsp butter, melted
- 1 tsp cayenne pepper
- 1 tsp garlic powder
- 2 tsp Cajun seasoning
- 1 tbsp lemon juice

Directions:
1. Preheat air fryer at 350ºF. Toss the shrimp, melted butter, cayenne pepper, garlic powder and cajun seasoning in a bowl, place them in the greased frying basket, and Air Fry for 6 minutes, flipping once. Transfer it to a plate. Squeeze lemon juice over shrimp and stir in Parmesan cheese. Serve immediately.

Crunchy And Buttery Cod With Ritz® Cracker Crust

Servings: 2
Cooking Time: 10 Minutes
Ingredients:
- 4 tablespoons butter, melted
- 8 to 10 RITZ® crackers, crushed into crumbs
- 2 (6-ounce) cod fillets
- salt and freshly ground black pepper
- 1 lemon

Directions:
1. Preheat the air fryer to 380°F (195°C).
2. Melt the butter in a small saucepan on the stovetop or in a microwavable dish in the microwave, and then transfer the butter to a shallow dish. Place the crushed RITZ® crackers into a second shallow dish.
3. Season the fish fillets with salt and freshly ground black pepper. Dip them into the butter and then coat both sides with the RITZ® crackers.
4. Place the fish into the air fryer basket and air-fry at 380°F (195°C) for 10 minutes, flipping the fish over halfway through the cooking time.
5. Serve with a wedge of lemon to squeeze over the top.

Crab Stuffed Salmon Roast

Servings: 4
Cooking Time: 20 Minutes
Ingredients:
- 1 (1½-pound) salmon fillet
- salt and freshly ground black pepper
- 6 ounces crabmeat
- 1 teaspoon finely chopped lemon zest
- 1 teaspoon Dijon mustard
- 1 tablespoon chopped fresh parsley, plus more for garnish
- 1 scallion, chopped
- ¼ teaspoon salt
- olive oil

Directions:
1. Prepare the salmon fillet by butterflying it. Slice into the thickest side of the salmon, parallel to the countertop and along the length of the fillet. Don't slice all the way through to the other side – stop about an inch from the edge. Open the salmon up like a book. Season the salmon with salt and freshly ground black pepper.
2. Make the crab filling by combining the crabmeat, lemon zest, mustard, parsley, scallion, salt and freshly ground black pepper in a bowl. Spread this filling in the center of the salmon. Fold one side of the salmon over the filling. Then fold the other side over on top.
3. Transfer the rolled salmon to the center of a piece of parchment paper that is roughly 6- to 7-inches wide and about 12-inches long. The parchment paper will act as a sling, making it easier to put the salmon into the air fryer.

Preheat the air fryer to 370°F (185°C). Use the parchment paper to transfer the salmon roast to the air fryer basket and tuck the ends of the paper down beside the salmon. Drizzle a little olive oil on top and season with salt and pepper.
4. Air-fry the salmon at 370°F (185°C) for 20 minutes.
5. Remove the roast from the air fryer and let it rest for a few minutes. Then, slice it, sprinkle some more lemon zest and parsley (or fresh chives) on top and serve.

Korean-style Fried Calamari
Servings: 4
Cooking Time: 25 Minutes
Ingredients:
- 2 tbsp tomato paste
- 1 tbsp gochujang
- 1 tbsp lime juice
- 1 tsp lime zest
- 1 tsp smoked paprika
- ½ tsp salt
- 1 cup bread crumbs
- 1/3 lb calamari rings

Directions:
1. Preheat air fryer to 400°F. Whisk tomato paste, gochujang, lime juice and zest, paprika, and salt in a bowl. In another bowl, add in the bread crumbs. Dredge calamari rings in the tomato mixture, shake off excess, then roll through the crumbs. Place calamari rings in the greased frying basket and Air Fry for 4-5 minutes, flipping once. Serve.

Stuffed Shrimp Wrapped In Bacon
Servings: 4
Cooking Time: 30 Minutes
Ingredients:
- 1 lb shrimp, deveined and shelled
- 3 tbsp crumbled goat cheese
- 2 tbsp panko bread crumbs
- ¼ tsp soy sauce
- ½ tsp prepared horseradish
- ¼ tsp garlic powder
- ½ tsp chili powder
- 2 tsp mayonnaise
- Black pepper to taste
- 5 slices bacon, quartered
- ¼ cup chopped parsley

Directions:
1. Preheat air fryer to 400°F. Butterfly shrimp by cutting down the spine of each shrimp without going all the way through. Combine the goat cheese, bread crumbs, soy sauce, horseradish, garlic powder, chili powder, mayonnaise, and black pepper in a bowl. Evenly press goat cheese mixture into shrimp. Wrap a piece of bacon around each piece of shrimp to hold in the cheese mixture. Place them in the frying basket and Air Fry for 8-10 minutes, flipping once. Top with parsley to serve.

Sriracha Salmon Melt Sandwiches
Servings: 4
Cooking Time: 20 Minutes
Ingredients:
- 2 tbsp butter, softened
- 2 cans pink salmon
- 2 English muffins
- 1/3 cup mayonnaise
- 2 tbsp Dijon mustard
- 1 tbsp fresh lemon juice
- 1/3 cup chopped celery
- ½ tsp sriracha sauce
- 4 slices tomato
- 4 slices Swiss cheese

Directions:
1. Preheat the air fryer to 370°F (185°C). Split the English muffins with a fork and spread butter on the 4 halves. Put the halves in the basket and Bake for 3-5 minutes, or until toasted. Remove and set aside. Combine the salmon, mayonnaise, mustard, lemon juice, celery, and sriracha in a bowl. Divide among the English muffin halves. Top each sandwich with tomato and cheese and put in the frying basket. Bake for 4-6 minutes or until the cheese is melted and starts to brown. Serve hot.

Chili Blackened Shrimp
Servings: 4
Cooking Time: 15 Minutes
Ingredients:
- 1 lb peeled shrimp, deveined
- 1 tsp paprika
- ½ tsp dried dill
- ½ tsp red chili flakes
- ½ lemon, juiced
- Salt and pepper to taste

Directions:
1. Preheat air fryer to 400°F (205°C). In a resealable bag, add shrimp, paprika, dill, red chili flakes, lemon juice, salt and pepper. Seal and shake well. Place the shrimp in the greased frying basket and Air Fry for 7-8 minutes, shaking the basket once until blackened. Let cool slightly and serve.

Classic Crab Cakes
Servings: 4
Cooking Time: 10 Minutes
Ingredients:
- 10 ounces Lump crabmeat, picked over for shell and cartilage
- 6 tablespoons Plain panko bread crumbs (gluten-free, if a concern)
- 6 tablespoons Chopped drained jarred roasted red peppers
- 4 Medium scallions, trimmed and thinly sliced
- ¼ cup Regular or low-fat mayonnaise (not fat-free; gluten-free, if a concern)
- ¼ teaspoon Dried dill
- ¼ teaspoon Dried thyme
- ¼ teaspoon Onion powder
- ¼ teaspoon Table salt
- ⅛ teaspoon Celery seeds
- Up to ⅛ teaspoon Cayenne
- Vegetable oil spray

Directions:
1. Preheat the air fryer to 400°F (205°C).
2. Gently mix the crabmeat, bread crumbs, red pepper, scallion, mayonnaise, dill, thyme, onion powder, salt, celery seeds, and cayenne in a bowl until well combined.

3. Use clean and dry hands to form ½ cup of this mixture into a tightly packed 1-inch-thick, 3- to 4-inch-wide patty. Coat the top and bottom of the patty with vegetable oil spray and set it aside. Continue making 1 more patty for a small batch, 3 more for a medium batch, or 5 more for a larger one, coating them with vegetable oil spray on both sides.
4. Set the patties in one layer in the basket and air-fry undisturbed for 10 minutes, or until lightly browned and cooked through.
5. Use a nonstick-safe spatula to transfer the crab cakes to a serving platter or plates. Wait a couple of minutes before serving.

Home-style Fish Sticks

Servings: 4
Cooking Time: 30 Minutes
Ingredients:
- 1 lb cod fillets, cut into sticks
- 1 cup flour
- 1 egg
- ¼ cup cornmeal
- Salt and pepper to taste
- ¼ tsp smoked paprika
- 1 lemon

Directions:
1. Preheat air fryer at 350ºF. In a bowl, add ½ cup of flour. In another bowl, beat the egg and in a third bowl, combine the remaining flour, cornmeal, salt, black pepper and paprika. Roll the sticks in the flour, shake off excess flour. Then, dip them in the egg, shake off excess egg. Finally, dredge them in the cornmeal mixture. Place fish fingers in the greased frying basket and Air Fry for 10 minutes, flipping once. Serve with squeezed lemon.

Saucy Shrimp

Servings: 4
Cooking Time: 30 Minutes
Ingredients:
- 1 lb peeled shrimp, deveined
- ½ cup grated coconut
- ¼ cup bread crumbs
- ¼ cup flour
- ¼ tsp smoked paprika
- Salt and pepper to taste
- 1 egg
- 2 tbsp maple syrup
- ½ tsp rice vinegar
- 1 tbsp hot sauce
- ⅛ tsp red pepper flakes
- ¼ cup orange juice
- 1 tsp cornstarch
- ½ cup banana ketchup
- 1 lemon, sliced

Directions:
1. Preheat air fryer to 350°F (175°C). Combine coconut, bread crumbs, flour, paprika, black pepper, and salt in a bowl. In a separate bowl, whisk egg and 1 teaspoon water. Dip one shrimp into the egg bowl and shake off excess drips. Dip the shrimp in the bread crumb mixture and coat it completely. Continue the process for all of the shrimp. Arrange the shrimp on the greased frying basket. Air Fry for 5 minutes, then use tongs to flip the shrimp. Cook for another 2-3 minutes.
2. To make the sauce, add maple syrup, banana ketchup, hot sauce, vinegar, and red pepper flakes in a small saucepan over medium heat. Make a slurry in a small bowl with orange juice and cornstarch. Stir in slurry and continue stirring. Bring the sauce to a boil and cook for 5 minutes. When the sauce begins to thicken, remove from heat and allow to sit for 5 minutes. Serve shrimp warm along with sauce and lemon slices on the side.

Shrimp Patties

Servings: 4
Cooking Time: 10 Minutes
Ingredients:
- ½ pound shelled and deveined raw shrimp
- ¼ cup chopped red bell pepper
- ¼ cup chopped green onion
- ¼ cup chopped celery
- 2 cups cooked sushi rice
- ½ teaspoon garlic powder
- ½ teaspoon Old Bay Seasoning
- ½ teaspoon salt
- 2 teaspoons Worcestershire sauce
- ½ cup plain breadcrumbs
- oil for misting or cooking spray

Directions:
1. Finely chop the shrimp. You can do this in a food processor, but it takes only a few pulses. Be careful not to overprocess into mush.
2. Place shrimp in a large bowl and add all other ingredients except the breadcrumbs and oil. Stir until well combined.
3. Preheat air fryer to 390°F (200°C).
4. Shape shrimp mixture into 8 patties, no more than ½-inch thick. Roll patties in breadcrumbs and mist with oil or cooking spray.
5. Place 4 shrimp patties in air fryer basket and cook at 390°F (200°C) for 10 minutes, until shrimp cooks through and outside is crispy.
6. Repeat step 5 to cook remaining shrimp patties.

Fish Nuggets With Broccoli Dip

Servings: 4
Cooking Time: 40 Minutes
Ingredients:
- 1 lb cod fillets, cut into chunks
- 1 ½ cups broccoli florets
- ¼ cup grated Parmesan
- 3 garlic cloves, peeled
- 3 tbsp sour cream
- 2 tbsp lemon juice
- 2 tbsp olive oil
- 2 egg whites
- 1 cup panko bread crumbs
- 1 tsp dried dill
- Salt and pepper to taste

Directions:
1. Preheat the air fryer to 400°F (205°C). Put the broccoli and garlic in the greased frying basket and Air Fry for 5-7 minutes or until tender. Remove to a blender and add sour cream, lemon juice, olive oil, and ½ tsp of salt and process

until smooth. Set the sauce aside. Beat the egg whites until frothy in a shallow bowl. On a plate, combine the panko, Parmesan, dill, pepper, and the remaining ½ tsp of salt. Dip the cod fillets in the egg whites, then the breadcrumbs, pressing to coat. Put half the cubes in the frying basket and spray with cooking oil. Air Fry for 6-8 minutes or until the fish is cooked through. Serve the fish with the sauce and enjoy!

Holliday Lobster Salad

Servings: 2
Cooking Time: 20 Minutes
Ingredients:
- 2 lobster tails
- ¼ cup mayonnaise
- 2 tsp lemon juice
- 1 stalk celery, sliced
- 2 tsp chopped chives
- 2 tsp chopped tarragon
- Salt and pepper to taste
- 2 tomato slices
- 4 cucumber slices
- 1 avocado, diced

Directions:
1. Preheat air fryer to 400°F. Using kitchen shears, cut down the middle of each lobster tail on the softer side. Carefully run your finger between the lobster meat and the shell to loosen meat. Place lobster tails, cut sides up, in the frying basket, and Air Fry for 8 minutes. Transfer to a large plate and let cool for 3 minutes until easy to handle, then pull lobster meat from the shell and roughly chop it. Combine chopped lobster, mayonnaise, lemon juice, celery, chives, tarragon, salt, and pepper in a bowl. Divide between 2 medium plates and top with tomato slices, cucumber and avocado cubes. Serve immediately.

Quick Shrimp Scampi

Servings: 2
Cooking Time: 5 Minutes
Ingredients:
- 16 to 20 raw large shrimp, peeled, deveined and tails removed
- ½ cup white wine
- freshly ground black pepper
- ¼ cup + 1 tablespoon butter, divided
- 1 clove garlic, sliced
- 1 teaspoon olive oil
- salt, to taste
- juice of ½ lemon, to taste
- ¼ cup chopped fresh parsley

Directions:
1. Start by marinating the shrimp in the white wine and freshly ground black pepper for at least 30 minutes, or as long as 2 hours in the refrigerator.
2. Preheat the air fryer to 400°F.
3. Melt ¼ cup of butter in a small saucepan on the stovetop. Add the garlic and let the butter simmer, but be sure to not let it burn.
4. Pour the shrimp and marinade into the air fryer, letting the marinade drain through to the bottom drawer. Drizzle the olive oil on the shrimp and season well with salt. Air-fry at 400°F (205°C) for 3 minutes. Turn the shrimp over (don't shake the basket because the marinade will splash around) and pour the garlic butter over the shrimp. Air-fry for another 2 minutes.
5. Remove the shrimp from the air fryer basket and transfer them to a bowl. Squeeze lemon juice over all the shrimp and toss with the chopped parsley and remaining tablespoon of butter. Season to taste with salt and serve immediately.

Salmon Croquettes

Servings: 4
Cooking Time: 8 Minutes
Ingredients:
- 1 tablespoon oil
- ½ cup breadcrumbs
- 1 14.75-ounce can salmon, drained and all skin and fat removed
- 1 egg, beaten
- ⅓ cup coarsely crushed saltine crackers (about 8 crackers)
- ½ teaspoon Old Bay Seasoning
- ½ teaspoon onion powder
- ½ teaspoon Worcestershire sauce

Directions:
1. Preheat air fryer to 390°F (20°C).
2. In a shallow dish, mix oil and breadcrumbs until crumbly.
3. In a large bowl, combine the salmon, egg, cracker crumbs, Old Bay, onion powder, and Worcestershire. Mix well and shape into 8 small patties about ½-inch thick.
4. Gently dip each patty into breadcrumb mixture and turn to coat well on all sides.
5. Cook at 390°F (200°C) for 8minutes or until outside is crispy and browned.

Popcorn Crawfish

Servings: 4
Cooking Time: 18 Minutes
Ingredients:
- ½ cup flour, plus 2 tablespoons
- ½ teaspoon garlic powder
- 1½ teaspoons Old Bay Seasoning
- ½ teaspoon onion powder
- ½ cup beer, plus 2 tablespoons
- 12-ounce package frozen crawfish tail meat, thawed and drained
- oil for misting or cooking spray
- Coating
- 1½ cups panko crumbs
- 1 teaspoon Old Bay Seasoning
- ½ teaspoon ground black pepper

Directions:
1. In a large bowl, mix together the flour, garlic powder, Old Bay Seasoning, and onion powder. Stir in beer to blend.
2. Add crawfish meat to batter and stir to coat.
3. Combine the coating ingredients in food processor and pulse to finely crush the crumbs. Transfer crumbs to shallow dish.
4. Preheat air fryer to 390°F (200°C).
5. Pour the crawfish and batter into a colander to drain. Stir with a spoon to drain excess batter.

Tower Air Fryer Cookbook

6. Working with a handful of crawfish at a time, roll in crumbs and place on a cookie sheet. It's okay if some of the smaller pieces of crawfish meat stick together.
7. Spray breaded crawfish with oil or cooking spray and place all at once into air fryer basket.
8. Cook at 390°F (200°C) for 5minutes. Shake basket or stir and mist again with olive oil or spray. Cook 5 moreminutes, shake basket again, and mist lightly again. Continue cooking 5 more minutes, until browned and crispy.

Fish Piccata With Crispy Potatoes
Servings: 4
Cooking Time: 30 Minutes
Ingredients:
- 4 cod fillets
- 1 tbsp butter
- 2 tsp capers
- 1 garlic clove, minced
- 2 tbsp lemon juice
- ½ lb asparagus, trimmed
- 2 large potatoes, cubed
- 1 tbsp olive oil
- Salt and pepper to taste
- ¼ tsp garlic powder
- 1 tsp dried rosemary
- 1 tsp dried parsley
- 1 tsp chopped dill

Directions:
1. Preheat air fryer to 380°F 195°C). Place each fillet on a large piece of foil. Top each fillet with butter, capers, dill, garlic, and lemon juice. Fold the foil over the fish and seal the edges to make a pouch. Mix asparagus, parsley, potatoes, olive oil, salt, rosemary, garlic powder, and pepper in a large bowl. Place asparagus in the frying basket. Roast for 4 minutes, then shake the basket. Top vegetable with foil packets and Roast for another 8 minutes. Turn off air fryer and let it stand for 5 minutes. Serve warm and enjoy.

Coconut Jerk Shrimp
Servings:3
Cooking Time: 8 Minutes
Ingredients:
- 1 Large egg white(s)
- 1 teaspoon Purchased or homemade jerk dried seasoning blend (see the headnote)
- ¾ cup Plain panko bread crumbs (gluten-free, if a concern)
- ¾ cup Unsweetened shredded coconut
- 12 Large shrimp (20–25 per pound), peeled and deveined
- Coconut oil spray

Directions:
1. Preheat the air fryer to 375°F (190°C).
2. Whisk the egg white(s) and seasoning blend in a bowl until foamy. Add the shrimp and toss well to coat evenly.
3. Mix the bread crumbs and coconut on a dinner plate until well combined. Use kitchen tongs to pick up a shrimp, letting the excess egg white mixture slip back into the rest. Set the shrimp in the bread-crumb mixture. Turn several times to coat evenly and thoroughly. Set on a cutting board and continue coating the remainder of the shrimp.
4. Lightly coat all the shrimp on both sides with the coconut oil spray. Set them in the basket in one layer with as much space between them as possible. (You can even stand some up along the basket's wall in some models.) Air-fry undisturbed for 6 minutes, or until the coating is lightly browned. If the air fryer is at 360°F (185°C), you may need to add 2 minutes to the cooking time.
5. Use clean kitchen tongs to transfer the shrimp to a wire rack. Cool for only a minute or two before serving.

Panko-breaded Cod Fillets
Servings:2
Cooking Time: 20 Minutes
Ingredients:
- 1 lemon wedge, juiced and zested
- ½ cup panko bread crumbs
- Salt to taste
- 1 tbsp Dijon mustard
- 1 tbsp butter, melted
- 2 cod fillets

Directions:
1. Preheat air fryer to 350ºF. Combine all ingredients, except for the fish, in a bowl. Press mixture evenly across tops of cod fillets. Place fillets in the greased frying basket and Air Fry for 10 minutes until the cod is opaque and flakes easily with a fork. Serve immediately.

Mediterranean Cod Croquettes
Servings: 4
Cooking Time: 30 Minutes
Ingredients:
- ½ cup instant mashed potatoes
- 12 oz raw cod fillet, flaked
- 2 large eggs, beaten
- ¼ cup sour cream
- 2 tsp olive oil
- 1/3 cup chopped thyme
- 1 shallot, minced
- 1 garlic clove, minced
- 1 cup bread crumbs
- 1 tsp lemon juice
- Salt and pepper to taste
- ½ tsp dried basil
- 5 tbsp Greek yogurt
- ½ tsp harissa paste
- 1 tbsp chopped dill

Directions:
1. In a bowl, combine the fish, 1 egg, sour cream, instant mashed potatoes, olive oil, thyme, shallot, garlic, 2 tbsp of the bread crumbs, salt, dill, lemon juice, and pepper; mix well. Refrigerate for 30 minutes. Mix yogurt, harissa paste, and basil in a bowl until blended. Set aside.
2. Preheat air fryer to 350°F (175°C). Take the fish mixture out of the refrigerator. Knead and shape the mixture into 12 longs. In a bowl, place the remaining egg. In a second bowl, add the remaining bread crumbs. Dip the croquettes into the egg and shake off the excess drips. Then roll the logs into the breadcrumbs. Place the croquettes in the greased frying basket. Air Fry for 10 minutes, flipping once until golden. Serve with the yogurt sauce.

Honey Pecan Shrimp

Servings: 4
Cooking Time: 10 Minutes
Ingredients:
- ¼ cup cornstarch
- ¾ teaspoon sea salt, divided
- ¼ teaspoon pepper
- 2 egg whites
- ⅔ cup finely chopped pecans
- 1 pound raw, peeled, and deveined shrimp
- ¼ cup honey
- 2 tablespoons mayonnaise

Directions:
1. In a small bowl, whisk together the cornstarch, ½ teaspoon of the salt, and the pepper.
2. In a second bowl, whisk together the egg whites until soft and foamy. (They don't need to be whipped to peaks or even soft peaks, just frothy.)
3. In a third bowl, mix together the pecans and the remaining ¼ teaspoon of sea salt.
4. Pat the shrimp dry with paper towels. Working in small batches, dip the shrimp into the cornstarch, then into the egg whites, and then into the pecans until all the shrimp are coated with pecans.
5. Preheat the air fryer to 330°F (165°C).
6. Place the coated shrimp inside the air fryer basket and spray with cooking spray. Cook for 5 minutes, toss the shrimp, and cook another 5 minutes.
7. Meanwhile, place the honey in a microwave-safe bowl and microwave for 30 seconds. Whisk in the mayonnaise until smooth and creamy. Pour the honey sauce into a serving bowl. Add the cooked shrimp to the serving bowl while hot and toss to coat. Serve immediately.

Cheesy Tuna Tower

Servings: 2
Cooking Time: 15 Minutes
Ingredients:
- ½ cup grated mozzarella
- 1 can tuna in water
- ¼ cup mayonnaise
- 2 tsp yellow mustard
- 1 tbsp minced dill pickle
- 1 tbsp minced celery
- 1 tbsp minced green onion
- Salt and pepper to taste
- 4 tomato slices
- 8 avocado slices

Directions:
1. Preheat air fryer to 350°F. In a bowl, combine tuna, mayonnaise, mustard, pickle, celery, green onion, salt, and pepper. Cut a piece of parchment paper to fit the bottom of the frying basket. Place tomato slices on paper in a single layer and top with 2 avocado slices. Share tuna salad over avocado slices and top with mozzarella cheese. Place the towers in the frying basket and Bake for 4 minutes until the cheese starts to brown. Serve warm.

Basil Crab Cakes With Fresh Salad

Servings: 2
Cooking Time: 25 Minutes
Ingredients:
- 8 oz lump crabmeat
- 2 tbsp mayonnaise
- ½ tsp Dijon mustard
- ½ tsp lemon juice
- ½ tsp lemon zest
- 2 tsp minced yellow onion
- ¼ tsp prepared horseradish
- ¼ cup flour
- 1 egg white, beaten
- 1 tbsp basil, minced
- 1 tbsp olive oil
- 2 tsp white wine vinegar
- Salt and pepper to taste
- 4 oz arugula
- ½ cup blackberries
- ¼ cup pine nuts
- 2 lemon wedges

Directions:
1. Preheat air fryer to 400°F. Combine the crabmeat, mayonnaise, mustard, lemon juice and zest, onion, horseradish, flour, egg white, and basil in a bowl. Form mixture into 4 patties. Place the patties in the lightly greased frying basket and Air Fry for 10 minutes, flipping once. Combine olive oil, vinegar, salt, and pepper in a bowl. Toss in the arugula and share into 2 medium bowls. Add 2 crab cakes to each bowl and scatter with blackberries, pine nuts, and lemon wedges. Serve warm.

Salmon Puttanesca En Papillotte With Zucchini

Servings: 2
Cooking Time: 17 Minutes
Ingredients:
- 1 small zucchini, sliced into ¼-inch thick half moons
- 1 teaspoon olive oil
- salt and freshly ground black pepper
- 2 (5-ounce) salmon fillets
- 1 beefsteak tomato, chopped (about 1 cup)
- 1 tablespoon capers, rinsed
- 10 black olives, pitted and sliced
- 2 tablespoons dry vermouth or white wine 2 tablespoons butter
- ¼ cup chopped fresh basil, chopped

Directions:
1. Preheat the air fryer to 400°F (205°C).
2. Toss the zucchini with the olive oil, salt and freshly ground black pepper. Transfer the zucchini into the air fryer basket and air-fry for 5 minutes, shaking the basket once or twice during the cooking process.
3. Cut out 2 large rectangles of parchment paper – about 13-inches by 15-inches each. Divide the air-fried zucchini between the two pieces of parchment paper, placing the vegetables in the center of each rectangle.
4. Place a fillet of salmon on each pile of zucchini. Season the fish very well with salt and pepper. Toss the tomato, capers, olives and vermouth (or white wine) together in a bowl. Divide the tomato mixture between the two fish packages, placing it on top of the fish fillets and pouring any juice out of the bowl onto the fish. Top each fillet with a tablespoon of butter.

5. Fold up each parchment square. Bring two edges together and fold them over a few times, leaving some space above the fish. Twist the open sides together and upwards so they can serve as handles for the packet, but don't let them extend beyond the top of the air fryer basket.

6. Place the two packages into the air fryer and air-fry at 400°F (205°C) for 12 minutes. The packages should be puffed up and slightly browned when fully cooked. Once cooked, let the fish sit in the parchment for 2 minutes.

7. Serve the fish in the parchment paper, or if desired, remove the parchment paper before serving. Garnish with a little fresh basil.

Potato-wrapped Salmon Fillets

Servings: 3
Cooking Time: 8 Minutes
Ingredients:
- 1 Large 1-pound elongated yellow potato(es), peeled
- 3 6-ounce, 1½-inch-wide, quite thick skinless salmon fillets
- Olive oil spray
- ¼ teaspoon Table salt
- ¼ teaspoon Ground black pepper

Directions:
1. Preheat the air fryer to 400°F (205°C).
2. Use a vegetable peeler or mandoline to make long strips from the potato(es). You'll need anywhere from 8 to 12 strips per fillet, depending on the shape of the potato and of the salmon fillet.
3. Drape potato strips over a salmon fillet, overlapping the strips to create an even "crust." Tuck the potato strips under the fillet, overlapping the strips underneath to create as smooth a bottom as you can. Wrap the remaining fillet(s) in the same way.
4. Gently turn the fillets over. Generously coat the bottoms with olive oil spray. Turn them back seam side down and generously coat the tops with the oil spray. Sprinkle the salt and pepper over the wrapped fillets.
5. Use a nonstick-safe spatula to gently transfer the fillets seam side down to the basket. It helps to remove the basket from the machine and set it on your work surface (keeping in mind that the basket's hot). Leave as much air space as possible between the fillets. Air-fry undisturbed for 8 minutes, or until golden brown and crisp.
6. Use a nonstick-safe spatula to gently transfer the fillets to serving plates. Cool for a couple of minutes before serving.

Almond-crusted Fish

Servings: 4
Cooking Time: 10 Minutes
Ingredients:
- 4 4-ounce fish fillets
- ¾ cup breadcrumbs
- ¼ cup sliced almonds, crushed
- 2 tablespoons lemon juice
- ⅛ teaspoon cayenne
- salt and pepper
- ¾ cup flour
- 1 egg, beaten with 1 tablespoon water
- oil for misting or cooking spray

Directions:

1. Split fish fillets lengthwise down the center to create 8 pieces.
2. Mix breadcrumbs and almonds together and set aside.
3. Mix the lemon juice and cayenne together. Brush on all sides of fish.
4. Season fish to taste with salt and pepper.
5. Place the flour on a sheet of wax paper.
6. Roll fillets in flour, dip in egg wash, and roll in the crumb mixture.
7. Mist both sides of fish with oil or cooking spray.
8. Spray air fryer basket and lay fillets inside.
9. Cook at 390°F (200°C) for 5 minutes, turn fish over, and cook for an additional 5 minutes or until fish is done and flakes easily.

Baltimore Crab Cakes

Servings: 4
Cooking Time: 35 Minutes
Ingredients:
- ½ lb lump crabmeat, shells discarded
- 2 tbsp mayonnaise
- ½ tsp yellow mustard
- ½ tsp lemon juice
- ½ tbsp minced shallot
- ¼ cup bread crumbs
- 1 egg
- Salt and pepper to taste
- 4 poached eggs
- ½ cup bechamel sauce
- 2 tsp chopped chives
- 1 lemon, cut into wedges

Directions:
1. Preheat air fryer at 400°F. Combine all ingredients, except eggs, sauce, and chives, in a bowl. Form mixture into 4 patties. Place crab cakes in the greased frying basket and Air Fry for 10 minutes, flipping once. Transfer them to a serving dish. Top each crab cake with 1 poached egg, drizzle with Bechamel sauce and scatter with chives and lemon wedges. Serve and enjoy!

Aromatic Ahi Tuna Steaks

Servings: 4
Cooking Time: 15 Minutes
Ingredients:
- 1 tsp garlic powder
- ½ tsp salt
- ¼ tsp dried thyme
- ¼ tsp dried oregano
- ¼ tsp cayenne pepper
- 4 ahi tuna steaks
- 2 tbsp olive oil
- 1 lemon, cut into wedges

Directions:
1. Preheat air fryer to 380°F (195°C). Stir together the garlic powder, salt, thyme, cayenne pepper and oregano in a bowl to combine. Coat the tuna steaks with olive oil. Season both sides of each steak with the seasoning mix. Put the steaks in the frying basket. Air Fry for 5 minutes, then flip and cook for an additional 3-4 minutes. Serve warm with lemon wedges on the side.

Caribbean Skewers

Servings: 4
Cooking Time: 25 Minutes
Ingredients:
- 1 ½ lb large shrimp, peeled and deveined
- 1 can pineapple chunks, drained, liquid reserved
- 1 red bell pepper, chopped
- 3 scallions, chopped
- 1 tbsp lemon juice
- 1 tbsp olive oil
- ½ tsp jerk seasoning
- ⅛ tsp cayenne pepper
- 2 tbsp cilantro, chopped

Directions:
1. Preheat the air fryer to 37°F (5°C). Thread the shrimp, pineapple, bell pepper, and scallions onto 8 bamboo skewers. Mix 3 tbsp of pineapple juice with lemon juice, olive oil, jerk seasoning, and cayenne pepper. Brush every bit of the mix over the skewers. Place 4 kebabs in the frying basket, add a rack, and put the rest of the skewers on top. Bake for 6-9 minutes and rearrange at about 4-5 minutes. Cook until the shrimp curl and pinken. Sprinkle with freshly chopped cilantro and serve.

Mediterranean Sea Scallops

Servings: 2
Cooking Time: 20 Minutes
Ingredients:
- 1 tbsp olive oil
- 1 shallot, minced
- 2 tbsp capers
- 2 cloves garlic, minced
- ½ cup heavy cream
- 3 tbsp butter
- 1 tbsp lemon juice
- Salt and pepper to taste
- ¼ tbsp cumin powder
- ¼ tbsp curry powder
- 1 lb jumbo sea scallops
- 2 tbsp chopped parsley
- 1 tbsp chopped cilantro

Directions:
1. Warm the olive oil in a saucepan over medium heat. Add shallot and stir-fry for 2 minutes until translucent. Stir in capers, cumin, curry, garlic, heavy cream, 1 tbsp of butter, lemon juice, salt, and pepper and cook for 2 minutes until rolling a boil. Low the heat and simmer for 3 minutes until the caper sauce thickens. Turn the heat off.
2. Preheat air fryer at 400ºF. In a bowl, add the remaining butter and scallops and toss to coat on all sides. Place scallops in the greased frying basket and Air Fry for 8 minutes, flipping once. Drizzle caper sauce over, scatter with parsley, cilantro and serve.

The Best Oysters Rockefeller

Servings: 2
Cooking Time: 30 Minutes
Ingredients:
- 4 tsp grated Parmesan
- 2 tbsp butter
- 1 sweet onion, minced
- 1 clove garlic, minced
- 1 cup baby spinach
- ⅛ tsp Tabasco hot sauce
- ½ tsp lemon juice
- ½ tsp lemon zest
- ¼ cup bread crumbs
- 12 oysters, on the half shell

Directions:
1. Melt butter in a skillet over medium heat. Stir in onion, garlic, and spinach and stir-fry for 3 minutes until the onion is translucent. Mix in Parmesan cheese, hot sauce, lemon juice, lemon zest, and bread crumbs. Divide this mixture between the tops of oysters.
2. Preheat air fryer to 400ºF. Place oysters in the frying basket and Air Fry for 6 minutes. Serve immediately.

Easy-peasy Shrimp

Servings: 2
Cooking Time: 15 Minutes
Ingredients:
- 1 lb tail-on shrimp, deveined
- 2 tbsp butter, melted
- 1 tbsp lemon juice
- 1 tbsp dill, chopped

Directions:
1. Preheat air fryer to 350ºF. Combine shrimp and butter in a bowl. Place shrimp in the greased frying basket and Air Fry for 6 minutes, flipping once. Squeeze lemon juice over and top with dill. Serve hot.

Fish Cakes

Servings: 4
Cooking Time: 10 Minutes
Ingredients:
- ¾ cup mashed potatoes (about 1 large russet potato)
- 12 ounces cod or other white fish
- salt and pepper
- oil for misting or cooking spray
- 1 large egg
- ¼ cup potato starch
- ½ cup panko breadcrumbs
- 1 tablespoon fresh chopped chives
- 2 tablespoons minced onion

Directions:
1. Peel potatoes, cut into cubes, and cook on stovetop till soft.
2. Salt and pepper raw fish to taste. Mist with oil or cooking spray, and cook in air fryer at 360°F (180°C) for 6 to 8minutes, until fish flakes easily. If fish is crowded, rearrange halfway through cooking to ensure all pieces cook evenly.
3. Transfer fish to a plate and break apart to cool.
4. Beat egg in a shallow dish.
5. Place potato starch in another shallow dish, and panko crumbs in a third dish.
6. When potatoes are done, drain in colander and rinse with cold water.
7. In a large bowl, mash the potatoes and stir in the chives and onion. Add salt and pepper to taste, then stir in the fish.
8. If needed, stir in a tablespoon of the beaten egg to help bind the mixture.

9. Shape into 8 small, fat patties. Dust lightly with potato starch, dip in egg, and roll in panko crumbs. Spray both sides with oil or cooking spray.
10. Cook at 360°F (180°C) for 10 minutes, until golden brown and crispy.

Mediterranean Salmon Burgers
Servings: 4
Cooking Time: 30 Minutes
Ingredients:
- 1 lb salmon fillets
- 1 scallion, diced
- 4 tbsp mayonnaise
- 1 egg
- 1 tsp capers, drained
- Salt and pepper to taste
- ¼ tsp paprika
- 1 lemon, zested
- 1 lemon, sliced
- 1 tbsp chopped dill
- ¼ cup bread crumbs
- 4 buns, toasted
- 4 tsp whole-grain mustard
- 4 lettuce leaves
- 1 small tomato, sliced

Directions:
1. Preheat air fryer to 400°F (205°C). Divide salmon in half. Cut one of the halves into chunks and transfer the chunks to the food processor. Also, add scallion, 2 tablespoons mayonnaise, egg, capers, dill, salt, pepper, paprika, and lemon zest. Pulse to puree. Dice the rest of the salmon into ¼-inch chunks. Combine chunks and puree along with bread crumbs in a large bowl. Shape the fish into 4 patties and transfer to the frying basket. Air Fry for 5 minutes, then flip the patties. Air Fry for another 5 to 7 minutes. Place the patties each on a bun along with 1 teaspoon mustard, mayonnaise, lettuce, lemon slices, and a slice of tomato. Serve and enjoy.

Seared Scallops In Beurre Blanc
Servings: 4
Cooking Time: 15 Minutes
Ingredients:
- 1 lb sea scallops
- Salt and pepper to taste
- 2 tbsp butter, melted
- 1 lemon, zested and juiced
- 2 tbsp dry white wine

Directions:
1. Preheat the air fryer to 400°F (205°C). Sprinkle the scallops with salt and pepper, then set in a bowl. Combine the butter, lemon zest, lemon juice, and white wine in another bowl; mix well. Put the scallops in a baking pan and drizzle over them the mixture. Air Fry for 8-11 minutes, flipping over at about 5 minutes until opaque. Serve and enjoy!

Family Fish Nuggets With Tartar Sauce
Servings: 4
Cooking Time: 30 Minutes
Ingredients:
- ½ cup mayonnaise
- 1 tbsp yellow mustard
- ½ cup diced dill pickles
- Salt and pepper to taste
- 1 egg, beaten
- ¼ cup cornstarch
- ¼ cup flour
- 1 lb cod, cut into sticks

Directions:
1. In a bowl, whisk the mayonnaise, mustard, pickles, salt, and pepper. Set aside the resulting tarter sauce.
2. Preheat air fryer to 350°F. Add the beaten egg to a bowl. In another bowl, combine cornstarch, flour, salt, and pepper. Dip fish nuggets in the egg and roll them in the flour mixture. Place fish nuggets in the lightly greased frying basket and Air Fry for 10 minutes, flipping once. Serve with the sauce on the side.

Fried Oysters
Servings: 12
Cooking Time: 8 Minutes
Ingredients:
- 1½ cups All-purpose flour
- 1½ cups Yellow cornmeal
- 1½ tablespoons Cajun dried seasoning blend (for a homemade blend, see here)
- 1¼ cups, plus more if needed Amber beer, pale ale, or IPA
- 12 Large shucked oysters, any liquid drained off
- Vegetable oil spray

Directions:
1. Preheat the air fryer to 400°F (205°C).
2. Whisk ⅔ cup of the flour, ½ cup of the cornmeal, and the seasoning blend in a bowl until uniform. Set aside.
3. Whisk the remaining ⅓ cup flour and the remaining ½ cup cornmeal with the beer in a second bowl, adding more beer in dribs and drabs until the mixture is the consistency of pancake batter.
4. Using a fork, dip a shucked oyster in the beer batter, coating it thoroughly. Gently shake off any excess batter, then set the oyster in the dry mixture and turn gently to coat well and evenly. Set the coated oyster on a cutting board and continue dipping and coating the remainder of the oysters.
5. Coat the oysters with vegetable oil spray, then set them in the basket with as much air space between them as possible. Air-fry undisturbed for 8 minutes, or until lightly browned and crisp.
6. Use a nonstick-safe spatula to transfer the oysters to a wire rack. Cool for a couple of minutes before serving.

Sweet Potato-wrapped Shrimp
Servings: 3
Cooking Time: 6 Minutes
Ingredients:
- 24 Long spiralized sweet potato strands
- Olive oil spray
- ¼ teaspoon Garlic powder
- ¼ teaspoon Table salt
- Up to a ⅛ teaspoon Cayenne
- 12 Large shrimp (20–25 per pound), peeled and deveined

Directions:

Tower Air Fryer Cookbook

1. Preheat the air fryer to 400°F (205°C).
2. Lay the spiralized sweet potato strands on a large swath of paper towels and straighten out the strands to long ropes. Coat them with olive oil spray, then sprinkle them with the garlic powder, salt, and cayenne.
3. Pick up 2 strands and wrap them around the center of a shrimp, with the ends tucked under what now becomes the bottom side of the shrimp. Continue wrapping the remainder of the shrimp.
4. Set the shrimp bottom side down in the basket with as much air space between them as possible. Air-fry undisturbed for 6 minutes, or until the sweet potato strands are crisp and the shrimp are pink and firm.
5. Use kitchen tongs to transfer the shrimp to a wire rack. Cool for only a minute or two before serving.

Black Cod With Grapes, Fennel, Pecans And Kale

Servings: 2
Cooking Time: 15 Minutes
Ingredients:
- 2 (6- to 8-ounce) fillets of black cod (or sablefish)
- salt and freshly ground black pepper
- olive oil
- 1 cup grapes, halved
- 1 small bulb fennel, sliced ¼-inch thick
- ½ cup pecans
- 3 cups shredded kale
- 2 teaspoons white balsamic vinegar or white wine vinegar
- 2 tablespoons extra virgin olive oil

Directions:
1. Preheat the air fryer to 400°F (205°C).
2. Season the cod fillets with salt and pepper and drizzle, brush or spray a little olive oil on top. Place the fish, presentation side up (skin side down), into the air fryer basket. Air-fry for 10 minutes.
3. When the fish has finished cooking, remove the fillets to a side plate and loosely tent with foil to rest.
4. Toss the grapes, fennel and pecans in a bowl with a drizzle of olive oil and season with salt and pepper. Add the grapes, fennel and pecans to the air fryer basket and air-fry for 5 minutes at 400°F (205°C), shaking the basket once during the cooking time.
5. Transfer the grapes, fennel and pecans to a bowl with the kale. Dress the kale with the balsamic vinegar and olive oil, season to taste with salt and pepper and serve along side the cooked fish.

Easy Scallops With Lemon Butter

Servings: 3
Cooking Time: 4 Minutes
Ingredients:
- 1 tablespoon Olive oil
- 2 teaspoons Minced garlic
- 1 teaspoon Finely grated lemon zest
- ½ teaspoon Red pepper flakes
- ¼ teaspoon Table salt
- 1 pound Sea scallops
- 3 tablespoons Butter, melted
- 1½ tablespoons Lemon juice

Directions:

1. Preheat the air fryer to 400°F (205°C).
2. Gently stir the olive oil, garlic, lemon zest, red pepper flakes, and salt in a bowl. Add the scallops and stir very gently until they are evenly and well coated.
3. When the machine is at temperature, arrange the scallops in a single layer in the basket. Some may touch. Air-fry undisturbed for 4 minutes, or until the scallops are opaque and firm.
4. While the scallops cook, stir the melted butter and lemon juice in a serving bowl. When the scallops are ready, pour them from the basket into this bowl. Toss well before serving.

Sweet & Spicy Swordfish Kebabs

Servings: 4
Cooking Time: 30 Minutes
Ingredients:
- ½ cup canned pineapple chunks, drained, juice reserved
- 1 lb swordfish steaks, cubed
- ½ cup large red grapes
- 1 tbsp honey
- 2 tsp grated fresh ginger
- 1 tsp olive oil
- Pinch cayenne pepper

Directions:
1. Preheat air fryer to 370°F (185°C). Poke 8 bamboo skewers through the swordfish, pineapple, and grapes. Mix the honey, 1 tbsp of pineapple juice, ginger, olive oil, and cayenne in a bowl, then use a brush to rub the mix on the kebabs. Allow the marinate to sit on the kebab for 10 minutes. Grill the kebabs for 8-12 minutes until the fish is cooked through and the fruit is soft and glazed. Brush the kebabs again with the mix, then toss the rest of the marinade. Serve warm and enjoy!

Crunchy Flounder Gratin

Servings: 4
Cooking Time: 20 Minutes
Ingredients:
- ¼ cup grated Parmesan
- 4 flounder fillets
- 4 tbsp butter, melted
- ¼ cup panko bread crumbs
- ½ tsp paprika
- 1 egg
- Salt and pepper to taste
- ½ tsp dried oregano
- ½ tsp dried basil
- 1 tsp dried thyme
- 1 lemon, quartered
- 1 tbsp chopped parsley

Directions:
1. Preheat air fryer to 375°F (190°C). In a bowl, whisk together egg until smooth. Brush the fillets on both sides with some of the butter. Combine the rest of the butter, bread crumbs, Parmesan cheese, salt, paprika, thyme, oregano, basil, and pepper in a small bowl until crumbly. Dip the fish into the egg and then into the bread crumb mixture and coat completely. Transfer the fish to the frying basket and bake for 5 minutes. Carefully flip the fillets and bake for another 6 minutes until crispy and golden on the outside. Garnish with lemon wedges and parsley. Serve and enjoy.

Salty German-style Shrimp Pancakes

Servings: 4
Cooking Time: 15 Minutes
Ingredients:
- 1 tbsp butter
- 3 eggs, beaten
- ½ cup flour
- ½ cup milk
- ⅛ tsp salt
- 1 cup salsa
- 1 cup cooked shrimp, minced
- 2 tbsp cilantro, chopped

Directions:
1. Preheat air fryer to 390°F (200°C). Mix the eggs, flour, milk, and salt in a bowl until frothy. Pour the batter into a greased baking pan and place in the air fryer. Bake for 15 minutes or until the pancake is puffed and golden. Flip the pancake onto a plate. Mix salsa, shrimp, and cilantro. Top the pancake and serve.

Horseradish Crusted Salmon

Servings: 2
Cooking Time: 14 Minutes
Ingredients:
- 2 (5-ounce) salmon fillets
- salt and freshly ground black pepper
- 2 teaspoons Dijon mustard
- ½ cup panko breadcrumbs*
- 2 tablespoons prepared horseradish
- ½ teaspoon finely chopped lemon zest
- 1 tablespoon olive oil
- 1 tablespoon chopped fresh parsley

Directions:
1. Preheat the air fryer to 360°F (180°C).
2. Season the salmon with salt and freshly ground black pepper. Then spread the Dijon mustard on the salmon, coating the entire surface.
3. Combine the breadcrumbs, horseradish, lemon zest and olive oil in a small bowl. Spread the mixture over the top of the salmon and press down lightly with your hands, adhering it to the salmon using the mustard as "glue".
4. Transfer the salmon to the air fryer basket and air-fry at 360°F (180°C) for 14 minutes (depending on how thick your fillet is) or until the fish feels firm to the touch. Sprinkle with the parsley.

Fried Scallops

Servings: 3
Cooking Time: 6 Minutes
Ingredients:
- ½ cup All-purpose flour or tapioca flour
- 1 Large egg(s), well beaten
- 2 cups Corn flake crumbs (gluten-free, if a concern)
- Up to 2 teaspoons Cayenne
- 1 teaspoon Celery seeds
- 1 teaspoon Table salt
- 1 pound Sea scallops
- Vegetable oil spray

Directions:
1. Preheat the air fryer to 400°F (205°C).
2. Set up and fill three shallow soup plates or small pie plates on your counter: one for the flour; one for the beaten egg(s); and one for the corn flake crumbs, stirred with the cayenne, celery seeds, and salt until well combined.
3. One by one, dip a scallop in the flour, turning it every way to coat it thoroughly. Gently shake off any excess flour, then dip the scallop in the egg(s), turning it again to coat all sides. Let any excess egg slip back into the rest, then set the scallop in the corn flake mixture. Turn it several times, pressing gently to get an even coating on the scallop all around. Generously coat the scallop with vegetable oil spray, then set it aside on a cutting board. Coat the remaining scallops in the same way.
4. Set the scallops in the basket with as much air space between them as possible. They should not touch. Air-fry undisturbed for 6 minutes, or until lightly browned and firm.
5. Use kitchen tongs to gently transfer the scallops to a wire rack. Cool for only a minute or two before serving.

Tex-mex Fish Tacos

Servings: 3
Cooking Time: 7 Minutes
Ingredients:
- ¾ teaspoon Chile powder
- ¼ teaspoon Ground cumin
- ¼ teaspoon Dried oregano
- 3 5-ounce skinless mahi-mahi fillets
- Vegetable oil spray
- 3 Corn or flour tortillas
- 6 tablespoons Diced tomatoes
- 3 tablespoons Regular, low-fat, or fat-free sour cream

Directions:
1. Preheat the air fryer to 400°F (205°C).
2. Stir the chile powder, cumin, and oregano in a small bowl until well combined.
3. Coat each piece of fish all over (even the sides and ends) with vegetable oil spray. Sprinkle the spice mixture evenly over all sides of the fillets. Lightly spray them again.
4. When the machine is at temperature, set the fillets in the basket with as much air space between them as possible. Air-fry undisturbed for 7 minutes, until lightly browned and firm but not hard.
5. Use a nonstick-safe spatula to transfer the fillets to a wire rack. Microwave the tortillas on high for a few seconds, until supple. Put a fillet in each tortilla and top each with 2 tablespoons diced tomatoes and 1 tablespoon sour cream.

Buttery Lobster Tails

Servings: 4
Cooking Time: 6 Minutes
Ingredients:
- 4 6- to 8-ounce shell-on raw lobster tails
- 2 tablespoons Butter, melted and cooled
- 1 teaspoon Lemon juice
- ½ teaspoon Finely grated lemon zest
- ½ teaspoon Garlic powder
- ½ teaspoon Table salt
- ½ teaspoon Ground black pepper

Directions:
1. Preheat the air fryer to 375°F (190°C).
2. To give the tails that restaurant look, you need to butterfly the meat. To do so, place a tail on a cutting board

so that the shell is convex. Use kitchen shears to cut a line down the middle of the shell from the larger end to the smaller, cutting only the shell and not the meat below, and stopping before the back fins. Pry open the shell, leaving it intact. Use your clean fingers to separate the meat from the shell's sides and bottom, keeping it attached to the shell at the back near the fins. Pull the meat up and out of the shell through the cut line, laying the meat on top of the shell and closing the shell (as well as you can) under the meat. Make two equidistant cuts down the meat from the larger end to near the smaller end, each about ¼ inch deep, for the classic restaurant look on the plate. Repeat this procedure with the remaining tail(s).

3. Stir the butter, lemon juice, zest, garlic powder, salt, and pepper in a small bowl until well combined. Brush this mixture over the lobster meat set atop the shells.

4. When the machine is at temperature, place the tails shell side down in the basket with as much air space between them as possible. Air-fry undisturbed for 6 minutes, or until the lobster meat has pink streaks over it and is firm.

5. Use kitchen tongs to transfer the tails to a wire rack. Cool for only a minute or two before serving.

Nutty Shrimp With Amaretto Glaze

Servings: 10
Cooking Time: 10 Minutes
Ingredients:
- 1 cup flour
- ½ teaspoon baking powder
- 1 teaspoon salt
- 2 eggs, beaten
- ½ cup milk
- 2 tablespoons olive or vegetable oil
- 2 cups sliced almonds
- 2 pounds large shrimp (about 32 to 40 shrimp), peeled and deveined, tails left on
- 2 cups amaretto liqueur

Directions:
1. Combine the flour, baking powder and salt in a large bowl. Add the eggs, milk and oil and stir until it forms a smooth batter. Coarsely crush the sliced almonds into a second shallow dish with your hands.
2. Dry the shrimp well with paper towels. Dip the shrimp into the batter and shake off any excess batter, leaving just enough to lightly coat the shrimp. Transfer the shrimp to the dish with the almonds and coat completely. Place the coated shrimp on a plate or baking sheet and when all the shrimp have been coated, freeze the shrimp for an 1 hour, or as long as a week before air-frying.
3. Preheat the air fryer to 400°F (205°C).
4. Transfer 8 frozen shrimp at a time to the air fryer basket. Air-fry for 6 minutes. Turn the shrimp over and air-fry for an additional 4 minutes. Repeat with the remaining shrimp.
5. While the shrimp are cooking, bring the Amaretto to a boil in a small saucepan on the stovetop. Lower the heat and simmer until it has reduced and thickened into a glaze – about 10 minutes.
6. Remove the shrimp from the air fryer and brush both sides with the warm amaretto glaze. Serve warm.

Chapter 8: Beef, pork & Lamb Recipes

Easy-peasy Beef Sliders

Servings: 4
Cooking Time: 25 Minutes
Ingredients:
- 1 lb ground beef
- ¼ tsp cumin
- ¼ tsp mustard power
- 1/3 cup grated yellow onion
- ½ tsp smoked paprika
- Salt and pepper to taste

Directions:
1. Preheat air fryer to 350ºF. Combine the ground beef, cumin, mustard, onion, paprika, salt, and black pepper in a bowl. Form mixture into 8 patties and make a slight indentation in the middle of each. Place beef patties in the greased frying basket and Air Fry for 8-10 minutes, flipping once. Serve right away and enjoy!

Beef Fajitas

Servings: 2
Cooking Time: 15 Minutes
Ingredients:
- 8 oz sliced mushrooms
- ½ onion, cut into half-moons
- 1 tbsp olive oil
- Salt and pepper to taste
- 1 strip steak
- ½ tsp smoked paprika
- ½ tsp fajita seasoning
- 2 tbsp corn

Directions:
1. Preheat air fryer to 400ºF. Combine the olive oil, onion, and salt in a bowl. Add the mushrooms and toss to coat. Spread in the frying basket. Sprinkle steak with salt, paprika, fajita seasoning and black pepper. Place steak on top of the mushroom mixture and Air Fry for 9 minutes, flipping steak once. Let rest onto a cutting board for 5 minutes before cutting in half. Divide steak, mushrooms, corn, and onions between 2 plates and serve.

Cheeseburger Sliders With Pickle Sauce

Servings: 4
Cooking Time: 20 Minutes
Ingredients:
- 4 iceberg lettuce leaves, each halved lengthwise
- 2 red onion slices, rings separated
- ¼ cup shredded Swiss cheese
- 1 lb ground beef
- 1 tbsp Dijon mustard
- Salt and pepper to taste
- ¼ tsp shallot powder
- 2 tbsp mayonnaise
- 2 tsp ketchup
- ½ tsp mustard powder
- ½ tsp dill pickle juice
- ⅛ tsp onion powder
- ⅛ tsp garlic powder
- ⅛ tsp sweet paprika
- 8 tomato slices
- ½ cucumber, thinly sliced

Directions:
1. In a large bowl, use your hands to mix beef, Swiss cheese, mustard, salt, shallot, and black pepper. Do not overmix. Form 8 patties ½-inch thick. Mix together mayonnaise, ketchup, mustard powder, pickle juice, onion and garlic powder, and paprika in a medium bowl. Stir until smooth.
2. Preheat air fryer to 400°F (205°C). Place the sliders in the greased frying basket and Air Fry for about 8-10 minutes, flipping once until preferred doneness. Serve on top of lettuce halves with a slice of tomato, a slider, onion, a smear of special sauce, and cucumber.

City "chicken"

Servings: 3
Cooking Time: 10 Minutes
Ingredients:
- 1 pound Pork tenderloin, cut into 2-inch cubes
- ½ cup All-purpose flour or tapioca flour
- 1 Large egg(s)
- 1 teaspoon Dried poultry seasoning blend
- 1¼ cups Plain panko bread crumbs (gluten-free, if a concern)
- Vegetable oil spray

Directions:
1. Preheat the air fryer to 350°F (175°C).
2. Thread 3 or 4 pieces of pork on a 4-inch bamboo skewer. You'll need 2 or 3 skewers for a small batch, 3 or 4 for a medium, and up to 6 for a large batch.
3. Set up and fill three shallow soup plates or small pie plates on your counter: one for the flour; one for the egg(s), beaten with the poultry seasoning until foamy; and one for the bread crumbs.
4. Dip and roll one skewer into the flour, coating all sides of the meat. Gently shake off any excess flour, then dip and roll the skewer in the egg mixture. Let any excess egg mixture slip back into the rest, then set the skewer in the bread crumbs and roll it around, pressing gently, until the exterior surfaces of the meat are evenly coated. Generously coat the meat on the skewer with vegetable oil spray. Set aside and continue dredging, dipping, coating, and spraying the remaining skewers.
5. Set the skewers in the basket in one layer and air-fry undisturbed for 10 minutes, or until brown and crunchy.
6. Use kitchen tongs to transfer the skewers to a wire rack. Cool for a minute or two before serving.

Beef & Sauerkraut Spring Rolls

Servings: 4
Cooking Time: 20 Minutes
Ingredients:
- 5 Colby cheese slices, cut into strips
- 2 tbsp Thousand Island Dressing for dipping
- 10 spring roll wrappers
- 1/3 lb corned beef
- 2 cups sauerkraut
- 1 tsp ground cumin
- ½ tsp ground nutmeg
- 1 egg, beaten
- 1 tsp corn starch

Directions:

1. Preheat air fryer to 360°F (180°C). Mix the egg and cornstarch in a bowl to thicken. Lay out the spring roll wrappers on a clean surface. Place a few strips of the cut-up corned beef in the middle of the wraps. Sprinkle with Colby cheese, cumin, and nutmeg and top with 1-2 tablespoons of sauerkraut. Roll up and seal the seams with the egg and cornstarch mixture. Place the rolls in the greased frying basket. Bake for 7 minutes, shaking the basket several times until the spring rolls are golden brown. Serve warm with Thousand Island for dipping.

Barbecue-style London Broil
Servings: 5
Cooking Time: 17 Minutes
Ingredients:
- ¾ teaspoon Mild smoked paprika
- ¾ teaspoon Dried oregano
- ¾ teaspoon Table salt
- ¾ teaspoon Ground black pepper
- ¼ teaspoon Garlic powder
- ¼ teaspoon Onion powder
- 1½ pounds Beef London broil (in one piece)
- Olive oil spray

Directions:
1. Preheat the air fryer to 400°F (205°C).
2. Mix the smoked paprika, oregano, salt, pepper, garlic powder, and onion powder in a small bowl until uniform.
3. Pat and rub this mixture across all surfaces of the beef. Lightly coat the beef on all sides with olive oil spray.
4. When the machine is at temperature, lay the London broil flat in the basket and air-fry undisturbed for 8 minutes for the small batch, 10 minutes for the medium batch, or 12 minutes for the large batch for medium-rare, until an instant-read meat thermometer inserted into the center of the meat registers 130°F (55°C) (not USDA-approved). Add 1, 2, or 3 minutes, respectively (based on the size of the cut) for medium, until an instant-read meat thermometer registers 135°F (55°C) (not USDA-approved). Or add 3, 4, or 5 minutes respectively for medium, until an instant-read meat thermometer registers 145°F (60°C) (USDA-approved).
5. Use kitchen tongs to transfer the London broil to a cutting board. Let the meat rest for 10 minutes. It needs a long time for the juices to be reincorporated into the meat's fibers. Carve it against the grain into very thin (less than ¼-inch-thick) slices to serve.

Lazy Mexican Meat Pizza
Servings: 4
Cooking Time: 35 Minutes
Ingredients:
- 1 ¼ cups canned refried beans
- 2 cups shredded cheddar
- ½ cup chopped cilantro
- 2/3 cup salsa
- 1 red bell pepper, chopped
- 1 sliced jalapeño
- 1 pizza crust
- 16 meatballs, halved

Directions:
1. Preheat the air fryer to 375°F (190°C). Combine the refried beans, salsa, jalapeño, and bell pepper in a bowl and spread on the pizza crust. Top with meatball halves and sprinkle with cheddar cheese. Put the pizza in the greased frying basket and Bake for 7-10 minutes until hot and the cheese is brown. Sprinkle with the fresh cilantro and serve.

Pork Tenderloin With Apples & Celery
Servings: 4
Cooking Time: 30 Minutes
Ingredients:
- 1 lb pork tenderloin, cut into 4 pieces
- 2 Granny Smith apples, sliced
- 1 tbsp butter, melted
- 2 tsp olive oil
- 3 celery stalks, sliced
- 1 onion, sliced
- 2 tsp dried thyme
- 1/3 cup apple juice

Directions:
1. Preheat air fryer to 400°F (205°C). Brush olive oil and butter all over the pork, then toss the pork, apples, celery, onion, thyme, and apple juice in a bowl and mix well. Put the bowl in the air fryer and Roast for 15-19 minutes until the pork is cooked through and the apples and veggies are soft, stirring once during cooking. Serve warm.

Sausage-cheese Calzone
Servings: 8
Cooking Time: 8 Minutes
Ingredients:
- Crust
- 2 cups white wheat flour, plus more for kneading and rolling
- 1 package (¼ ounce) RapidRise yeast
- 1 teaspoon salt
- ½ teaspoon dried basil
- 1 cup warm water (115°F (45°C) to 125°F (50°C))
- 2 teaspoons olive oil
- Filling
- ¼ pound Italian sausage
- ½ cup ricotta cheese
- 4 ounces mozzarella cheese, shredded
- ¼ cup grated Parmesan cheese
- oil for misting or cooking spray
- marinara sauce for serving

Directions:
1. Crumble Italian sausage into air fryer baking pan and cook at 390°F (200°C) for 5minutes. Stir, breaking apart, and cook for 3 to 4minutes, until well done. Remove and set aside on paper towels to drain.
2. To make dough, combine flour, yeast, salt, and basil. Add warm water and oil and stir until a soft dough forms. Turn out onto lightly floured board and knead for 3 or 4minutes. Let dough rest for 10minutes.
3. To make filling, combine the three cheeses in a medium bowl and mix well. Stir in the cooked sausage.
4. Cut dough into 8 pieces.
5. Working with 4 pieces of the dough, press each into a circle about 5 inches in diameter. Top each dough circle with 2 heaping tablespoons of filling. Fold over to create a half-moon shape and press edges firmly together. Be sure that edges are firmly sealed to prevent leakage. Spray both sides with oil or cooking spray.

6. Place 4 calzones in air fryer basket and cook at 360°F (180°C) for 5minutes. Mist with oil and cook for 3 minutes, until crust is done and nicely browned.
7. While the first batch is cooking, press out the remaining dough, fill, and shape into calzones.
8. Spray both sides with oil and cook for 5minutes. If needed, mist with oil and continue cooking for 3 minutes longer. This second batch will cook a little faster than the first because your air fryer is already hot.
9. Serve with marinara sauce on the side for dipping.

Cheesy Mushroom-stuffed Pork Loins
Servings:3
Cooking Time: 30 Minutes
Ingredients:
- ¾ cup diced mushrooms
- 2 tsp olive oil
- 1 shallot, diced
- Salt and pepper to taste
- 3 center-cut pork loins
- 6 Gruyère cheese slices

Directions:
1. Warm the olive oil in a skillet over medium heat. Add in shallot and mushrooms and stir-fry for 3 minutes. Sprinkle with salt and pepper and cook for 1 minute.
2. Preheat air fryer to 350°F. Cut a pocket into each pork loin and set aside. Stuff an even amount of mushroom mixture into each chop pocket and top with 2 Gruyere cheese slices into each pocket. Place the pork in the lightly greased frying basket and Air Fry for 11 minutes cooked through and the cheese has melted. Let sit onto a cutting board for 5 minutes before serving.

Bacon Wrapped Filets Mignons
Servings: 4
Cooking Time: 18 Minutes
Ingredients:
- 4 slices bacon (not thick cut)
- 4 (8-ounce) filets mignons
- 1 tablespoon fresh thyme leaves
- salt and freshly ground black pepper

Directions:
1. Preheat the air fryer to 400°F (205°C).
2. Lay the bacon slices down on a cutting board and sprinkle the thyme leaves on the bacon slices. Remove any string tying the filets and place the steaks down on their sides on top of the bacon slices. Roll the bacon around the side of the filets and secure the bacon to the fillets with a toothpick or two.
3. Season the steaks generously with salt and freshly ground black pepper and transfer the steaks to the air fryer.
4. Air-fry for 18 minutes, turning the steaks over halfway through the cooking process. This should cook your steaks to about medium, depending on how thick they are. If you'd prefer your steaks medium-rare or medium-well, simply add or subtract two minutes from the cooking time. Remove the steaks from the air fryer and let them rest for 5 minutes before removing the toothpicks and serving. (Just enough time to quickly air-fry some vegetables to go with them!)

Sweet Potato-crusted Pork Rib Chops
Servings: 2
Cooking Time: 14 Minutes

Ingredients:
- 2 Large egg white(s), well beaten
- 1½ cups (about 6 ounces) Crushed sweet potato chips (certified gluten-free, if a concern)
- 1 teaspoon Ground cinnamon
- 1 teaspoon Ground dried ginger
- 1 teaspoon Table salt (optional)
- 2 10-ounce, 1-inch-thick bone-in pork rib chop(s)

Directions:
1. Preheat the air fryer to 375°F (190°C).
2. Set up and fill two shallow soup plates or small pie plates on your counter: one for the beaten egg white(s); and one for the crushed chips, mixed with the cinnamon, ginger, and salt (if using).
3. Dip a chop in the egg white(s), coating it on both sides as well as the edges. Let the excess egg white slip back into the rest, then set it in the crushed chip mixture. Turn it several times, pressing gently, until evenly coated on both sides and the edges. If necessary, set the chop aside and coat the remaining chop(s).
4. Set the chop(s) in the basket with as much air space between them as possible. Air-fry undisturbed for 12 minutes, or until crunchy and browned and an instant-read meat thermometer inserted into the center of a chop (without touching bone) registers 145°F (60°C). If the machine is at 360°F (180°C), you may need to add 2 minutes to the cooking time.
5. Use kitchen tongs to transfer the chop(s) to a wire rack. Cool for 2 or 3 minutes before serving.

Blossom Bbq Pork Chops
Servings: 2
Cooking Time: 20 Minutes
Ingredients:
- 2 tbsp cherry preserves
- 1 tbsp honey
- 1 tbsp Dijon mustard
- 2 tsp light brown sugar
- 1 tsp Worcestershire sauce
- 1 tbsp lime juice
- 1 tbsp olive oil
- 2 cloves garlic, minced
- 1 tbsp chopped parsley
- 2 pork chops

Directions:
1. Mix all ingredients in a bowl. Toss in pork chops. Let marinate covered in the fridge for 30 minutes.
2. Preheat air fryer at 350°F. Place pork chops in the greased frying basket and Air Fry for 12 minutes, turning once. Let rest onto a cutting board for 5 minutes. Serve.

Lamb Koftas Meatballs
Servings: 3
Cooking Time: 8 Minutes
Ingredients:
- 1 pound ground lamb
- 1 teaspoon ground cumin
- 1 teaspoon ground coriander
- 2 tablespoons chopped fresh mint
- 1 egg, beaten
- ½ teaspoon salt
- freshly ground black pepper

Directions:
1. Combine all ingredients in a bowl and mix together well. Divide the mixture into 10 portions. Roll each portion into a ball and then by cupping the meatball in your hand, shape it into an oval.
2. Preheat the air fryer to 400°F (205°C).
3. Air-fry the koftas for 8 minutes.
4. Serve warm with the cucumber-yogurt dip.

Peppered Steak Bites
Servings: 4
Cooking Time: 14 Minutes
Ingredients:
- 1 pound sirloin steak, cut into 1-inch cubes
- ½ teaspoon coarse sea salt
- 1 teaspoon coarse black pepper
- 2 teaspoons Worcestershire sauce
- ½ teaspoon garlic powder
- ¼ teaspoon red pepper flakes
- ¼ cup chopped parsley

Directions:
1. Preheat the air fryer to 390°F (200°C).
2. In a large bowl, place the steak cubes and toss with the salt, pepper, Worcestershire sauce, garlic powder, and red pepper flakes.
3. Pour the steak into the air fryer basket and cook for 10 to 14 minutes, depending on how well done you prefer your bites. Starting at the 8-minute mark, toss the steak bites every 2 minutes to check for doneness.
4. When the steak is cooked, remove it from the basket to a serving bowl and top with the chopped parsley. Allow the steak to rest for 5 minutes before serving.

Fried Spam
Servings: 2
Cooking Time: 12 Minutes
Ingredients:
- ½ cup All-purpose flour or gluten-free all-purpose flour
- 1 Large egg(s)
- 1 tablespoon Wasabi paste
- 1⅓ cups Plain panko bread crumbs (gluten-free, if a concern)
- 4 ½-inch-thick Spam slices
- Vegetable oil spray

Directions:
1. Preheat the air fryer to 400°F (205°C).
2. Set up and fill three shallow soup plates or small pie plates on your counter: one for the flour; one for the egg(s), whisked with the wasabi paste until uniform; and one for the bread crumbs.
3. Dip a slice of Spam in the flour, coating both sides. Slip it into the egg mixture and turn to coat on both sides, even along the edges. Let any excess egg mixture slip back into the rest, then set the slice in the bread crumbs. Turn it several times, pressing gently to make an even coating on both sides. Generously coat both sides of the slice with vegetable oil spray. Set aside so you can dip, coat, and spray the remaining slice(s).
4. Set the slices in the basket in a single layer so that they don't touch (even if they're close together). Air-fry undisturbed for 12 minutes, or until very brown and quite crunchy.
5. Use kitchen tongs to transfer the slices to a wire rack. Cool for a minute or two before serving.

Pork Loin
Servings: 8
Cooking Time: 50 Minutes
Ingredients:
- 1 tablespoon lime juice
- 1 tablespoon orange marmalade
- 1 teaspoon coarse brown mustard
- 1 teaspoon curry powder
- 1 teaspoon dried lemongrass
- 2-pound boneless pork loin roast
- salt and pepper
- cooking spray

Directions:
1. Mix together the lime juice, marmalade, mustard, curry powder, and lemongrass.
2. Rub mixture all over the surface of the pork loin. Season to taste with salt and pepper.
3. Spray air fryer basket with nonstick spray and place pork roast diagonally in basket.
4. Cook at 360°F (180°C) for approximately 50 minutes, until roast registers 130°F (55°C) on a meat thermometer.
5. Wrap roast in foil and let rest for 10minutes before slicing.

Taco Pie With Meatballs
Servings: 4
Cooking Time: 40 Minutes + Cooling Time
Ingredients:
- 1 cup shredded quesadilla cheese
- 1 cup shredded Colby cheese
- 10 cooked meatballs, halved
- 1 cup salsa
- 1 cup canned refried beans
- 2 tsp chipotle powder
- ½ tsp ground cumin
- 4 corn tortillas

Directions:
1. Preheat the air fryer to 375°F 190°C). Combine the meatball halves, salsa, refried beans, chipotle powder, and cumin in a bowl. In a baking pan, add a tortilla and top with one-quarter of the meatball mixture. Sprinkle one-quarter of the cheeses on top and repeat the layers three more times, ending with cheese. Put the pan in the fryer. Bake for 15-20 minutes until the pie is bubbling and the cheese has melted. Let cool on a wire rack for 10 minutes. Run a knife around the edges of the pan and remove the sides of the pan, then cut into wedges to serve.

Tuscan Chimichangas
Servings: 2
Cooking Time: 8 Minutes
Ingredients:
- ¼ pound Thinly sliced deli ham, chopped
- 1 cup Drained and rinsed canned white beans
- ½ cup (about 2 ounces) Shredded semi-firm mozzarella
- ¼ cup Chopped sun-dried tomatoes
- ¼ cup Bottled Italian salad dressing, vinaigrette type
- 2 Burrito-size (12-inch) flour tortilla(s)
- Olive oil spray

Directions:
1. Preheat the air fryer to 375°F (190°C).
2. Mix the ham, beans, cheese, tomatoes, and salad dressing in a bowl.
3. Lay a tortilla on a clean, dry work surface. Put all of the ham mixture in a narrow oval in the middle of the tortilla, if making one burrito; or half of this mixture, if making two. Fold the parts of the tortilla that are closest to the ends of the filling oval up and over the filling, then roll the tortilla tightly closed, but don't press down hard. Generously coat the tortilla with olive oil spray. Make a second filled tortilla, if necessary.
4. Set the filled tortilla(s) seam side down in the basket, with at least ½ inch between them, if making two. Air-fry undisturbed for 8 minutes, or until crisp and lightly browned.
5. Use kitchen tongs and a nonstick-safe spatula to transfer the chimichanga(s) to a wire rack. Cool for 5 minutes before serving.

Cowboy Rib Eye Steak
Servings: 2
Cooking Time: 20 Minutes
Ingredients:
- ¼ cup barbecue sauce
- 1 clove garlic, minced
- ⅛ tsp chili pepper
- ¼ tsp sweet paprika
- ¼ tsp cumin
- 1 rib-eye steak

Directions:
1. Preheat air fryer to 400°F. In a bowl, whisk the barbecue sauce, garlic, chili pepper, paprika, and cumin. Divide in half and brush the steak with half of the sauce. Add steak to the lightly greased frying basket and Air Fry for 10 minutes until you reach your desired doneness, turning once and brushing with the remaining sauce. Let rest for 5 minutes onto a cutting board before slicing. Serve warm.

Fusion Tender Flank Steak
Servings: 4
Cooking Time: 25 Minutes
Ingredients:
- 2 tbsp cilantro, chopped
- 2 tbsp chives, chopped
- ¼ tsp red pepper flakes
- 1 jalapeño pepper, minced
- 1 lime, juiced
- 3 tbsp olive oil
- Salt and pepper to taste
- 2 tbsp sesame oil
- 5 tbsp tamari sauce
- 3 tsp honey
- 1 tbsp grated fresh ginger
- 2 green onions, minced
- 2 garlic cloves, minced
- 1 ¼ pounds flank steak

Directions:
1. Combine the jalapeño pepper, cilantro, chives, lime juice, olive oil, salt, and pepper in a bowl. Set aside. Mix the sesame oil, tamari sauce, honey, ginger, green onions, garlic, and pepper flakes in another bowl. Stir until the honey is dissolved. Put the steak into the bowl and massage the marinade onto the meat. Marinate for 2 hours in the fridge. Preheat air fryer to 390 F.
2. Remove the steak from the marinade and place it in the greased frying basket. Air Fry for about 6 minutes, flip, and continue cooking for 6-8 more minutes. Allow to rest for a few minutes, slice thinly against the grain and top with the prepared dressing. Serve and enjoy!

Sirloin Steak Flatbread
Servings: 2
Cooking Time: 40 Minutes
Ingredients:
- 1 premade flatbread dough
- 1 sirloin steak, cubed
- 2 cups breadcrumbs
- 2 eggs, beaten
- Salt and pepper to taste
- 2 tsp onion powder
- 1 tsp garlic powder
- 1 tsp dried thyme
- ½ onion, sliced
- 2 Swiss cheese slices

Directions:
1. Preheat air fryer to 360°F (180°C). Place the breadcrumbs, onion powder, garlic powder, thyme, salt, and pepper in a bowl and stir to combine. Add in the steak cubes, coating all sides. Dip into the beaten eggs, then dip again into the crumbs. Lay the coated steak pieces on half of the greased fryer basket. Place the onion slices on the other half of the basket. Air Fry 6 minutes. Turn the onions over and flip the steak pieces. Continue cooking for another 6 minutes. Roll the flatbread out and pierce it several times with a fork. Cover with Swiss cheese slices.
2. When the steak and onions are ready, remove them to the cheese-covered flatbread dough. Fold the flatbread over. Arrange the folded flatbread on the frying basket. Bake for 10 minutes, flipping once until golden brown. Serve.

Lamb Burger With Feta And Olives
Servings: 3
Cooking Time: 16 Minutes
Ingredients:
- 2 teaspoons olive oil
- ⅓ onion, finely chopped
- 1 clove garlic, minced
- 1 pound ground lamb
- 2 tablespoons fresh parsley, finely chopped
- 1½ teaspoons fresh oregano, finely chopped
- ½ cup black olives, finely chopped
- ⅓ cup crumbled feta cheese
- ½ teaspoon salt
- freshly ground black pepper
- 4 thick pita breads
- toppings and condiments

Directions:
1. Preheat a medium skillet over medium-high heat on the stovetop. Add the olive oil and cook the onion until tender, but not browned – about 4 to 5 minutes. Add the garlic and cook for another minute. Transfer the onion and garlic to a mixing bowl and add the ground lamb, parsley, oregano, olives, feta cheese, salt and pepper. Gently mix the ingredients together.

2. Divide the mixture into 3 or 4 equal portions and then form the hamburgers, being careful not to over-handle the meat. One good way to do this is to throw the meat back and forth between your hands like a baseball, packing the meat each time you catch it. Flatten the balls into patties, making an indentation in the center of each patty. Flatten the sides of the patties as well to make it easier to fit them into the air fryer basket.
3. Preheat the air fryer to 370°F (185°C).
4. If you don't have room for all four burgers, air-fry two or three burgers at a time for 8 minutes at 370°F (185°C). Flip the burgers over and air-fry for another 8 minutes. If you cooked your burgers in batches, return the first batch of burgers to the air fryer for the last two minutes of cooking to re-heat. This should give you a medium-well burger. If you'd prefer a medium-rare burger, shorten the cooking time to about 13 minutes. Remove the burgers to a resting plate and let the burgers rest for a few minutes before dressing and serving.
5. While the burgers are resting, toast the pita breads in the air fryer for 2 minutes. Tuck the burgers into the toasted pita breads, or wrap the pitas around the burgers and serve with a tzatziki sauce or some mayonnaise.

Apple Cornbread Stuffed Pork Loin With Apple Gravy

Servings: 4
Cooking Time: 61 Minutes
Ingredients:
- 4 strips of bacon, chopped
- 1 Granny Smith apple, peeled, cored and finely chopped
- 2 teaspoons fresh thyme leaves
- ¼ cup chopped fresh parsley
- 2 cups cubed cornbread
- ½ cup chicken stock
- salt and freshly ground black pepper
- 1 (2-pound) boneless pork loin
- kitchen twine
- Apple Gravy:
- 2 tablespoons butter
- 1 shallot, minced
- 1 Granny Smith apple, peeled, cored and finely chopped
- 3 sprigs fresh thyme
- 2 tablespoons flour
- 1 cup chicken stock
- ½ cup apple cider
- salt and freshly ground black pepper, to taste

Directions:
1. Preheat the air fryer to 400°F (205°C).
2. Add the bacon to the air fryer and air-fry for 6 minutes until crispy. While the bacon is cooking, combine the apple, fresh thyme, parsley and cornbread in a bowl and toss well. Moisten the mixture with the chicken stock and season to taste with salt and freshly ground black pepper. Add the cooked bacon to the mixture.
3. Butterfly the pork loin by holding it flat on the cutting board with one hand, while slicing into the pork loin parallel to the cutting board with the other. Slice into the longest side of the pork loin, but stop before you cut all the way through. You should then be able to open the pork loin up like a book, making it twice as wide as it was when you started. Season the inside of the pork with salt and freshly ground black pepper.
4. Spread the cornbread mixture onto the butterflied pork loin, leaving a one-inch border around the edge of the pork. Roll the pork loin up around the stuffing to enclose the stuffing, and tie the rolled pork in several places with kitchen twine or secure with toothpicks. Try to replace any stuffing that falls out of the roast as you roll it, by stuffing it into the ends of the rolled pork. Season the outside of the pork with salt and freshly ground black pepper.
5. Preheat the air fryer to 360°F (180°C).
6. Place the stuffed pork loin into the air fryer, seam side down. Air-fry the pork loin for 15 minutes at 360°F (180°C). Turn the pork loin over and air-fry for an additional 15 minutes. Turn the pork loin a quarter turn and air-fry for an additional 15 minutes. Turn the pork loin over again to expose the fourth side, and air-fry for an additional 10 minutes. The pork loin should register 155°F (70°C) on an instant read thermometer when it is finished.
7. While the pork is cooking, make the apple gravy. Preheat a saucepan over medium heat on the stovetop and melt the butter. Add the shallot, apple and thyme sprigs and sauté until the apple starts to soften and brown a little. Add the flour and stir for a minute or two. Whisk in the stock and apple cider vigorously to prevent the flour from forming lumps. Bring the mixture to a boil to thicken and season to taste with salt and pepper.
8. Transfer the pork loin to a resting plate and loosely tent with foil, letting the pork rest for at least 5 minutes before slicing and serving with the apple gravy poured over the top.

Greek Pita Pockets

Servings: 4
Cooking Time: 7 Minutes
Ingredients:
- Dressing
- 1 cup plain yogurt
- 1 tablespoon lemon juice
- 1 teaspoon dried dill weed, crushed
- 1 teaspoon ground oregano
- ½ teaspoon salt
- Meatballs
- ½ pound ground lamb
- 1 tablespoon diced onion
- 1 teaspoon dried parsley
- 1 teaspoon dried dill weed, crushed
- ¼ teaspoon oregano
- ¼ teaspoon coriander
- ¼ teaspoon ground cumin
- ¼ teaspoon salt
- 4 pita halves
- Suggested Toppings
- red onion, slivered
- seedless cucumber, thinly sliced
- crumbled Feta cheese
- sliced black olives
- chopped fresh peppers

Directions:
1. Stir dressing ingredients together and refrigerate while preparing lamb.
2. Combine all meatball ingredients in a large bowl and stir to distribute seasonings.

3. Shape meat mixture into 12 small meatballs, rounded or slightly flattened if you prefer.
4. Cook at 390°F (200°C) for 7minutes, until well done. Remove and drain on paper towels.
5. To serve, pile meatballs and your choice of toppings in pita pockets and drizzle with dressing.

Baharat Lamb Kebab With Mint Sauce
Servings: 6
Cooking Time: 50 Minutes
Ingredients:
- 1 lb ground lamb
- ¼ cup parsley, chopped
- 3 garlic cloves, minced
- 1 shallot, diced
- Salt and pepper to taste
- 1 tsp ground cumin
- ¼ tsp ground cinnamon
- ¼ tsp baharat seasoning
- ¼ tsp chili powder
- ¼ tsp ground ginger
- 3 tbsp olive oil
- 1 cup Greek yogurt
- ½ cup mint, chopped
- 2 tbsp lemon juice
- ¼ tsp hot paprika

Directions:
1. Preheat air fryer to 360°F (180°C). Mix the ground lamb, parsley, 2 garlic cloves, shallot, 2 tbsp olive oil, salt, black pepper, cumin, cinnamon, baharat seasoning, chili powder, and ginger in a bowl. Divide the mixture into 4 equal quantities, and roll each into a long oval. Drizzle with the remaining olive oil, place them in a single layer in the frying basket and Air Fry for 10 minutes. While the kofta is cooking, mix together the Greek yogurt, mint, remaining garlic, lemon juice, hot paprika, salt, and pepper in a bowl. Serve the kofta with mint sauce.

Pork Kabobs With Pineapple
Servings: 4
Cooking Time: 30 Minutes
Ingredients:
- 2 cans juice-packed pineapple chunks, juice reserved
- 1 green bell pepper, cut into ½-inch chunks
- 1 red bell pepper, cut into ½-inch chunks
- 1 lb pork tenderloin, cubed
- Salt and pepper to taste
- 1 tbsp honey
- ½ tsp ground ginger
- ½ tsp ground coriander
- 1 red chili, minced

Directions:
1. Preheat the air fryer to 375°F (190°C). Mix the coriander, chili, salt, and pepper in a bowl. Add the pork and toss to coat. Then, thread the pork pieces, pineapple chunks, and bell peppers onto skewers. Combine the pineapple juice, honey, and ginger and mix well. Use all the mixture as you brush it on the kebabs. Put the kebabs in the greased frying basket and Air Fry for 10-14 minutes or until cooked through. Serve and enjoy!

Tender Steak With Salsa Verde
Servings:4
Cooking Time: 20 Minutes
Ingredients:
- 1 flank steak, halved
- 1 ½ cups salsa verde
- ½ tsp black pepper

Directions:
1. Toss steak and 1 cup of salsa verde in a bowl and refrigerate covered for 2 hours. Preheat air fryer to 400°F. Add steaks to the lightly greased frying basket and Air Fry for 10-12 minutes or until you reach your desired doneness, flipping once. Let sit onto a cutting board for 5 minutes. Thinly slice against the grain and divide between 4 plates. Spoon over the remaining salsa verde and serve sprinkled with black pepper to serve.

T-bone Steak With Roasted Tomato, Corn And Asparagus Salsa
Servings: 2
Cooking Time: 15-20 Minutes
Ingredients:
- 1 (20-ounce) T-bone steak
- salt and freshly ground black pepper
- Salsa
- 1½ cups cherry tomatoes
- ¾ cup corn kernels (fresh, or frozen and thawed)
- 1½ cups sliced asparagus (1-inch slices) (about ½ bunch)
- 1 tablespoon + 1 teaspoon olive oil, divided
- salt and freshly ground black pepper
- 1½ teaspoons red wine vinegar
- 3 tablespoons chopped fresh basil
- 1 tablespoon chopped fresh chives

Directions:
1. Preheat the air fryer to 400°F (205°C).
2. Season the steak with salt and pepper and air-fry at 400°F (205°C) for 10 minutes (medium-rare), 12 minutes (medium), or 15 minutes (well-done), flipping the steak once halfway through the cooking time.
3. In the meantime, toss the tomatoes, corn and asparagus in a bowl with a teaspoon or so of olive oil, salt and freshly ground black pepper.
4. When the steak has finished cooking, remove it to a cutting board, tent loosely with foil and let it rest. Transfer the vegetables to the air fryer and air-fry at 400°F (205°C) for 5 minutes, shaking the basket once or twice during the cooking process. Transfer the cooked vegetables back into the bowl and toss with the red wine vinegar, remaining olive oil and fresh herbs.
5. To serve, slice the steak on the bias and serve with some of the salsa on top.

Friday Night Cheeseburgers
Servings: 4
Cooking Time: 20 Minutes
Ingredients:
- 1 lb ground beef
- 1 tsp Worcestershire sauce
- 1 tbsp allspice
- Salt and pepper to taste
- 4 cheddar cheese slices
- 4 buns

Directions:
1. Preheat air fryer to 360°F (180°C). Combine beef, Worcestershire sauce, allspice, salt and pepper in a large bowl. Divide into 4 equal portions and shape into patties. Place the burgers in the greased frying basket and Air Fry for 8 minutes. Flip and cook for another 3-4 minutes. Top each burger with cheddar cheese and cook for another minute so the cheese melts. Transfer to a bun and serve.

Mustard-crusted Rib-eye
Servings: 2
Cooking Time: 9 Minutes
Ingredients:
- Two 6-ounce rib-eye steaks, about 1-inch thick
- 1 teaspoon coarse salt
- ½ teaspoon coarse black pepper
- 2 tablespoons Dijon mustard

Directions:
1. Rub the steaks with the salt and pepper. Then spread the mustard on both sides of the steaks. Cover with foil and let the steaks sit at room temperature for 30 minutes.
2. Preheat the air fryer to 390°F (200°C).
3. Cook the steaks for 9 minutes. Check for an internal temperature of 140°F (60°C) and immediately remove the steaks and let them rest for 5 minutes before slicing.

Perfect Strip Steaks
Servings: 2
Cooking Time: 17 Minutes
Ingredients:
- 1½ tablespoons Olive oil
- 1½ tablespoons Minced garlic
- 2 teaspoons Ground black pepper
- 1 teaspoon Table salt
- 2 ¾-pound boneless beef strip steak(s)

Directions:
1. Preheat the air fryer to 375°F (190°C) (or 380°F (195°C) or 390°F (200°C), if one of these is the closest setting).
2. Mix the oil, garlic, pepper, and salt in a small bowl, then smear this mixture over both sides of the steak(s).
3. When the machine is at temperature, put the steak(s) in the basket with as much air space as possible between them for the larger batch. They should not overlap or even touch. That said, even just a ¼-inch between them will work. Air-fry for 12 minutes, turning once, until an instant-read meat thermometer inserted into the thickest part of a steak registers 127°F (52°C) for rare (not USDA-approved). Or air-fry for 15 minutes, turning once, until an instant-read meat thermometer registers 145°F (60°C) for medium (USDA-approved). If the machine is at 390°F (200°C), the steaks may cook 2 minutes more quickly than the stated timing.
4. Use kitchen tongs to transfer the steak(s) to a wire rack. Cool for 5 minutes before serving.

Calf's Liver
Servings: 4
Cooking Time: 5 Minutes
Ingredients:
- 1 pound sliced calf's liver
- salt and pepper
- 2 eggs
- 2 tablespoons milk
- ½ cup whole wheat flour
- 1½ cups panko breadcrumbs
- ½ cup plain breadcrumbs
- ½ teaspoon salt
- ¼ teaspoon pepper
- oil for misting or cooking spray

Directions:
1. Cut liver slices crosswise into strips about ½-inch wide. Sprinkle with salt and pepper to taste.
2. Beat together egg and milk in a shallow dish.
3. Place wheat flour in a second shallow dish.
4. In a third shallow dish, mix together panko, plain breadcrumbs, ½ teaspoon salt, and ¼ teaspoon pepper.
5. Preheat air fryer to 390°F (200°C).
6. Dip liver strips in flour, egg wash, and then breadcrumbs, pressing in coating slightly to make crumbs stick.
7. Cooking half the liver at a time, place strips in air fryer basket in a single layer, close but not touching. Cook at 390°F (200°C) for 5 minutes or until done to your preference.
8. Repeat step 7 to cook remaining liver.

Mongolian Beef
Servings: 4
Cooking Time: 15 Minutes
Ingredients:
- 1½ pounds flank steak, thinly sliced on the bias into ¼-inch strips
- Marinade
- 2 tablespoons soy sauce*
- 1 clove garlic, smashed
- big pinch crushed red pepper flakes
- Sauce
- 1 tablespoon vegetable oil
- 2 cloves garlic, minced
- 1 tablespoon finely grated fresh ginger
- 3 dried red chili peppers
- ¾ cup soy sauce*
- ¾ cup chicken stock
- 5 to 6 tablespoons brown sugar (depending on how sweet you want the sauce)
- ½ cup cornstarch, divided
- 1 bunch scallions, sliced into 2-inch pieces

Directions:
1. Marinate the beef in the soy sauce, garlic and red pepper flakes for one hour.
2. In the meantime, make the sauce. Preheat a small saucepan over medium heat on the stovetop. Add the oil, garlic, ginger and dried chili peppers and sauté for just a minute or two. Add the soy sauce, chicken stock and brown sugar and continue to simmer for a few minutes. Dissolve 3 tablespoons of cornstarch in 3 tablespoons of water and stir this into the saucepan. Stir the sauce over medium heat until it thickens. Set this aside.
3. Preheat the air fryer to 400°F (205°C).
4. Remove the beef from the marinade and transfer it to a zipper sealable plastic bag with the remaining cornstarch. Shake it around to completely coat the beef and transfer the coated strips of beef to a baking sheet or plate, shaking off any excess cornstarch. Spray the strips with vegetable oil on all sides and transfer them to the air fryer basket.

Tower Air Fryer Cookbook

5. Air-fry at 400°F (205°C) for 15 minutes, shaking the basket to toss and rotate the beef strips throughout the cooking process. Add the scallions for the last 4 minutes of the cooking. Transfer the hot beef strips and scallions to a bowl and toss with the sauce (warmed on the stovetop if necessary), coating all the beef strips with the sauce. Serve warm over white rice.

Wasabi-coated Pork Loin Chops

Servings: 3
Cooking Time: 14 Minutes
Ingredients:
- 1½ cups Wasabi peas
- ¼ cup Plain panko bread crumbs
- 1 Large egg white(s)
- 2 tablespoons Water
- 3 5- to 6-ounce boneless center-cut pork loin chops (about ½ inch thick)

Directions:
1. Preheat the air fryer to 375°F (190°C).
2. Put the wasabi peas in a food processor. Cover and process until finely ground, about like panko bread crumbs. Add the bread crumbs and pulse a few times to blend.
3. Set up and fill two shallow soup plates or small pie plates on your counter: one for the egg white(s), whisked with the water until uniform; and one for the wasabi pea mixture.
4. Dip a pork chop in the egg white mixture, coating the chop on both sides as well as around the edge. Allow any excess egg white mixture to slip back into the rest, then set the chop in the wasabi pea mixture. Press gently and turn it several times to coat evenly on both sides and around the edge. Set aside, then dip and coat the remaining chop(s).
5. Set the chops in the basket with as much air space between them as possible. Air-fry, turning once at the 6-minute mark, for 12 minutes, or until the chops are crisp and browned and an instant-read meat thermometer inserted into the center of a chop registers 145°F (60°C). If the machine is at 360°F (180°C), you may need to add 2 minutes to the cooking time.
6. Use kitchen tongs to transfer the chops to a wire rack. Cool for a couple of minutes before serving.

Crispy Pork Medallions With Radicchio And Endive Salad

Servings: 4
Cooking Time: 7 Minutes
Ingredients:
- 1 (8-ounce) pork tenderloin
- salt and freshly ground black pepper
- ¼ cup flour
- 2 eggs, lightly beaten
- ¾ cup cracker meal
- 1 teaspoon paprika
- 1 teaspoon dry mustard
- 1 teaspoon garlic powder
- 1 teaspoon dried thyme
- 1 teaspoon salt
- vegetable or canola oil, in spray bottle
- Vinaigrette
- ¼ cup white balsamic vinegar
- 2 tablespoons agave syrup (or honey or maple syrup)
- 1 tablespoon Dijon mustard
- juice of ½ lemon
- 2 tablespoons chopped chervil or flat-leaf parsley
- salt and freshly ground black pepper
- ½ cup extra-virgin olive oil
- Radicchio and Endive Salad
- 1 heart romaine lettuce, torn into large pieces
- ½ head radicchio, coarsely chopped
- 2 heads endive, sliced
- ½ cup cherry tomatoes, halved
- 3 ounces fresh mozzarella, diced
- salt and freshly ground black pepper

Directions:
1. Slice the pork tenderloin into 1-inch slices. Using a meat pounder, pound the pork slices into thin ½-inch medallions. Generously season the pork with salt and freshly ground black pepper on both sides.
2. Set up a dredging station using three shallow dishes. Place the flour in one dish and the beaten eggs in a second dish. Combine the cracker meal, paprika, dry mustard, garlic powder, thyme and salt in a third dish.
3. Preheat the air fryer to 400°F (205°C).
4. Dredge the pork medallions in flour first and then into the beaten egg. Let the excess egg drip off and coat both sides of the medallions with the cracker meal crumb mixture. Spray both sides of the coated medallions with vegetable or canola oil.
5. Air-fry the medallions in two batches at 400°F (205°C) for 5 minutes. Once you have air-fried all the medallions, flip them all over and return the first batch of medallions back into the air fryer on top of the second batch. Air-fry at 400°F (205°C) for an additional 2 minutes.
6. While the medallions are cooking, make the salad and dressing. Whisk the white balsamic vinegar, agave syrup, Dijon mustard, lemon juice, chervil, salt and pepper together in a small bowl. Whisk in the olive oil slowly until combined and thickened.
7. Combine the romaine lettuce, radicchio, endive, cherry tomatoes, and mozzarella cheese in a large salad bowl. Drizzle the dressing over the vegetables and toss to combine. Season with salt and freshly ground black pepper.
8. Serve the pork medallions warm on or beside the salad.

Pork Schnitzel With Dill Sauce

Servings: 4
Cooking Time: 4 Minutes
Ingredients:
- 6 boneless, center cut pork chops (about 1½ pounds)
- ½ cup flour
- 1½ teaspoons salt
- freshly ground black pepper
- 2 eggs
- ½ cup milk
- 1½ cups toasted fine breadcrumbs
- 1 teaspoon paprika
- 3 tablespoons butter, melted
- 2 tablespoons vegetable or olive oil
- lemon wedges
- Dill Sauce:
- 1 cup chicken stock
- 1½ tablespoons cornstarch

- ⅓ cup sour cream
- 1½ tablespoons chopped fresh dill
- salt and pepper

Directions:
1. Trim the excess fat from the pork chops and pound each chop with a meat mallet between two pieces of plastic wrap until they are ½-inch thick.
2. Set up a dredging station. Combine the flour, salt, and black pepper in a shallow dish. Whisk the eggs and milk together in a second shallow dish. Finally, combine the breadcrumbs and paprika in a third shallow dish.
3. Dip each flattened pork chop in the flour. Shake off the excess flour and dip each chop into the egg mixture. Finally dip them into the breadcrumbs and press the breadcrumbs onto the meat firmly. Place each finished chop on a baking sheet until they are all coated.
4. Preheat the air fryer to 400°F (205°C).
5. Combine the melted butter and the oil in a small bowl and lightly brush both sides of the coated pork chops. Do not brush the chops too heavily or the breading will not be as crispy.
6. Air-fry one schnitzel at a time for 4 minutes, turning it over halfway through the cooking time. Hold the cooked schnitzels warm on a baking pan in a 170°F (75°C) oven while you finish air-frying the rest.
7. While the schnitzels are cooking, whisk the chicken stock and cornstarch together in a small saucepan over medium-high heat on the stovetop. Bring the mixture to a boil and simmer for 2 minutes. Remove the saucepan from heat and whisk in the sour cream. Add the chopped fresh dill and season with salt and pepper.
8. Transfer the pork schnitzel to a platter and serve with dill sauce and lemon wedges. For a traditional meal, serve this along side some egg noodles, spätzle or German potato salad.

Tacos Norteños

Servings: 4
Cooking Time: 25 Minutes
Ingredients:
- ½ cup minced purple onions
- 5 radishes, julienned
- 2 tbsp white wine vinegar
- ½ tsp granulated sugar
- Salt and pepper to taste
- ¼ cup olive oil
- ½ tsp ground cumin
- 1 flank steak
- 10 mini flour tortillas
- 1 cup shredded red cabbage
- ½ cup cucumber slices
- ½ cup fresh radish slices

Directions:
1. Combine the radishes, vinegar, sugar, and salt in a bowl. Let sit covered in the fridge until ready to use. Whisk the olive oil, salt, black pepper and cumin in a bowl. Toss in flank steak and let marinate in the fridge for 30 minutes.
2. Preheat air fryer at 325ºF. Place flank steak in the frying basket and Bake for 18-20 minutes, tossing once. Let rest onto a cutting board for 5 minutes before slicing thinly against the grain. Add steak slices to flour tortillas along with red cabbage, chopped purple onions, cucumber slices, radish slices and fresh radish slices. Serve warm.

Venison Backstrap

Servings: 4
Cooking Time: 10 Minutes
Ingredients:
- 2 eggs
- ¼ cup milk
- 1 cup whole wheat flour
- ½ teaspoon salt
- ¼ teaspoon pepper
- 1 pound venison backstrap, sliced
- salt and pepper
- oil for misting or cooking spray

Directions:
1. Beat together eggs and milk in a shallow dish.
2. In another shallow dish, combine the flour, salt, and pepper. Stir to mix well.
3. Sprinkle venison steaks with additional salt and pepper to taste. Dip in flour, egg wash, then in flour again, pressing in coating.
4. Spray steaks with oil or cooking spray on both sides.
5. Cooking in 2 batches, place steaks in the air fryer basket in a single layer. Cook at 360°F (180°C) for 8minutes. Spray with oil, turn over, and spray other side. Cook for 2 minutes longer, until coating is crispy brown and meat is done to your liking.
6. Repeat to cook remaining venison.

Citrus Pork Lettuce Wraps

Servings:4
Cooking Time: 35 Minutes
Ingredients:
- Salt and white pepper to taste
- 1 tbsp cornstarch
- 1 tbsp red wine vinegar
- 2 tbsp orange marmalade
- 1 tsp pulp-free orange juice
- 2 tsp olive oil
- ¼ tsp chili pepper
- ¼ tsp ground ginger
- 1 lb pork loin, cubed
- 8 iceberg lettuce leaves

Directions:
1. Create a slurry by whisking cornstarch and 1 tbsp of water in a bowl. Set aside. Place a small saucepan over medium heat. Add the red wine vinegar, orange marmalade, orange juice, olive oil, chili pepper, and ginger and cook for 3 minutes, stirring continuously. Mix in the slurry and simmer for 1 more minute. Turn the heat off and let it thicken, about3 minutes.
2. Preheat air fryer to 350ºF. Sprinkle the pork with salt and white pepper. Place them in the greased frying basket and Air Fry for 8-10 minutes until cooked through and browned, turning once. Transfer pork cubes to a bowl with the sauce and toss to coat. Serve in lettuce leaves.

Sriracha Short Ribs

Servings: 4
Cooking Time: 15 Minutes
Ingredients:
- 2 tsp sesame seeds
- 8 pork short ribs
- ½ cup soy sauce
- ¼ cup rice wine vinegar
- ½ cup chopped onion
- 2 garlic cloves, minced
- 1 tbsp sesame oil
- 1 tsp sriracha
- 4 scallions, thinly sliced
- Salt and pepper to taste

Directions:
1. Put short ribs in a resealable bag along with soy sauce, vinegar, onion, garlic, sesame oil, Sriracha, half of the scallions, salt, and pepper. Seal the bag and toss to coat. Refrigerate for one hour.
2. Preheat air fryer to 380°F (195°C). Place the short ribs in the air fryer. Bake for 8-10 minutes, flipping once until crisp. When the ribs are done, garnish with remaining scallions and sesame seeds. Serve and enjoy!

Beef Meatballs With Herbs

Servings: 6
Cooking Time: 30 Minutes
Ingredients:
- 1 medium onion, minced
- 2 garlic cloves, minced
- 1 tsp olive oil
- 1 bread slice, crumbled
- 3 tbsp milk
- 1 tsp dried sage
- 1 tsp dried thyme
- 1 lb ground beef

Directions:
1. Preheat air fryer to 380°F (195°C). Toss the onion, garlic, and olive oil in a baking pan, place it in the air fryer, and Air Fry for 2-4 minutes. The veggies should be crispy but tender. Transfer the veggies to a bowl and add in the breadcrumbs, milk, thyme, and sage, then toss gently to combine. Add in the ground beef and mix with your hands. Shape the mixture into 24 meatballs. Put them in the frying basket and Air Fry for 12-16 minutes or until the meatballs are browned on all sides. Serve and enjoy!

Pork Cutlets With Almond-lemon Crust

Servings: 3
Cooking Time: 14 Minutes
Ingredients:
- ¾ cup Almond flour
- ¾ cup Plain dried bread crumbs (gluten-free, if a concern)
- 1½ teaspoons Finely grated lemon zest
- 1¼ teaspoons Table salt
- ¾ teaspoon Garlic powder
- ¾ teaspoon Dried oregano
- 1 Large egg white(s)
- 2 tablespoons Water
- 3 6-ounce center-cut boneless pork loin chops (about ¾ inch thick)
- Olive oil spray

Directions:
1. Preheat the air fryer to 375°F (190°C).
2. Mix the almond flour, bread crumbs, lemon zest, salt, garlic powder, and dried oregano in a large bowl until well combined.
3. Whisk the egg white(s) and water in a shallow soup plate or small pie plate until uniform.
4. Dip a chop in the egg white mixture, turning it to coat all sides, even the ends. Let any excess egg white mixture slip back into the rest, then set it in the almond flour mixture. Turn it several times, pressing gently to coat it evenly. Generously coat the chop with olive oil spray, then set aside to dip and coat the remaining chop(s).
5. Set the chops in the basket with as much air space between them as possible. Air-fry undisturbed for 12 minutes, or until browned and crunchy. You may need to add 2 minutes to the cooking time if the machine is at 360°F 180°C).
6. Use kitchen tongs to transfer the chops to a wire rack. Cool for a few minutes before serving.

Creamy Horseradish Roast Beef

Servings: 6
Cooking Time: 65 Minutes + Chilling Time
Ingredients:
- 1 topside roast, tied
- Salt to taste
- 1 tsp butter, melted
- 2 tbsp Dijon mustard
- 3 tbsp prepared horseradish
- 1 garlic clove, minced
- 2/3 cup buttermilk
- 2 tsp red wine
- 1 tbsp minced chives
- Salt and pepper to taste

Directions:
1. Preheat air fryer to 320°F (160°C). Mix salt, butter, half of the mustard, 1 tsp of horseradish, and garlic until blended. Rub all over the roast. Bake the roast in the air fryer for 30-35 minutes, flipping once until browned. Transfer to a cutting board and cover with foil. Let rest for 15 minutes.
2. In a bowl, mix buttermilk, horseradish, remaining mustard, chives, wine, salt, and pepper until smooth. Refrigerate. When ready to serve, carve the roast into thin slices and serve with horseradish cream on the side.

Meatball Subs

Servings: 4
Cooking Time: 11 Minutes
Ingredients:
- Marinara Sauce
- 1 15-ounce can diced tomatoes
- 1 teaspoon garlic powder
- 1 teaspoon dried basil
- ½ teaspoon oregano
- ⅛ teaspoon salt
- 1 tablespoon robust olive oil
- Meatballs
- ¼ pound ground turkey

- ¾ pound very lean ground beef
- 1 tablespoon milk
- ½ cup torn bread pieces
- 1 egg
- ¼ teaspoon salt
- ½ teaspoon dried onion
- 1 teaspoon garlic powder
- ¼ teaspoon smoked paprika
- ¼ teaspoon crushed red pepper
- 1½ teaspoons dried parsley
- ¼ teaspoon oregano
- 2 teaspoons Worcestershire sauce
- Sandwiches
- 4 large whole-grain sub or hoagie rolls, split
- toppings, sliced or chopped:
- mushrooms
- jalapeño or banana peppers
- red or green bell pepper
- red onions
- grated cheese

Directions:
1. Place all marinara ingredients in saucepan and bring to a boil. Lower heat and simmer 10 minutes, uncovered.
2. Combine all meatball ingredients in large bowl and stir. Mixture should be well blended but don't overwork it. Excessive mixing will toughen the meatballs.
3. Divide meat into 16 equal portions and shape into balls.
4. Cook the balls at 360°F (180°C) until meat is done and juices run clear, about 11 minutes.
5. While meatballs are cooking, taste marinara. If you prefer stronger flavors, add more seasoning and simmer another 5 minutes.
6. When meatballs finish cooking, drain them on paper towels.
7. To assemble subs, place 4 meatballs on each sub roll, spoon sauce over meat, and add preferred toppings. Serve with additional marinara for dipping.

Extra Crispy Country-style Pork Riblets

Servings: 3
Cooking Time: 30 Minutes
Ingredients:
- ⅓ cup Tapioca flour
- 2½ tablespoons Chile powder
- ¾ teaspoon Table salt (optional)
- 1¼ pounds Boneless country-style pork ribs, cut into 1½-inch chunks
- Vegetable oil spray

Directions:
1. Preheat the air fryer to 375°F (190°C).
2. Mix the tapioca flour, chile powder, and salt (if using) in a large bowl until well combined. Add the country-style rib chunks and toss well to coat thoroughly.
3. When the machine is at temperature, gently shake off any excess tapioca coating from the chunks. Generously coat them on all sides with vegetable oil spray. Arrange the chunks in the basket in one (admittedly fairly tight) layer. The pieces may touch. Air-fry for 30 minutes, rearranging the pieces at the 10- and 20-minute marks to expose any touching bits, until very crisp and well browned.
4. Gently pour the contents of the basket onto a wire rack. Cool for 5 minutes before serving.

Brie And Cranberry Burgers

Servings: 3
Cooking Time: 9 Minutes
Ingredients:
- 1 pound ground beef (80% lean)
- 1 tablespoon chopped fresh thyme
- 1 tablespoon Worcestershire sauce
- ½ teaspoon salt
- freshly ground black pepper
- 1 (4-ounce) wheel of Brie cheese, sliced
- handful of arugula
- 3 or 4 brioche hamburger buns (or potato hamburger buns), toasted
- ¼ to ½ cup whole berry cranberry sauce

Directions:
1. Combine the beef, thyme, Worcestershire sauce, salt and pepper together in a large bowl and mix well. Divide the meat into 4 (¼-pound) portions or 3 larger portions and then form them into burger patties, being careful not to over-handle the meat.
2. Preheat the air fryer to 390°F (200°C) and pour a little water into the bottom of the air fryer drawer. (This will help prevent the grease that drips into the bottom drawer from burning and smoking.)
3. Transfer the burgers to the air fryer basket. Air-fry the burgers at 390°F (200°C) for 5 minutes. Flip the burgers over and air-fry for another 2 minutes. Top each burger with a couple slices of brie and air-fry for another minute or two, just to soften the cheese.
4. Build the burgers by placing a few leaves of arugula on the bottom bun, adding the burger and a spoonful of cranberry sauce on top. Top with the other half of the hamburger bun and enjoy.

Barbecue-style Beef Cube Steak

Servings: 2
Cooking Time: 14 Minutes
Ingredients:
- 2 4-ounce beef cube steak(s)
- 2 cups (about 8 ounces) Fritos (original flavor) or a generic corn chip equivalent, crushed to crumbs (see here)
- 6 tablespoons Purchased smooth barbecue sauce, any flavor (gluten-free, if a concern)

Directions:
1. Preheat the air fryer to 375°F (190°C).
2. Spread the Fritos crumbs in a shallow soup plate or a small pie plate. Rub the barbecue sauce onto both sides of the steak(s). Dredge the steak(s) in the Fritos crumbs to coat well and thoroughly, turning several times and pressing down to get the little bits to adhere to the meat.
3. When the machine is at temperature, set the steak(s) in the basket. Leave as much air space between them as possible if you're working with more than one piece of beef. Air-fry undisturbed for 12 minutes, or until lightly brown and crunchy. If the machine is at 360°F (180°C), you may need to add 2 minutes to the cooking time.
4. Use kitchen tongs to transfer the steak(s) to a wire rack. Cool for 5 minutes before serving.

Greek-style Pork Stuffed Jalapeño Poppers

Servings: 6
Cooking Time: 30 Minutes
Ingredients:
- 6 jalapeños, halved lengthwise
- 3 tbsp diced Kalamata olives
- 3 tbsp olive oil
- ¼ lb ground pork
- 2 tbsp feta cheese
- 1 oz cream cheese, softened
- ½ tsp dried mint
- ½ cup Greek yogurt

Directions:
1. Warm 2 tbsp of olive oil in a skillet over medium heat. Stir in ground pork and cook for 6 minutes until no longer pink. Preheat air fryer to 350°F. Mix the cooked pork, olives, feta cheese, and cream cheese in a bowl. Divide the pork mixture between the peppers. Place them in the frying basket and Air Fry for 6 minutes. Mix the Greek yogurt with the remaining olive oil and mint in a small bowl. Serve with the poppers.

Cajun Pork Loin Chops

Servings: 4
Cooking Time: 25 Minutes
Ingredients:
- 8 thin boneless pork loin chops
- ¾ tsp Coarse sea salt
- 1 egg, beaten
- 1 tsp Cajun seasoning
- ½ cup bread crumbs
- 1 cucumber, sliced
- 1 tomato, sliced

Directions:
1. Place the chops between two sheets of parchment paper. Pound the pork to ¼-inch thickness using a meat mallet or rolling pin. Season with sea salt. In a shallow bowl, beat the egg with 1 tsp of water and Cajun seasoning. In a second bowl, add the breadcrumbs. Dip the chops into the egg mixture, shake, and dip into the crumbs.
2. Preheat air fryer to 400°F (205°C). Place the chops in the greased frying basket and Air Fry for 6-8 minutes, flipping once until golden and cooked through. Serve immediately with cucumber and tomato.

Mini Meatloaves With Pancetta

Servings: 4
Cooking Time: 40 Minutes
Ingredients:
- ¼ cup grated Parmesan
- 1/3 cup quick-cooking oats
- 2 tbsp milk
- 3 tbsp ketchup
- 3 tbsp Dijon mustard
- 1 egg
- 1 tsp dried oregano
- Salt and pepper to taste
- 1 lb lean ground beef
- 4 pancetta slices, uncooked

Directions:
1. Preheat the air fryer to 375°F (190°C). Combine the oats, milk, 1 tbsp of ketchup, 1 tbsp of mustard, the egg, oregano, Parmesan cheese, salt, and pepper, and mix. Add the beef and mix with your hands, then form 4 mini loaves. Wrap each mini loaf with pancetta, covering the meat.
2. Combine the remaining ketchup and mustard and set aside. Line the frying basket with foil and poke holes in it, then set the loaves in the basket. Brush with the ketchup/mustard mix. Bake for 17-22 minutes or until cooked and golden. Serve and enjoy!

Honey Mesquite Pork Chops

Servings: 2
Cooking Time: 10 Minutes
Ingredients:
- 2 tablespoons mesquite seasoning
- ¼ cup honey
- 1 tablespoon olive oil
- 1 tablespoon water
- freshly ground black pepper
- 2 bone-in center cut pork chops (about 1 pound)

Directions:
1. Whisk the mesquite seasoning, honey, olive oil, water and freshly ground black pepper together in a shallow glass dish. Pierce the chops all over and on both sides with a fork or meat tenderizer. Add the pork chops to the marinade and massage the marinade into the chops. Cover and marinate for 30 minutes.
2. Preheat the air fryer to 330°F (165°C).
3. Transfer the pork chops to the air fryer basket and pour half of the marinade over the chops, reserving the remaining marinade. Air-fry the pork chops for 6 minutes. Flip the pork chops over and pour the remaining marinade on top. Air-fry for an additional 3 minutes at 330°F (165°C). Then, increase the air fryer temperature to 400°F (205°C) and air-fry the pork chops for an additional minute.
4. Transfer the pork chops to a serving plate, and let them rest for 5 minutes before serving. If you'd like a sauce for these chops, pour the cooked marinade from the bottom of the air fryer over the top.

Mushroom & Quinoa-stuffed Pork Loins

Servings: 3
Cooking Time: 25 Minutes
Ingredients:
- 3 boneless center-cut pork loins, pocket cut in each loin
- ½ cup diced white mushrooms
- 1 tsp vegetable oil
- 3 bacon slices, diced
- ½ onion, peeled and diced
- 1 cup baby spinach
- Salt and pepper to taste
- ½ cup cooked quinoa
- ½ cup mozzarella cheese

Directions:
1. Warm the oil in a skillet over medium heat. Add the bacon and cook for 3 minutes until the fat is rendered but not crispy. Add in onion and mushrooms and stir-fry for 3 minutes until the onions are translucent. Stir in spinach, salt, and pepper and cook for 1 minute until the spinach wilts. Set aside and toss in quinoa.
2. Preheat air fryer at 350°F. Stuff quinoa mixture into each pork loin and sprinkle with mozzarella cheese. Place them in the frying basket and Air Fry for 11 minutes. Let rest onto a cutting board for 5 minutes before serving.

Pork Cutlets With Aloha Salsa

Servings: 4
Cooking Time: 9 Minutes
Ingredients:
- Aloha Salsa
- 1 cup fresh pineapple, chopped in small pieces
- ¼ cup red onion, finely chopped
- ¼ cup green or red bell pepper, chopped
- ½ teaspoon ground cinnamon
- 1 teaspoon low-sodium soy sauce
- ⅛ teaspoon crushed red pepper
- ⅛ teaspoon ground black pepper
- 2 eggs
- 2 tablespoons milk
- ¼ cup flour
- ¼ cup panko breadcrumbs
- 4 teaspoons sesame seeds
- 1 pound boneless, thin pork cutlets (⅜- to ½-inch thick)
- lemon pepper and salt
- ¼ cup cornstarch
- oil for misting or cooking spray

Directions:
1. In a medium bowl, stir together all ingredients for salsa. Cover and refrigerate while cooking pork.
2. Preheat air fryer to 390°F (200°C).
3. Beat together eggs and milk in shallow dish.
4. In another shallow dish, mix together the flour, panko, and sesame seeds.
5. Sprinkle pork cutlets with lemon pepper and salt to taste. Most lemon pepper seasoning contains salt, so go easy adding extra.
6. Dip pork cutlets in cornstarch, egg mixture, and then panko coating. Spray both sides with oil or cooking spray.
7. Cook cutlets for 3minutes. Turn cutlets over, spraying both sides, and continue cooking for 6 minutes or until well done.
8. Serve fried cutlets with salsa on the side.

Spicy Hoisin Bbq Pork Chops

Servings: 2
Cooking Time: 12 Minutes
Ingredients:
- 3 tablespoons hoisin sauce
- ¼ cup honey
- 1 tablespoon soy sauce
- 3 tablespoons rice vinegar
- 2 tablespoons brown sugar
- 1½ teaspoons grated fresh ginger
- 1 to 2 teaspoons Sriracha sauce, to taste
- 2 to 3 bone-in center cut pork chops, 1-inch thick (about 1¼ pounds)
- chopped scallions, for garnish

Directions:
1. Combine the hoisin sauce, honey, soy sauce, rice vinegar, brown sugar, ginger, and Sriracha sauce in a small saucepan. Whisk the ingredients together and bring the mixture to a boil over medium-high heat on the stovetop. Reduce the heat and simmer the sauce until it has reduced in volume and thickened slightly – about 10 minutes.
2. Preheat the air fryer to 400°F (205°C).
3. Place the pork chops into the air fryer basket and pour half the hoisin BBQ sauce over the top. Air-fry for 6 minutes. Then, flip the chops over, pour the remaining hoisin BBQ sauce on top and air-fry for 6 more minutes, depending on the thickness of the pork chops. The internal temperature of the pork chops should be 155°F (70°C) when tested with an instant read thermometer.
4. Let the pork chops rest for 5 minutes before serving. You can spoon a little of the sauce from the bottom drawer of the air fryer over the top if desired. Sprinkle with chopped scallions and serve.

Chapter 9: Sandwiches And Burgers Recipes

Lamb Burgers

Servings: 3
Cooking Time: 17 Minutes
Ingredients:
- 1 pound 2 ounces Ground lamb
- 3 tablespoons Crumbled feta
- 1 teaspoon Minced garlic
- 1 teaspoon Tomato paste
- ¾ teaspoon Ground coriander
- ¾ teaspoon Ground dried ginger
- Up to ⅛ teaspoon Cayenne
- Up to a ⅛ teaspoon Table salt (optional)
- 3 Kaiser rolls or hamburger buns (gluten-free, if a concern), split open

Directions:
1. Preheat the air fryer to 375°F (190°C).
2. Gently mix the ground lamb, feta, garlic, tomato paste, coriander, ginger, cayenne, and salt (if using) in a bowl until well combined, trying to keep the bits of cheese intact. Form this mixture into two 5-inch patties for the small batch, three 5-inch patties for the medium, or four 5-inch patties for the large.
3. Set the patties in the basket in one layer and air-fry undisturbed for 16 minutes, or until an instant-read meat thermometer inserted into one burger registers 160°F (70°C). (The cheese is not an issue with the temperature probe in this recipe as it was for the Inside-Out Cheeseburgers, because the feta is so well mixed into the ground meat.)
4. Use a nonstick-safe spatula, and perhaps a flatware fork for balance, to transfer the burgers to a cutting board. Set the buns cut side down in the basket in one layer (working in batches as necessary) and air-fry undisturbed for 1 minute, to toast a bit and warm up. Serve the burgers warm in the buns.

Thai-style Pork Sliders

Servings: 4
Cooking Time: 15 Minutes
Ingredients:
- 11 ounces Ground pork
- 2½ tablespoons Very thinly sliced scallions, white and green parts
- 4 teaspoons Minced peeled fresh ginger
- 2½ teaspoons Fish sauce (gluten-free, if a concern)
- 2 teaspoons Thai curry paste (see the headnote; gluten-free, if a concern)
- 2 teaspoons Light brown sugar
- ¾ teaspoon Ground black pepper
- 4 Slider buns (gluten-free, if a concern)

Directions:
1. Preheat the air fryer to 375°F (190°C).
2. Gently mix the pork, scallions, ginger, fish sauce, curry paste, brown sugar, and black pepper in a bowl until well combined. With clean, wet hands, form about ⅓ cup of the pork mixture into a slider about 2½ inches in diameter. Repeat until you use up all the meat—3 sliders for the small batch, 4 for the medium, and 6 for the large. (Keep wetting your hands to help the patties adhere.)
3. When the machine is at temperature, set the sliders in the basket in one layer. Air-fry undisturbed for 14 minutes, or until the sliders are golden brown and caramelized at their edges and an instant-read meat thermometer inserted into the center of a slider registers 160°F (70°C).
4. Use a nonstick-safe spatula, and perhaps a flatware fork for balance, to transfer the sliders to a cutting board. Set the buns cut side down in the basket in one layer (working in batches as necessary) and air-fry undisturbed for 1 minute, to toast a bit and warm up. Serve the sliders warm in the buns.

Black Bean Veggie Burgers

Servings: 3
Cooking Time: 10 Minutes
Ingredients:
- 1 cup Drained and rinsed canned black beans
- ⅓ cup Pecan pieces
- ⅓ cup Rolled oats (not quick-cooking or steel-cut; gluten-free, if a concern)
- 2 tablespoons (or 1 small egg) Pasteurized egg substitute, such as Egg Beaters (gluten-free, if a concern)
- 2 teaspoons Red ketchup-like chili sauce, such as Heinz
- ¼ teaspoon Ground cumin
- ¼ teaspoon Dried oregano
- ¼ teaspoon Table salt
- ¼ teaspoon Ground black pepper
- Olive oil
- Olive oil spray

Directions:
1. Preheat the air fryer to 400°F (205°C).
2. Put the beans, pecans, oats, egg substitute or egg, chili sauce, cumin, oregano, salt, and pepper in a food processor. Cover and process to a coarse paste that will hold its shape like sugar-cookie dough, adding olive oil in 1-teaspoon increments to get the mixture to blend smoothly. The amount of olive oil is actually dependent on the internal moisture content of the beans and the oats. Figure on about 1 tablespoon (three 1-teaspoon additions) for the smaller batch, with proportional increases for the other batches. A little too much olive oil can't hurt, but a dry paste will fall apart as it cooks and a far-too-wet paste will stick to the basket.
3. Scrape down and remove the blade. Using clean, wet hands, form the paste into two 4-inch patties for the small batch, three 4-inch patties for the medium, or four 4-inch patties for the large batch, setting them one by one on a cutting board. Generously coat both sides of the patties with olive oil spray.
4. Set them in the basket in one layer. Air-fry undisturbed for 10 minutes, or until lightly browned and crisp at the edges.
5. Use a nonstick-safe spatula, and perhaps a flatware fork for balance, to transfer the burgers to a wire rack. Cool for 5 minutes before serving.

Inside-out Cheeseburgers

Servings: 3
Cooking Time: 9-11 Minutes
Ingredients:
- 1 pound 2 ounces 90% lean ground beef
- ¾ teaspoon Dried oregano
- ¾ teaspoon Table salt
- ¾ teaspoon Ground black pepper
- ¼ teaspoon Garlic powder
- 6 tablespoons (about 1½ ounces) Shredded Cheddar, Swiss, or other semi-firm cheese, or a purchased blend of shredded cheeses
- 3 Hamburger buns (gluten-free, if a concern), split open

Directions:
1. Preheat the air fryer to 375°F (190°C).
2. Gently mix the ground beef, oregano, salt, pepper, and garlic powder in a bowl until well combined without turning the mixture to mush. Form it into two 6-inch patties for the small batch, three for the medium, or four for the large.
3. Place 2 tablespoons of the shredded cheese in the center of each patty. With clean hands, fold the sides of the patty up to cover the cheese, then pick it up and roll it gently into a ball to seal the cheese inside. Gently press it back into a 5-inch burger without letting any cheese squish out. Continue filling and preparing more burgers, as needed.
4. Place the burgers in the basket in one layer and air-fry undisturbed for 8 minutes for medium or 10 minutes for well-done. (An instant-read meat thermometer won't work for these burgers because it will hit the mostly melted cheese inside and offer a hotter temperature than the surrounding meat.)
5. Use a nonstick-safe spatula, and perhaps a flatware fork for balance, to transfer the burgers to a cutting board. Set the buns cut side down in the basket in one layer (working in batches as necessary) and air-fry undisturbed for 1 minute, to toast a bit and warm up. Cool the burgers a few minutes more, then serve them warm in the buns.

White Bean Veggie Burgers

Servings: 3
Cooking Time: 13 Minutes
Ingredients:
- 1⅓ cups Drained and rinsed canned white beans
- 3 tablespoons Rolled oats (not quick-cooking or steel-cut; gluten-free, if a concern)
- 3 tablespoons Chopped walnuts
- 2 teaspoons Olive oil
- 2 teaspoons Lemon juice
- 1½ teaspoons Dijon mustard (gluten-free, if a concern)
- ¾ teaspoon Dried sage leaves
- ¼ teaspoon Table salt
- Olive oil spray
- 3 Whole-wheat buns or gluten-free whole-grain buns (if a concern), split open

Directions:
1. Preheat the air fryer to 400°F (205°C).
2. Place the beans, oats, walnuts, oil, lemon juice, mustard, sage, and salt in a food processor. Cover and process to make a coarse paste that will hold its shape, about like wet sugar-cookie dough, stopping the machine to scrape down the inside of the canister at least once.
3. Scrape down and remove the blade. With clean and wet hands, form the bean paste into two 4-inch patties for the small batch, three 4-inch patties for the medium, or four 4-inch patties for the large batch. Generously coat the patties on both sides with olive oil spray.
4. Set them in the basket with some space between them and air-fry undisturbed for 12 minutes, or until lightly brown and crisp at the edges. The tops of the burgers will feel firm to the touch.
5. Use a nonstick-safe spatula, and perhaps a flatware fork for balance, to transfer the burgers to a cutting board. Set the buns cut side down in the basket in one layer (working in batches as necessary) and air-fry undisturbed for 1 minute, to toast a bit and warm up. Serve the burgers warm in the buns.

Mexican Cheeseburgers

Servings: 4
Cooking Time: 22 Minutes
Ingredients:
- 1¼ pounds ground beef
- ¼ cup finely chopped onion
- ½ cup crushed yellow corn tortilla chips
- 1 (1.25-ounce) packet taco seasoning
- ¼ cup canned diced green chilies
- 1 egg, lightly beaten
- 4 ounces pepper jack cheese, grated
- 4 (12-inch) flour tortillas
- shredded lettuce, sour cream, guacamole, salsa (for topping)

Directions:
1. Combine the ground beef, minced onion, crushed tortilla chips, taco seasoning, green chilies, and egg in a large bowl. Mix thoroughly until combined – your hands are good tools for this. Divide the meat into four equal portions and shape each portion into an oval-shaped burger.
2. Preheat the air fryer to 370°F (185°C).
3. Air-fry the burgers for 18 minutes, turning them over halfway through the cooking time. Divide the cheese between the burgers, lower fryer to 340°F (170°C) and air-fry for an additional 4 minutes to melt the cheese. (This will give you a burger that is medium-well. If you prefer your cheeseburger medium-rare, shorten the cooking time to about 15 minutes and then add the cheese and proceed with the recipe.)
4. While the burgers are cooking, warm the tortillas wrapped in aluminum foil in a 350°F (175°C) oven, or in a skillet with a little oil over medium-high heat for a couple of minutes. Keep the tortillas warm until the burgers are ready.
5. To assemble the burgers, spread sour cream over three quarters of the tortillas and top each with some shredded lettuce and salsa. Place the Mexican cheeseburgers on the lettuce and top with guacamole. Fold the tortillas around the burger, starting with the bottom and then folding the sides in over the top. (A little sour cream can help hold the seam of the tortilla together.) Serve immediately.

Best-ever Roast Beef Sandwiches

Servings: 6
Cooking Time: 30-50 Minutes
Ingredients:
- 2½ teaspoons Olive oil
- 1½ teaspoons Dried oregano
- 1½ teaspoons Dried thyme
- 1½ teaspoons Onion powder
- 1½ teaspoons Table salt
- 1½ teaspoons Ground black pepper
- 3 pounds Beef eye of round
- 6 Round soft rolls, such as Kaiser rolls or hamburger buns (gluten-free, if a concern), split open lengthwise
- ¾ cup Regular, low-fat, or fat-free mayonnaise (gluten-free, if a concern)
- 6 Romaine lettuce leaves, rinsed
- 6 Round tomato slices (¼ inch thick)

Directions:
1. Preheat the air fryer to 350°F (175°C).

2. Mix the oil, oregano, thyme, onion powder, salt, and pepper in a small bowl. Spread this mixture all over the eye of round.
3. When the machine is at temperature, set the beef in the basket and air-fry for 30 to 50 minutes (the range depends on the size of the cut), turning the meat twice, until an instant-read meat thermometer inserted into the thickest piece of the meat registers 130°F (55°C) for rare, 140°F (60°C) for medium, or 150°F (65C) for well-done.
4. Use kitchen tongs to transfer the beef to a cutting board. Cool for 10 minutes. If serving now, carve into ⅛-inch-thick slices. Spread each roll with 2 tablespoons mayonnaise and divide the beef slices between the rolls. Top with a lettuce leaf and a tomato slice and serve. Or set the beef in a container, cover, and refrigerate for up to 3 days to make cold roast beef sandwiches anytime.

Sausage And Pepper Heros
Servings: 3
Cooking Time: 11 Minutes
Ingredients:
- 3 links (about 9 ounces total) Sweet Italian sausages (gluten-free, if a concern)
- 1½ Medium red or green bell pepper(s), stemmed, cored, and cut into ½-inch-wide strips
- 1 medium Yellow or white onion(s), peeled, halved, and sliced into thin half-moons
- 3 Long soft rolls, such as hero, hoagie, or Italian sub rolls (gluten-free, if a concern), split open lengthwise
- For garnishing Balsamic vinegar
- For garnishing Fresh basil leaves

Directions:
1. Preheat the air fryer to 400°F (205°C).
2. When the machine is at temperature, set the sausage links in the basket in one layer and air-fry undisturbed for 5 minutes.
3. Add the pepper strips and onions. Continue air-frying, tossing and rearranging everything about once every minute, for 5 minutes, or until the sausages are browned and an instant-read meat thermometer inserted into one of the links registers 160°F (70°C).
4. Use a nonstick-safe spatula and kitchen tongs to transfer the sausages and vegetables to a cutting board. Set the rolls cut side down in the basket in one layer (working in batches as necessary) and air-fry undisturbed for 1 minute, to toast the rolls a bit and warm them up. Set 1 sausage with some pepper strips and onions in each warm roll, sprinkle balsamic vinegar over the sandwich fillings, and garnish with basil leaves.

Salmon Burgers
Servings: 3
Cooking Time: 8 Minutes
Ingredients:
- 1 pound 2 ounces Skinless salmon fillet, preferably fattier Atlantic salmon
- 1½ tablespoons Minced chives or the green part of a scallion
- ½ cup Plain panko bread crumbs (gluten-free, if a concern)
- 1½ teaspoons Dijon mustard (gluten-free, if a concern)
- 1½ teaspoons Drained and rinsed capers, minced
- 1½ teaspoons Lemon juice
- ¼ teaspoon Table salt
- ¼ teaspoon Ground black pepper
- Vegetable oil spray

Directions:
1. Preheat the air fryer to 375°F (190°C).
2. Cut the salmon into pieces that will fit in a food processor. Cover and pulse until coarsely chopped. Add the chives and pulse to combine, until the fish is ground but not a paste. Scrape down and remove the blade. Scrape the salmon mixture into a bowl. Add the bread crumbs, mustard, capers, lemon juice, salt, and pepper. Stir gently until well combined.
3. Use clean and dry hands to form the mixture into two 5-inch patties for a small batch, three 5-inch patties for a medium batch, or four 5-inch patties for a large one.
4. Coat both sides of each patty with vegetable oil spray. Set them in the basket in one layer and air-fry undisturbed for 8 minutes, or until browned and an instant-read meat thermometer inserted into the center of a burger registers 145°F (60°C).
5. Use a nonstick-safe spatula, and perhaps a flatware fork for balance, to transfer the burgers to a wire rack. Cool for 2 or 3 minutes before serving.

Reuben Sandwiches
Servings: 2
Cooking Time: 11 Minutes
Ingredients:
- ½ pound Sliced deli corned beef
- 4 teaspoons Regular or low-fat mayonnaise (not fat-free)
- 4 Rye bread slices
- 2 tablespoons plus 2 teaspoons Russian dressing
- ½ cup Purchased sauerkraut, squeezed by the handful over the sink to get rid of excess moisture
- 2 ounces (2 to 4 slices) Swiss cheese slices (optional)

Directions:
1. Set the corned beef in the basket, slip the basket into the machine, and heat the air fryer to 400°F (205°C). Air-fry undisturbed for 3 minutes from the time the basket is put in the machine, just to warm up the meat.
2. Use kitchen tongs to transfer the corned beef to a cutting board. Spread 1 teaspoon mayonnaise on one side of each slice of rye bread, rubbing the mayonnaise into the bread with a small flatware knife.
3. Place the bread slices mayonnaise side down on a cutting board. Spread the Russian dressing over the "dry" side of each slice. For one sandwich, top one slice of bread with the corned beef, sauerkraut, and cheese (if using). For two sandwiches, top two slices of bread each with half of the corned beef, sauerkraut, and cheese (if using). Close the sandwiches with the remaining bread, setting it mayonnaise side up on top.
4. Set the sandwich(es) in the basket and air-fry undisturbed for 8 minutes, or until browned and crunchy.
5. Use a nonstick-safe spatula, and perhaps a flatware fork for balance, to transfer the sandwich(es) to a cutting board. Cool for 2 or 3 minutes before slicing in half and serving.

Chicken Gyros

Servings: 4
Cooking Time: 14 Minutes
Ingredients:
- 4 4- to 5-ounce boneless skinless chicken thighs, trimmed of any fat blobs
- 2 tablespoons Lemon juice
- 2 tablespoons Red wine vinegar
- 2 tablespoons Olive oil
- 2 teaspoons Dried oregano
- 2 teaspoons Minced garlic
- 1 teaspoon Table salt
- 1 teaspoon Ground black pepper
- 4 Pita pockets (gluten-free, if a concern)
- ½ cup Chopped tomatoes
- ½ cup Bottled regular, low-fat, or fat-free ranch dressing (gluten-free, if a concern)

Directions:
1. Mix the thighs, lemon juice, vinegar, oil, oregano, garlic, salt, and pepper in a zip-closed bag. Seal, gently massage the marinade into the meat through the plastic, and refrigerate for at least 2 hours or up to 6 hours. (Longer than that and the meat can turn rubbery.)
2. Set the plastic bag out on the counter (to make the contents a little less frigid). Preheat the air fryer to 375°F (190°C).
3. When the machine is at temperature, use kitchen tongs to place the thighs in the basket in one layer. Discard the marinade. Air-fry the chicken thighs undisturbed for 12 minutes, or until browned and an instant-read meat thermometer inserted into the thickest part of one thigh registers 165°F (75°C). You may need to air-fry the chicken 2 minutes longer if the machine's temperature is 360°F (180°C).
4. Use kitchen tongs to transfer the thighs to a cutting board. Cool for 5 minutes, then set one thigh in each of the pita pockets. Top each with 2 tablespoons chopped tomatoes and 2 tablespoons dressing. Serve warm.

Chicken Saltimbocca Sandwiches

Servings: 3
Cooking Time: 11 Minutes
Ingredients:
- 3 5- to 6-ounce boneless skinless chicken breasts
- 6 Thin prosciutto slices
- 6 Provolone cheese slices
- 3 Long soft rolls, such as hero, hoagie, or Italian sub rolls (gluten-free, if a concern), split open lengthwise
- 3 tablespoons Pesto, purchased or homemade (see the headnote)

Directions:
1. Preheat the air fryer to 400°F (205°C).
2. Wrap each chicken breast with 2 prosciutto slices, spiraling the prosciutto around the breast and overlapping the slices a bit to cover the breast. The prosciutto will stick to the chicken more readily than bacon does.
3. When the machine is at temperature, set the wrapped chicken breasts in the basket and air-fry undisturbed for 10 minutes, or until the prosciutto is frizzled and the chicken is cooked through.
4. Overlap 2 cheese slices on each breast. Air-fry undisturbed for 1 minute, or until melted. Take the basket out of the machine.
5. Smear the insides of the rolls with the pesto, then use kitchen tongs to put a wrapped and cheesy chicken breast in each roll.

Perfect Burgers

Servings: 3
Cooking Time: 13 Minutes
Ingredients:
- 1 pound 2 ounces 90% lean ground beef
- 1½ tablespoons Worcestershire sauce (gluten-free, if a concern)
- ½ teaspoon Ground black pepper
- 3 Hamburger buns (gluten-free if a concern), split open

Directions:
1. Preheat the air fryer to 375°F (190°C).
2. Gently mix the ground beef, Worcestershire sauce, and pepper in a bowl until well combined but preserving as much of the meat's fibers as possible. Divide this mixture into two 5-inch patties for the small batch, three 5-inch patties for the medium, or four 5-inch patties for the large. Make a thumbprint indentation in the center of each patty, about halfway through the meat.
3. Set the patties in the basket in one layer with some space between them. Air-fry undisturbed for 10 minutes, or until an instant-read meat thermometer inserted into the center of a burger registers 160°F (70°C) (a medium-well burger). You may need to add 2 minutes cooking time if the air fryer is at 360°F (180°C).
4. Use a nonstick-safe spatula, and perhaps a flatware fork for balance, to transfer the burgers to a cutting board. Set the buns cut side down in the basket in one layer (working in batches as necessary) and air-fry undisturbed for 1 minute, to toast a bit and warm up. Serve the burgers in the warm buns.

Dijon Thyme Burgers

Servings: 3
Cooking Time: 18 Minutes
Ingredients:
- 1 pound lean ground beef
- ⅓ cup panko breadcrumbs
- ¼ cup finely chopped onion
- 3 tablespoons Dijon mustard
- 1 tablespoon chopped fresh thyme
- 4 teaspoons Worcestershire sauce
- 1 teaspoon salt
- freshly ground black pepper
- Topping (optional):
- 2 tablespoons Dijon mustard
- 1 tablespoon dark brown sugar
- 1 teaspoon Worcestershire sauce
- 4 ounces sliced Swiss cheese, optional

Directions:
1. Combine all the burger ingredients together in a large bowl and mix well. Divide the meat into 4 equal portions and then form the burgers, being careful not to over-handle the meat. One good way to do this is to throw the meat back and forth from one hand to another, packing the meat each time you catch it. Flatten the balls into patties, making an indentation in the center of each patty with your thumb (this

will help it stay flat as it cooks) and flattening the sides of the burgers so that they will fit nicely into the air fryer basket.
2. Preheat the air fryer to 370°F (185°C).
3. If you don't have room for all four burgers, air-fry two or three burgers at a time for 8 minutes. Flip the burgers over and air-fry for another 6 minutes.
4. While the burgers are cooking combine the Dijon mustard, dark brown sugar, and Worcestershire sauce in a small bowl and mix well. This optional topping to the burgers really adds a boost of flavor at the end. Spread the Dijon topping evenly on each burger. If you cooked the burgers in batches, return the first batch to the cooker at this time – it's ok to place the fourth burger on top of the others in the center of the basket. Air-fry the burgers for another 3 minutes.
5. Finally, if desired, top each burger with a slice of Swiss cheese. Lower the air fryer temperature to 330°F (165°C) and air-fry for another minute to melt the cheese. Serve the burgers on toasted brioche buns, dressed the way you like them.

Inside Out Cheeseburgers

Servings: 2
Cooking Time: 20 Minutes
Ingredients:
- ¾ pound lean ground beef
- 3 tablespoons minced onion
- 4 teaspoons ketchup
- 2 teaspoons yellow mustard
- salt and freshly ground black pepper
- 4 slices of Cheddar cheese, broken into smaller pieces
- 8 hamburger dill pickle chips

Directions:
1. Combine the ground beef, minced onion, ketchup, mustard, salt and pepper in a large bowl. Mix well to thoroughly combine the ingredients. Divide the meat into four equal portions.
2. To make the stuffed burgers, flatten each portion of meat into a thin patty. Place 4 pickle chips and half of the cheese onto the center of two of the patties, leaving a rim around the edge of the patty exposed. Place the remaining two patties on top of the first and press the meat together firmly, sealing the edges tightly. With the burgers on a flat surface, press the sides of the burger with the palm of your hand to create a straight edge. This will help keep the stuffing inside the burger while it cooks.
3. Preheat the air fryer to 370°F (185°C).
4. Place the burgers inside the air fryer basket and air-fry for 20 minutes, flipping the burgers over halfway through the cooking time.
5. Serve the cheeseburgers on buns with lettuce and tomato.

Chapter 10: Appetizers And Snacks Recipes

Chicken Shawarma Bites

Servings: 6
Cooking Time: 22 Minutes
Ingredients:
- 1½ pounds Boneless skinless chicken thighs, trimmed of any fat and cut into 1-inch pieces
- 1½ tablespoons Olive oil
- Up to 1½ tablespoons Minced garlic
- ½ teaspoon Table salt
- ¼ teaspoon Ground cardamom
- ¼ teaspoon Ground cinnamon
- ¼ teaspoon Ground cumin
- ¼ teaspoon Mild paprika
- Up to a ¼ teaspoon Grated nutmeg
- ¼ teaspoon Ground black pepper

Directions:
1. Preheat the air fryer to 400°F (205°C).
2. Mix all the ingredients in a large bowl until the chicken is thoroughly and evenly coated in the oil and spices.
3. When the machine is at temperature, scrape the coated chicken pieces into the basket and spread them out into one layer as much as you can. Air-fry for 22 minutes, shaking the basket at least three times during cooking to rearrange the pieces, until well browned and crisp.
4. Pour the chicken pieces onto a wire rack. Cool for 5 minutes before serving.

Beer Battered Onion Rings

Servings: 2
Cooking Time: 16 Minutes
Ingredients:
- ⅔ cup flour
- ½ teaspoon baking soda
- 1 teaspoon paprika
- 1 teaspoon salt
- ½ teaspoon freshly ground black pepper
- ¾ cup beer
- 1 egg, beaten
- 1½ cups fine breadcrumbs
- 1 large Vidalia onion, peeled and sliced into ½-inch rings
- vegetable oil

Directions:
1. Set up a dredging station. Mix the flour, baking soda, paprika, salt and pepper together in a bowl. Pour in the beer, add the egg and whisk until smooth. Place the breadcrumbs in a cake pan or shallow dish.
2. Separate the onion slices into individual rings. Dip each onion ring into the batter with a fork. Lift the onion ring out of the batter and let any excess batter drip off. Then place the onion ring in the breadcrumbs and shake the cake pan back and forth to coat the battered onion ring. Pat the ring gently with your hands to make sure the breadcrumbs stick and that both sides of the ring are covered. Place the coated onion ring on a sheet pan and repeat with the rest of the onion rings.
3. Preheat the air fryer to 360°F (180°C).
4. Lightly spray the onion rings with oil, coating both sides. Layer the onion rings in the air fryer basket, stacking them on top of each other in a haphazard manner.
5. Air-fry for 10 minutes at 360°F (180°C). Flip the onion rings over and rotate the onion rings from the bottom of the basket to the top. Air-fry for an additional 6 minutes.
6. Serve immediately with your favorite dipping sauce.

Avocado Fries

Servings: 8
Cooking Time: 8 Minutes
Ingredients:
- 2 medium avocados, firm but ripe
- 1 large egg
- ½ teaspoon garlic powder
- ¼ teaspoon cayenne pepper
- ¼ teaspoon salt
- ¾ cup almond flour
- ½ cup finely grated Parmesan cheese
- ½ cup gluten-free breadcrumbs

Directions:
1. Preheat the air fryer to 370°F (185°C).
2. Rinse the outside of the avocado with water. Slice the avocado in half, slice it in half again, and then slice it in half once more to get 8 slices. Remove the outer skin. Repeat for the other avocado. Set the avocado slices aside.
3. In a small bowl, whisk the egg, garlic powder, cayenne pepper, and salt in a small bowl. Set aside.
4. In a separate bowl, pour the almond flour.
5. In a third bowl, mix the Parmesan cheese and breadcrumbs.
6. Carefully roll the avocado slices in the almond flour, then dip them in the egg wash, and coat them in the cheese and breadcrumb topping. Repeat until all 16 fries are coated.
7. Liberally spray the air fryer basket with olive oil spray and place the avocado fries into the basket, leaving a little space around the sides between fries. Depending on the size of your air fryer, you may need to cook these in batches.
8. Cook fries for 8 minutes, or until the outer coating turns light brown.
9. Carefully remove, repeat with remaining slices, and then serve warm.

Cauliflower "tater" Tots

Servings: 6
Cooking Time: 10 Minutes
Ingredients:
- 1 head of cauliflower
- 2 eggs
- ¼ cup all-purpose flour*
- ½ cup grated Parmesan cheese
- 1 teaspoon salt
- freshly ground black pepper
- vegetable or olive oil, in a spray bottle

Directions:
1. Grate the head of cauliflower with a box grater or finely chop it in a food processor. You should have about 3½ cups. Place the chopped cauliflower in the center of a clean kitchen towel and twist the towel tightly to squeeze all the water out of the cauliflower. (This can be done in two batches to make it easier to drain all the water from the cauliflower.)
2. Place the squeezed cauliflower in a large bowl. Add the eggs, flour, Parmesan cheese, salt and freshly ground black pepper. Shape the cauliflower into small cylinders or "tater

Tower Air Fryer Cookbook

tot" shapes, rolling roughly one tablespoon of the mixture at a time. Place the tots on a cookie sheet lined with paper towel to absorb any residual moisture. Spray the cauliflower tots all over with oil.
3. Preheat the air fryer to 400°F (205°C).
4. Air-fry the tots at 400°F (205°C), one layer at a time for 10 minutes, turning them over for the last few minutes of the cooking process for even browning. Season with salt and black pepper. Serve hot with your favorite dipping sauce.

Carrot Chips

Servings: 4
Cooking Time: 10 Minutes
Ingredients:
- 1 pound carrots, thinly sliced
- 2 tablespoons extra-virgin olive oil
- ¼ teaspoon garlic powder
- ¼ teaspoon black pepper
- ½ teaspoon salt

Directions:
1. Preheat the air fryer to 390°F (200°C).
2. In a medium bowl, toss the carrot slices with the olive oil, garlic powder, pepper, and salt.
3. Liberally spray the air fryer basket with olive oil mist.
4. Place the carrot slices in the air fryer basket. To allow for even cooking, don't overlap the carrots; cook in batches if necessary.
5. Cook for 5 minutes, shake the basket, and cook another 5 minutes.
6. Remove from the basket and serve warm. Repeat with the remaining carrot slices until they're all cooked.

Crunchy Pickle Chips

Servings: 4
Cooking Time: 20 Minutes
Ingredients:
- 1 lb dill pickles, sliced
- 2 eggs
- 1/3 cup flour
- 1/3 cup bread crumbs
- 1 tsp Italian seasoning

Directions:
1. Preheat air fryer to 400°F (205°C). Set out three small bowls. In the first bowl, add flour. In the second bowl, beat eggs. In the third bowl, mix bread crumbs with Italian seasoning. Dip the pickle slices in the flour. Shake, then dredge in egg. Roll in bread crumbs and shake excess. Place the pickles in the greased frying basket and Air Fry for 6 minutes. Flip them halfway through cooking and fry for another 3 minutes until crispy. Serve warm.

Paprika Onion Blossom

Servings: 4
Cooking Time: 35 Minutes + Cooling Time
Ingredients:
- 1 large onion
- 1 ½ cups flour
- 1 tsp garlic powder
- 1 tsp paprika
- ½ tsp bell pepper powder
- Salt and pepper to taste
- 2 eggs
- 1 cup milk

Directions:
1. Remove the tip of the onion but leave the root base intact. Peel the onion to the root and remove skin. Place the onion cut-side down on a cutting board. Starting ½-inch down from the root, cut down to the bottom. Repeat until the onion is divided into quarters. Starting ½-inch down from the root, repeat the cuts in between the first cuts. Repeat this process in between the cuts until you have 16 cuts in the onion. Flip the onion onto the root and carefully spread the inner layers. Set aside.
2. In a bowl, add flour, garlic, paprika, bell pepper, salt, and pepper, then stir. In another large bowl, whisk eggs and milk. Place the onion in the flour bowl and cover with flour mixture. Transfer the onion into the egg mixture and coat completely with either a spoon or basting brush. Return the onion to the flour bowl and cover completely. Take a sheet of foil and wrap the onion with the foil. Freeze for 45 minutes.
3. Preheat air fryer to 400°F (205°C). Remove the onion from the foil and place in the greased frying basket. Air Fry for 10 minutes. Lightly spray the onion with cooking oil, then cook for another 10-15 minutes. Serve immediately.

Asian Five-spice Wings

Servings: 4
Cooking Time: 15 Minutes
Ingredients:
- 2 pounds chicken wings
- ½ cup Asian-style salad dressing
- 2 tablespoons Chinese five-spice powder

Directions:
1. Cut off wing tips and discard or freeze for stock. Cut remaining wing pieces in two at the joint.
2. Place wing pieces in a large sealable plastic bag. Pour in the Asian dressing, seal bag, and massage the marinade into the wings until well coated. Refrigerate for at least an hour.
3. Remove wings from bag, drain off excess marinade, and place wings in air fryer basket.
4. Cook at 360°F (180°C) for 15minutes or until juices run clear. About halfway through cooking time, shake the basket or stir wings for more even cooking.
5. Transfer cooked wings to plate in a single layer. Sprinkle half of the Chinese five-spice powder on the wings, turn, and sprinkle other side with remaining seasoning.

Seafood Egg Rolls

Servings: 6
Cooking Time: 35 Minutes
Ingredients:
- 2 tbsp olive oil
- 1 shallot, chopped
- 2 garlic cloves, minced
- ½ cup shredded carrots
- 1 lb cooked shrimp, chopped
- 1 cup corn kernels
- 1/3 cup chopped cashews
- 1 tbsp soy sauce
- 2 tsp fish sauce
- 12 egg roll wrappers

Directions:

1. Preheat the air fryer to 400°F (205°C). Combine the olive oil, shallot, garlic, and carrots in a 6-inch. Put the pan in the frying basket and Air Fry for 3-5 minutes, stirring once. Remove the pan and put the veggies in a bowl. Add shrimp, corn, cashews, soy sauce, and fish sauce to the veggies and combine. Lay the egg roll wrappers on the clean work surface and brush the edges with water. Divide the filling equally and fill them, then brush the edges with water again. Roll up, folding in the side, enclosing the filling inside. Place 4 egg rolls in the basket and spray with cooking oil. Air Fry for 10-12 minutes, rotating once halfway through cooking until golden and crispy. Repeat with remaining rolls. Serve hot.

Parmesan Pizza Nuggets

Servings: 8
Cooking Time: 6 Minutes
Ingredients:
- ¾ cup warm filtered water
- 1 package fast-rising yeast
- ½ teaspoon salt
- 2 cups all-purpose flour
- ¼ cup finely grated Parmesan cheese
- 1 teaspoon Italian seasoning
- 2 tablespoon extra-virgin olive oil
- 1 teaspoon kosher salt

Directions:
1. Preheat the air fryer to 370°F (185°C).
2. In a large microwave-safe bowl, add the water. Heat for 40 seconds in the microwave. Remove and mix in the yeast and salt. Let sit 5 minutes.
3. Meanwhile, in a medium bowl, mix the flour with the Parmesan cheese and Italian seasoning. Set aside.
4. Using a stand mixer with a dough hook attachment, add the yeast liquid and then mix in the flour mixture ⅓ cup at a time until all the flour mixture is added and a dough is formed.
5. Remove the bowl from the stand, and then let the dough rise for 1 hour in a warm space, covered with a kitchen towel.
6. After the dough has doubled in size, remove it from the bowl and punch it down a few times on a lightly floured flat surface.
7. Divide the dough into 4 balls, and then roll each ball out into a long, skinny, sticklike shape.
8. Using a sharp knife, cut each dough stick into 6 pieces. Repeat for the remaining dough balls until you have about 24 nuggets formed.
9. Lightly brush the top of each bite with the egg whites and cover with a pinch of sea salt.
10. Spray the air fryer basket with olive oil spray and place the pizza nuggets on top. Cook for 6 minutes, or until lightly browned. Remove and keep warm.
11. Repeat until all the nuggets are cooked.
12. Serve warm.

Greek Street Tacos

Servings: 8
Cooking Time: 3 Minutes
Ingredients:
- 8 small flour tortillas (4-inch diameter)
- 8 tablespoons hummus
- 4 tablespoons crumbled feta cheese
- 4 tablespoons chopped kalamata or other olives (optional)
- olive oil for misting

Directions:
1. Place 1 tablespoon of hummus or tapenade in the center of each tortilla. Top with 1 teaspoon of feta crumbles and 1 teaspoon of chopped olives, if using.
2. Using your finger or a small spoon, moisten the edges of the tortilla all around with water.
3. Fold tortilla over to make a half-moon shape. Press center gently. Then press the edges firmly to seal in the filling.
4. Mist both sides with olive oil.
5. Place in air fryer basket very close but try not to overlap.
6. Cook at 390°F (200°C) for 3minutes, just until lightly browned and crispy.

Garlic Wings

Servings: 4
Cooking Time: 15 Minutes
Ingredients:
- 2 pounds chicken wings
- oil for misting
- cooking spray
- Marinade
- 1 cup buttermilk
- 2 cloves garlic, mashed flat
- 1 teaspoon Worcestershire sauce
- 1 bay leaf
- Coating
- 1½ cups grated Parmesan cheese
- ¾ cup breadcrumbs
- 1½ tablespoons garlic powder
- ½ teaspoon salt

Directions:
1. Mix all marinade ingredients together.
2. Remove wing tips (the third joint) and discard or freeze for stock. Cut the remaining wings at the joint and toss them into the marinade, stirring to coat well. Refrigerate for at least an hour but no more than 8 hours.
3. When ready to cook, combine all coating ingredients in a shallow dish.
4. Remove wings from marinade, shaking off excess, and roll in coating mixture. Press coating into wings so that it sticks well. Spray wings with oil.
5. Spray air fryer basket with cooking spray. Place wings in basket in single layer, close but not touching.
6. Cook at 360°F (180°C) for 15minutes or until chicken is done and juices run clear.
7. Repeat previous step to cook remaining wings.

Zucchini Chips

Servings: 3
Cooking Time: 17 Minutes
Ingredients:
- 1½ small (about 1½ cups) Zucchini, washed but not peeled, and cut into ¼-inch-thick rounds
- Olive oil spray
- ¼ teaspoon Table salt

Directions:
1. Preheat the air fryer to 375°F (190°C).

2. Lay some paper towels on your work surface. Set the zucchini rounds on top, then set more paper towels over the rounds. Press gently to remove some of the moisture. Remove the top layer of paper towels and lightly coat the rounds with olive oil spray on both sides.
3. When the machine is at temperature, set the rounds in the basket, overlapping them a bit as needed. (They'll shrink as they cook.) Air-fry for 15 minutes, tossing and rearranging the rounds at the 5- and 10-minute marks, until browned, soft, yet crisp at the edges. (You'll need to air-fry the rounds 2 minutes more if the temperature is set at 360°F (180°C).)
4. Gently pour the contents of the basket onto a wire rack. Cool for at least 10 minutes or up to 2 hours before serving.

Wrapped Smokies In Bacon
Servings: 4
Cooking Time: 15 Minutes
Ingredients:
- 8 small smokies
- 8 bacon strips, sliced
- Salt and pepper to taste

Directions:
1. Preheat air fryer to 350°F (175°C). Wrap the bacon slices around smokies. Arrange the rolls, seam side down, on the greased frying basket. Sprinkle with salt and pepper and Air Fry for 5-8 minutes, turning once until the bacon is crisp and juicy around them. Serve and enjoy!

Oregano Cheese Rolls
Servings: 4
Cooking Time: 25 Minutes
Ingredients:
- ¼ cup grated cheddar cheese
- ¼ cup blue cheese, crumbled
- 8 flaky pastry dough sheets
- 1 tbsp vegetable oil
- 1 tsp dry oregano

Directions:
1. Preheat air fryer to 350°F (175°C). Mix the cheddar cheese, blue cheese, and oregano in a bowl. Divide the cheese mixture between pastry sheets and seal the seams with a touch of water. Brush the pastry rolls with vegetable oil. Arrange them on the greased frying basket and Bake for 15 minutes or until the pastry crust is golden brown and the cheese is melted. Serve hot.

Za'atar Garbanzo Beans
Servings: 6
Cooking Time: 12 Minutes
Ingredients:
- One 14.5-ounce can garbanzo beans, drained and rinsed
- 1 tablespoon extra-virgin olive oil
- 6 teaspoons za'atar seasoning mix
- 2 tablespoons chopped parsley
- Salt and pepper, to taste

Directions:
1. Preheat the air fryer to 390°F (200°C).
2. In a medium bowl, toss the garbanzo beans with olive oil and za'atar seasoning.
3. Pour the beans into the air fryer basket and cook for 12 minutes, or until toasted as you like. Stir every 3 minutes while roasting.
4. Remove the beans from the air fryer basket into a serving bowl, top with fresh chopped parsley, and season with salt and pepper.

Beet Chips
Servings: 4
Cooking Time: 20 Minutes
Ingredients:
- 2 large red beets, washed and skinned
- 1 tablespoon avocado oil
- ¼ teaspoon salt

Directions:
1. Preheat the air fryer to 330°F (165°C).
2. Using a mandolin or sharp knife, slice the beets in ⅛-inch slices. Place them in a bowl of water and let them soak for 30 minutes. Drain the water and pat the beets dry with a paper towel or kitchen cloth.
3. In a medium bowl, toss the beets with avocado oil and sprinkle them with salt.
4. Lightly spray the air fryer basket with olive oil mist and place the beet chips into the basket. To allow for even cooking, don't overlap the beets; cook in batches if necessary.
5. Cook the beet chips 15 to 20 minutes, shaking the basket every 5 minutes, until the outer edges of the beets begin to flip up like a chip. Remove from the basket and serve warm. Repeat with the remaining chips until they're all cooked.

Buffalo Chicken Wings
Servings: 6
Cooking Time: 60 Minutes
Ingredients:
- 2 lb chicken wings, split at the joint
- 1 tbsp butter, softened
- ½ cup buffalo wing sauce
- 1 tbs salt
- 1 tsp black pepper
- 1 tsp red chili powder
- 1 tsp garlic-ginger puree

Directions:
1. Preheat air fryer at 400ºF. Sprinkle the chicken wings with salt, pepper, red chili powder, grated garlic, and ginger. Place the chicken wings in the greased frying basket and Air Fry for 12 minutes, tossing once. Whisk butter and buffalo sauce in a large bowl. Air Fry for 10 more minutes, shaking once. Once done, transfer it into the bowl with the sauce. Serve immediately.

Crabby Fries
Servings: 2
Cooking Time: 30 Minutes
Ingredients:
- 2 to 3 large russet potatoes, peeled and cut into ½-inch sticks
- 2 tablespoons vegetable oil
- 2 tablespoons butter
- 2 tablespoons flour
- 1 to 1½ cups milk
- ½ cup grated white Cheddar cheese
- pinch of nutmeg
- ½ teaspoon salt

- freshly ground black pepper
- 1 tablespoon Old Bay® Seasoning

Directions:
1. Bring a large saucepan of salted water to a boil on the stovetop while you peel and cut the potatoes. Blanch the potatoes in the boiling salted water for 4 minutes while you Preheat the air fryer to 400°F (205°C). Strain the potatoes and rinse them with cold water. Dry them well with a clean kitchen towel.
2. Toss the dried potato sticks gently with the oil and place them in the air fryer basket. Air-fry for 25 minutes, shaking the basket a few times while the fries cook to help them brown evenly.
3. While the fries are cooking, melt the butter in a medium saucepan. Whisk in the flour and cook for one minute. Slowly add 1 cup of milk, whisking constantly. Bring the mixture to a simmer and continue to whisk until it thickens. Remove the pan from the heat and stir in the Cheddar cheese. Add a pinch of nutmeg and season with salt and freshly ground black pepper. Transfer the warm cheese sauce to a serving dish. Thin with more milk if you want the sauce a little thinner.
4. As soon as the French fries have finished air-frying transfer them to a large bowl and season them with the Old Bay® Seasoning. Return the fries to the air fryer basket and air-fry for an additional 3 to 5 minutes. Serve immediately with the warm white Cheddar cheese sauce.

Cheesy Green Wonton Triangles

Servings: 20 Wontons
Cooking Time: 55 Minutes
Ingredients:
- 6 oz marinated artichoke hearts
- 6 oz cream cheese
- ¼ cup sour cream
- ¼ cup grated Parmesan
- ¼ cup grated cheddar
- 5 oz chopped kale
- 2 garlic cloves, chopped
- Salt and pepper to taste
- 20 wonton wrappers

Directions:
1. Microwave cream cheese in a bowl for 20 seconds. Combine with sour cream, Parmesan, cheddar, kale, artichoke hearts, garlic, salt, and pepper. Lay out the wrappers on a cutting board. Scoop 1 ½ tsp of cream cheese mixture on top of the wrapper. Fold up diagonally to form a triangle. Bring together the two bottom corners. Squeeze out any air and press together to seal the edges.
2. Preheat air fryer to 375°F (190°C). Place a batch of wonton in the greased frying basket and Bake for 10 minutes. Flip them and cook for 5-8 minutes until crisp and golden. Serve.

Cheesy Zucchini Chips

Servings: 4
Cooking Time: 35 Minutes
Ingredients:
- 1 lb thin zucchini chips
- 2 eggs
- ½ cup bread crumbs
- ½ cup grated Pecorino cheese
- Salt and pepper to taste
- ½ cup mayonnaise
- ½ tbsp olive oil
- ½ lemon. juiced
- 1 tsp garlic powder
- Salt and pepper to taste

Directions:
1. Preheat air fryer to 350°F (175°C). Beat eggs in a small bowl, then set aside. In another small bowl, stir together bread crumbs, Pecorino, salt, and pepper. Dip zucchini slices into the egg mixture, then in the crumb mixture. Place them in the greased frying basket and Air Fry for 10 minutes. Remove and set aside to cool. Mix the mayonnaise, olive oil, lemon juice, garlic, salt, and pepper in a bowl to make aioli. Serve aioli with chips and enjoy.

Fried Apple Wedges

Servings: 4
Cooking Time: 9 Minutes
Ingredients:
- ¼ cup panko breadcrumbs
- ¼ cup pecans
- 1½ teaspoons cinnamon
- 1½ teaspoons brown sugar
- ¼ cup cornstarch
- 1 egg white
- 2 teaspoons water
- 1 medium apple
- oil for misting or cooking spray

Directions:
1. In a food processor, combine panko, pecans, cinnamon, and brown sugar. Process to make small crumbs.
2. Place cornstarch in a plastic bag or bowl with lid. In a shallow dish, beat together the egg white and water until slightly foamy.
3. Preheat air fryer to 390°F (200°C).
4. Cut apple into small wedges. The thickest edge should be no more than ⅜- to ½-inch thick. Cut away the core, but do not peel.
5. Place apple wedges in cornstarch, reseal bag or bowl, and shake to coat.
6. Dip wedges in egg wash, shake off excess, and roll in crumb mixture. Spray with oil.
7. Place apples in air fryer basket in single layer and cook for 5 minutes. Shake basket and break apart any apples that have stuck together. Mist lightly with oil and cook 4 minutes longer, until crispy.

Sweet Plantain Chips

Servings: 4
Cooking Time: 11 Minutes
Ingredients:
- 2 Very ripe plantain(s), peeled and sliced into 1-inch pieces
- Vegetable oil spray
- 3 tablespoons Maple syrup
- For garnishing Coarse sea salt or kosher salt

Directions:
1. Pour about ½ cup water into the bottom of your air fryer basket or into a metal tray on a lower rack in some models. Preheat the air fryer to 400°F (205°C).

Tower Air Fryer Cookbook

2. Put the plantain pieces in a bowl, coat them with vegetable oil spray, and toss gently, spraying at least one more time and tossing repeatedly, until the pieces are well coated.
3. When the machine is at temperature, arrange the plantain pieces in the basket in one layer. Air-fry undisturbed for 5 minutes.
4. Remove the basket from the machine and spray the back of a metal spatula with vegetable oil spray. Use the spatula to press down on the plantain pieces, spraying it again as needed, to flatten the pieces to about half their original height. Brush the plantain pieces with maple syrup, then return the basket to the machine and continue air-frying undisturbed for 6 minutes, or until the plantain pieces are soft and caramelized.
5. Use kitchen tongs to transfer the pieces to a serving platter. Sprinkle the pieces with salt and cool for a couple of minutes before serving. Or cool to room temperature before serving, about 1 hour.

Rich Clam Spread

Servings: 6
Cooking Time: 40 Minutes
Ingredients:
- 2 cans chopped clams in clam juice
- 1/3 cup panko bread crumbs
- 1 garlic clove, minced
- 1 tbsp olive oil
- 1 tbsp lemon juice
- ¼ tsp hot sauce
- 1 tsp Worcestershire sauce
- ½ tsp shallot powder
- ¼ tsp dried dill
- Salt and pepper to taste
- ½ tsp sweet paprika
- 4 tsp grated Parmesan cheese
- 2 celery stalks, chopped

Directions:
1. Completely drain one can of clams. Add them to a bowl along with the entire can of clams, breadcrumbs, garlic, olive oil, lemon juice, Worcestershire sauce, hot sauce, shallot powder, dill, pepper, salt, paprika, and 2 tbsp Parmesan. Combine well and set aside for 10 minutes. After that time, put the mixture in a greased baking dish.
2. Preheat air fryer to 325°F (160°C). Put the dish in the air fryer and Bake for 10 minutes. Sprinkle the remaining paprika and Parmesan, and continue to cook until golden brown on top, 8-10 minutes. Serve hot along with celery sticks.

Garam Masala Cauliflower Pakoras

Servings: 4
Cooking Time: 30 Minutes
Ingredients:
- ½ cup chickpea flour
- 1 tbsp cornstarch
- Salt to taste
- 2 tsp cumin powder
- ½ tsp coriander powder
- ½ tsp turmeric
- 1 tsp garam masala
- ⅛ tsp baking soda
- ⅛ tsp cayenne powder
- 1 ½ cups minced onion
- ½ cup chopped cilantro
- ½ cup chopped cauliflower
- ¼ cup lime juice

Directions:
1. Preheat air fryer to 350°F (175°C). Combine the flour, cornstarch, salt, cumin, coriander, turmeric, garam masala, baking soda, and cayenne in a bowl. Stir well. Mix in the onion, cilantro, cauliflower, and lime juice. Using your hands, stir the mix, massaging the flour and spices into the vegetables. Form the mixture into balls and place them in the greased frying basket. Spray the tops of the pakoras in the air fryer with oil and Air Fry for 15-18 minutes, turning once until browned and crispy. Serve hot.

Spicy Sweet Potato Tater-tots

Servings: 6
Cooking Time: 10 Minutes
Ingredients:
- 6 cups filtered water
- 2 medium sweet potatoes, peeled and cut in half
- 1 teaspoon garlic powder
- ½ teaspoon black pepper, divided
- ½ teaspoon salt, divided
- 1 cup panko breadcrumbs
- 1 teaspoon blackened seasoning

Directions:
1. In a large stovetop pot, bring the water to a boil. Add the sweet potatoes and let boil about 10 minutes, until a metal fork prong can be inserted but the potatoes still have a slight give (not completely mashed).
2. Carefully remove the potatoes from the pot and let cool.
3. When you're able to touch them, grate the potatoes into a large bowl. Mix the garlic powder, ¼ teaspoon of the black pepper, and ¼ teaspoon of the salt into the potatoes. Place the mixture in the refrigerator and let set at least 45 minutes (if you're leaving them longer than 45 minutes, cover the bowl).
4. Before assembling, mix the breadcrumbs and blackened seasoning in a small bowl.
5. Remove the sweet potatoes from the refrigerator and preheat the air fryer to 400°F (205°C).
6. Assemble the tater-tots by using a teaspoon to portion batter evenly and form into a tater-tot shape. Roll each tater-tot in the breadcrumb mixture. Then carefully place the tater-tots in the air fryer basket. Be sure that you've liberally sprayed the air fryer basket with an olive oil mist. Repeat until tater-tots fill the basket without touching one another. You'll need to do multiple batches, depending on the size of your air fryer.
7. Cook the tater-tots for 3 to 6 minutes, flip, and cook another 3 to 6 minutes.
8. Remove from the air fryer carefully and keep warm until ready to serve.

Parmesan Crackers

Servings: 6
Cooking Time: 6 Minutes
Ingredients:
- 2 cups finely grated Parmesan cheese
- ¼ teaspoon paprika

- ¼ teaspoon garlic powder
- ½ teaspoon dried thyme
- 1 tablespoon all-purpose flour

Directions:
1. Preheat the air fryer to 380°F (195°C).
2. In a medium bowl, stir together the Parmesan, paprika, garlic powder, thyme, and flour.
3. Line the air fryer basket with parchment paper.
4. Using a tablespoon measuring tool, create 1-tablespoon mounds of seasoned cheese on the parchment paper, leaving 2 inches between the mounds to allow for spreading.
5. Cook the crackers for 6 minutes. Allow the cheese to harden and cool before handling. Repeat in batches with the remaining cheese.

"fried" Pickles With Homemade Ranch

Servings: 8
Cooking Time: 8 Minutes
Ingredients:
- 1 cup all-purpose flour
- 2 teaspoons dried dill
- ½ teaspoon paprika
- ¾ cup buttermilk
- 1 egg
- 4 large kosher dill pickles, sliced ¼-inch thick
- 2 cups panko breadcrumbs

Directions:
1. Preheat the air fryer to 380°F (195°C).
2. In a medium bowl, whisk together the flour, dill, paprika, buttermilk, and egg.
3. Dip and coat thick slices of dill pickles into the batter. Next, dredge into the panko breadcrumbs.
4. Place a single layer of breaded pickles into the air fryer basket. Spray the pickles with cooking spray. Cook for 4 minutes, turn over, and cook another 4 minutes. Repeat until all the pickle chips have been cooked.

Crab Rangoon Dip With Wonton Chips

Servings: 6
Cooking Time: 18 Minutes
Ingredients:
- Wonton Chips:
- 1 (12-ounce) package wonton wrappers
- vegetable oil
- sea salt
- Crab Rangoon Dip:
- 8 ounces cream cheese, softened
- ¾ cup sour cream
- 1 teaspoon Worcestershire sauce
- 1½ teaspoons soy sauce
- 1 teaspoon sesame oil
- ⅛ teaspoon ground cayenne pepper
- ¼ teaspoon salt
- freshly ground black pepper
- 8 ounces cooked crabmeat
- 1 cup grated white Cheddar cheese
- ⅓ cup chopped scallions
- paprika (for garnish)

Directions:
1. Cut the wonton wrappers in half diagonally to form triangles. Working in batches, lay the wonton triangles on a flat surface and brush or spray both sides with vegetable oil.
2. Preheat the air fryer to 370°F (185°C).
3. Place about 10 to 12 wonton triangles in the air fryer basket, letting them overlap slightly. Air-fry for just 2 minutes, shaking the basket halfway through the cooking time. Transfer the wonton chips to a large bowl and season immediately with sea salt. (You'll hear the chips start to spin around in the air fryer when they are almost done.) Repeat with the rest of wontons (keeping those fishing hands at bay!).
4. To make the dip, combine the cream cheese, sour cream, Worcestershire sauce, soy sauce, sesame oil, cayenne pepper, salt, and freshly ground black pepper in a bowl. Mix well and then fold in the crabmeat, Cheddar cheese, and scallions.
5. Transfer the dip to a 7-inch ceramic baking pan or shallow casserole dish. Sprinkle paprika on top and cover the dish with aluminum foil. Lower the dish into the air fryer basket using a sling made of aluminum foil (fold a piece of aluminum foil into a strip about 2-inches wide by 24-inches long). Air-fry for 11 minutes. Remove the aluminum foil and air-fry for another 5 minutes to finish cooking and brown the top. Serve hot with the wonton chips.

Corn Dog Muffins

Servings: 8
Cooking Time: 10 Minutes
Ingredients:
- 1¼ cups sliced kosher hotdogs (3 or 4, depending on size)
- ½ cup flour
- ½ cup yellow cornmeal
- 2 teaspoons baking powder
- ½ cup skim milk
- 1 egg
- 2 tablespoons canola oil
- 8 foil muffin cups, paper liners removed
- cooking spray
- mustard or your favorite dipping sauce

Directions:
1. Slice each hot dog in half lengthwise, then cut in ¼-inch half-moon slices. Set aside.
2. Preheat air fryer to 390°F (200°C).
3. In a large bowl, stir together flour, cornmeal, and baking powder.
4. In a small bowl, beat together the milk, egg, and oil until just blended.
5. Pour egg mixture into dry ingredients and stir with a spoon to mix well.
6. Stir in sliced hot dogs.
7. Spray the foil cups lightly with cooking spray.
8. Divide mixture evenly into muffin cups.
9. Place 4 muffin cups in the air fryer basket and cook for 5 minutes.
10. Reduce temperature to 360°F (180°C) and cook 5 minutes or until toothpick inserted in center of muffin comes out clean.
11. Repeat steps 9 and 10 to bake remaining corn dog muffins.
12. Serve with mustard or other sauces for dipping.

Cinnamon Apple Crisps

Servings: 1
Cooking Time: 22 Minutes
Ingredients:
- 1 large apple
- ½ teaspoon ground cinnamon
- 2 teaspoons avocado oil or coconut oil

Directions:
1. Preheat the air fryer to 300°F (150°C).
2. Using a mandolin or knife, slice the apples to ¼-inch thickness. Pat the apples dry with a paper towel or kitchen cloth. Sprinkle the apple slices with ground cinnamon. Spray or drizzle the oil over the top of the apple slices and toss to coat.
3. Place the apple slices in the air fryer basket. To allow for even cooking, don't overlap the slices; cook in batches if necessary.
4. Cook for 20 minutes, shaking the basket every 5 minutes. After 20 minutes, increase the air fryer temperature to 330°F (165°C) and cook another 2 minutes, shaking the basket every 30 seconds. Remove the apples from the basket before they get too dark.
5. Spread the chips out onto paper towels to cool completely, at least 5 minutes. Repeat with the remaining apple slices until they're all cooked.

Grilled Cheese Sandwich Deluxe

Servings: 4
Cooking Time: 6 Minutes
Ingredients:
- 8 ounces Brie
- 8 slices oat nut bread
- 1 large ripe pear, cored and cut into ½-inch-thick slices
- 2 tablespoons butter, melted

Directions:
1. Spread a quarter of the Brie on each of four slices of bread.
2. Top Brie with thick slices of pear, then the remaining 4 slices of bread.
3. Lightly brush both sides of each sandwich with melted butter.
4. Cooking 2 at a time, place sandwiches in air fryer basket and cook at 360°F (180C) for 6minutes or until cheese melts and outside looks golden brown.

Warm Spinach Dip With Pita Chips

Servings: 6
Cooking Time: 40 Minutes
Ingredients:
- Pita Chips:
- 4 pita breads
- 1 tablespoon olive oil
- ½ teaspoon paprika
- salt and freshly ground black pepper
- Spinach Dip:
- 8 ounces cream cheese, softened at room, Temperature: 1 cup ricotta cheese
- 1 cup grated Fontina cheese
- ½ teaspoon Italian seasoning
- ½ teaspoon garlic powder
- ¾ teaspoon salt
- freshly ground black pepper
- 16 ounces frozen chopped spinach, thawed and squeezed dry
- ¼ cup grated Parmesan cheese
- ½ tomato, finely diced
- ¼ teaspoon dried oregano

Directions:
1. Preheat the air fryer to 390°F (200°C).
2. Split the pita breads open so you have 2 circles. Cut each circle into 8 wedges. Place all the wedges into a large bowl and toss with the olive oil. Season with the paprika, salt and pepper and toss to coat evenly. Air-fry the pita triangles in two batches for 5 minutes each, shaking the basket once or twice while they cook so they brown and crisp evenly.
3. Combine the cream cheese, ricotta cheese, Fontina cheese, Italian seasoning, garlic powder, salt and pepper in a large bowl. Fold in the spinach and mix well.
4. Transfer the spinach-cheese mixture to a 7-inch ceramic baking dish or cake pan. Sprinkle the Parmesan cheese on top and wrap the dish with aluminum foil. Transfer the dish to the basket of the air fryer, lowering the dish into the basket using a sling made of aluminum foil (fold a piece of aluminum foil into a strip about 2-inches wide by 24-inches long). Fold the ends of the aluminum foil over the top of the dish before returning the basket to the air fryer. Air-fry for 30 minutes at 390°F (200°C). With 4 minutes left on the air fryer timer, remove the foil and let the cheese brown on top.
5. Sprinkle the diced tomato and oregano on the warm dip and serve immediately with the pita chips.

Polenta Fries With Chili-lime Mayo

Servings: 4
Cooking Time: 28 Minutes
Ingredients:
- 2 teaspoons vegetable or olive oil
- ¼ teaspoon paprika
- 1 pound prepared polenta, cut into 3-inch x ½-inch sticks
- salt and freshly ground black pepper
- Chili-Lime Mayo
- ½ cup mayonnaise
- 1 teaspoon chili powder
- ¼ teaspoon ground cumin
- juice of half a lime
- 1 teaspoon chopped fresh cilantro
- salt and freshly ground black pepper

Directions:
1. Preheat the air fryer to 400°F (205°C).
2. Combine the oil and paprika and then carefully toss the polenta sticks in the mixture.
3. Air-fry the polenta fries at 400°F (205°C) for 15 minutes. Gently shake the basket to rotate the fries and continue to air-fry for another 13 minutes or until the fries have browned nicely. Season to taste with salt and freshly ground black pepper.
4. To make the chili-lime mayo, combine all the ingredients in a small bowl and stir well.
5. Serve the polenta fries warm with chili-lime mayo on the side for dipping.

Granola Three Ways

Servings: 4
Cooking Time: 10 Minutes
Ingredients:
- Nantucket Granola
- ¼ cup maple syrup
- ¼ cup dark brown sugar
- 1 tablespoon butter
- 1 teaspoon vanilla extract
- 1 cup rolled oats
- ½ cup dried cranberries
- ½ cup walnuts, chopped
- ¼ cup pumpkin seeds
- ¼ cup shredded coconut
- Blueberry Delight
- ¼ cup honey
- ¼ cup light brown sugar
- 1 tablespoon butter
- 1 teaspoon lemon extract
- 1 cup rolled oats
- ½ cup sliced almonds
- ½ cup dried blueberries
- ¼ cup pumpkin seeds
- ¼ cup sunflower seeds
- Cherry Black Forest Mix
- ¼ cup honey
- ¼ cup light brown sugar
- 1 tablespoon butter
- 1 teaspoon almond extract
- 1 cup rolled oats
- ½ cup sliced almonds
- ½ cup dried cherries
- ¼ cup shredded coconut
- ¼ cup dark chocolate chips
- oil for misting or cooking spray

Directions:
1. Combine the syrup or honey, brown sugar, and butter in a small saucepan or microwave-safe bowl. Heat and stir just until butter melts and sugar dissolves. Stir in the extract.
2. Place all other dry ingredients in a large bowl. (For the Cherry Black Forest Mix, don't add the chocolate chips yet.)
3. Pour melted butter mixture over dry ingredients and stir until oat mixture is well coated.
4. Lightly spray a baking pan with oil or cooking spray.
5. Pour granola into pan and cook at 390°F (200°C) for 5minutes. Stir. Continue cooking for 5minutes, stirring every minute or two, until golden brown. Watch closely. Once the mixture begins to brown, it will cook quickly.
6. Remove granola from pan and spread on wax paper. It will become crispier as it cools.
7. For the Cherry Black Forest Mix, stir in chocolate chips after granola has cooled completely.
8. Store in an airtight container.

Chapter 14: Desserts And Sweets Recipes

Spiced Fruit Skewers

Servings: 4
Cooking Time: 15 Minutes
Ingredients:
- 2 peeled peaches, thickly sliced
- 3 plums, halved and pitted
- 3 peeled kiwi, quartered
- 1 tbsp honey
- ½ tsp ground cinnamon
- ¼ tsp ground allspice
- ¼ tsp cayenne pepper

Directions:
1. Preheat air fryer to 400°F (205°C). Combine the honey, cinnamon, allspice, and cayenne and set aside. Alternate fruits on 8 bamboo skewers, then brush the fruit with the honey mix. Lay the skewers in the air fryer and Air Fry for 3-5 minutes. Allow to chill for 5 minutes before serving.

Home-style Pumpkin Pie Pudding

Servings: 4
Cooking Time: 30 Minutes
Ingredients:
- 1 cup canned pumpkin purée
- ¼ cup sugar
- 3 tbsp all-purpose flour
- 1 tbsp butter, melted
- 1 egg
- 1 orange, zested
- 2 tbsp milk
- 1 tsp vanilla extract
- 4 vanilla wafers, crumbled

Directions:
1. Preheat air fryer to 350°F (175°C). Beat the pumpkin puree, sugar, flour, butter, egg, orange zest, milk, and vanilla until well-mixed. Spritz a baking pan with the cooking spray, then pour the pumpkin mix in. Place it in the air fryer and Bake for 11-17 minutes or until golden brown. Take the pudding out of the fryer and let it chill. Serve with vanilla wager crumbs.

Nutty Banana Bread

Servings: 6
Cooking Time: 30 Minutes
Ingredients:
- 2 bananas
- 2 tbsp ground flaxseed
- ¼ cup milk
- 1 tbsp apple cider vinegar
- 1 tbsp vanilla extract
- ½ tsp ground cinnamon
- 2 tbsp honey
- ½ cup oat flour
- ½ tsp baking soda
- 3 tbsp butter

Directions:
1. Preheat air fryer to 320°F (160°C). Using a fork, mash the bananas until chunky. Mix in flaxseed, milk, apple vinegar, vanilla extract, cinnamon, and honey. Finally, toss in oat flour and baking soda until smooth but still chunky. Divide the batter between 6 cupcake molds. Top with one and a half teaspoons of butter each and swirl it a little. Bake for 18 minutes until golden brown and puffy. Let cool completely before serving.

Cinnamon Pear Cheesecake

Servings: 6
Cooking Time: 60 Minutes + Cooling Time
Ingredients:
- 16 oz cream cheese, softened
- 1 cup crumbled graham crackers
- 4 peeled pears, sliced
- 1 tsp vanilla extract
- 1 tbsp brown sugar
- 1 tsp ground cinnamon
- 1 egg
- 1 cup condensed milk
- 2 tbsp white sugar
- 1 ½ tsp butter, melted

Directions:
1. Preheat air fryer to 350°F (175°C). Place the crumbled graham cracker, white sugar, and butter in a large bowl and stir to combine. Spoon the mixture into a greased pan and press around the edges to flatten it against the dish. Place the pan into the frying basket and Bake for 5 minutes. Remove and let it cool for 30 minutes to harden.
2. Place the cream cheese, vanilla extract, brown sugar, cinnamon, condensed milk and egg in a large bowl and whip until the ingredients are thoroughly mixed. Arrange the pear slices on the cooled crust and spoon the wet mixture over. Level the top with a spatula. Place the pan in the frying basket. Bake for 40 minutes. Allow to cool completely. Serve and enjoy!

Almond-roasted Pears

Servings: 4
Cooking Time: 15 Minutes
Ingredients:
- Yogurt Topping
- 1 container vanilla Greek yogurt (5–6 ounces)
- ¼ teaspoon almond flavoring
- 2 whole pears
- ¼ cup crushed Biscoff cookies (approx. 4 cookies)
- 1 tablespoon sliced almonds
- 1 tablespoon butter

Directions:
1. Stir almond flavoring into yogurt and set aside while preparing pears.
2. Halve each pear and spoon out the core.
3. Place pear halves in air fryer basket.
4. Stir together the cookie crumbs and almonds. Place a quarter of this mixture into the hollow of each pear half.
5. Cut butter into 4 pieces and place one piece on top of crumb mixture in each pear.
6. Cook at 360°F (180°C) for 15 minutes or until pears have cooked through but are still slightly firm.
7. Serve pears warm with a dollop of yogurt topping.

Cheesecake Wontons

Servings: 16
Cooking Time: 6 Minutes
Ingredients:
- ¼ cup Regular or low-fat cream cheese (not fat-free)
- 2 tablespoons Granulated white sugar

Tower Air Fryer Cookbook

- 1½ tablespoons Egg yolk
- ¼ teaspoon Vanilla extract
- ⅛ teaspoon Table salt
- 1½ tablespoons All-purpose flour
- 16 Wonton wrappers (vegetarian, if a concern)
- Vegetable oil spray

Directions:
1. Preheat the air fryer to 400°F (205°C).
2. Using a flatware fork, mash the cream cheese, sugar, egg yolk, and vanilla in a small bowl until smooth. Add the salt and flour and continue mashing until evenly combined.
3. Set a wonton wrapper on a clean, dry work surface so that one corner faces you (so that it looks like a diamond on your work surface). Set 1 teaspoon of the cream cheese mixture in the middle of the wrapper but just above a horizontal line that would divide the wrapper in half. Dip your clean finger in water and run it along the edges of the wrapper. Fold the corner closest to you up and over the filling, lining it up with the corner farthest from you, thereby making a stuffed triangle. Press gently to seal. Wet the two triangle tips nearest you, then fold them up and together over the filling. Gently press together to seal and fuse. Set aside and continue making more stuffed wontons, 11 more for the small batch, 15 more for the medium batch, or 23 more for the large one.
4. Lightly coat the stuffed wrappers on all sides with vegetable oil spray. Set them with the fused corners up in the basket with as much air space between them as possible. Air-fry undisturbed for 6 minutes, or until golden brown and crisp.
5. Gently dump the contents of the basket onto a wire rack. Cool for at least 5 minutes before serving.

Healthy Berry Crumble

Servings: 4
Cooking Time: 30 Minutes
Ingredients:
- ½ cup fresh blackberries
- ½ cup chopped strawberries
- 1/3 cup frozen raspberries
- ½ lemon, juiced and zested
- 1 tbsp honey
- 2/3 cup flour
- 3 tbsp sugar
- 2 tbsp butter, melted

Directions:
1. Add the strawberries, blackberries, and raspberries to a baking pan, then sprinkle lemon juice and honey over the berries. Combine the flour, lemon zest, and sugar, then add the butter and mix; the mixture won't be smooth. Drizzle this all over the berries. Preheat air fryer to 370°F (185°C). Put the pan in the fryer and Bake for 12-17 minutes. The berries should be softened and the top golden. Serve hot.

Coconut Cream Roll-ups

Servings: 4
Cooking Time: 20 Minutes
Ingredients:
- ½ cup cream cheese, softened
- 1 cup fresh raspberries
- ¼ cup brown sugar
- ¼ cup coconut cream
- 1 egg
- 1 tsp corn starch
- 6 spring roll wrappers

Directions:
1. Preheat air fryer to 350°F (175°C). Add the cream cheese, brown sugar, coconut cream, cornstarch, and egg to a bowl and whisk until all ingredients are completely mixed and fluffy, thick and stiff. Spoon even amounts of the creamy filling into each spring roll wrapper, then top each dollop of filling with several raspberries. Roll up the wraps around the creamy raspberry filling, and seal the seams with a few dabs of water.
2. Place each roll on the foil-lined frying basket, seams facing down. Bake for 10 minutes, flipping them once until golden brown and perfect on the outside, while the raspberries and cream filling will have cooked together in a glorious fusion. Remove with tongs and serve hot or cold. Serve and enjoy!

Cinnamon Sugar Banana Rolls

Servings: 6
Cooking Time: 8 Minutes
Ingredients:
- ¼ cup Granulated white sugar
- 2 teaspoons Ground cinnamon
- 2 tablespoons Peach or apricot jam or orange marmalade
- 6 Spring roll wrappers, thawed if necessary
- 2 Ripe banana(s), peeled and cut into 3-inch-long sections
- 1 Large egg, well beaten
- Vegetable oil spray

Directions:
1. Preheat the air fryer to 400°F (205°C).
2. Stir the sugar and cinnamon in a small bowl until well combined. Stir the jam or marmalade with a fork to loosen it up.
3. Set a spring roll wrapper on a clean, dry work surface. Roll a banana section in the sugar mixture until evenly and well coated. Set the coated banana along one edge of the wrapper. Top it with about 1 teaspoon of the jam or marmalade. Fold the sides of the wrapper perpendicular to the banana up and over the banana, partially covering it. Brush beaten egg over the side of the wrapper farthest from the banana. Starting with the banana, roll the wrapper closed, ending at the part with the beaten egg. Press gently to seal. Set the roll aside seam side down and continue filling and rolling the remaining wrappers in the same way.
4. Lightly coat the wrappers with vegetable oil spray. Set them seam side down in the basket with as much air space between them as possible. Air-fry undisturbed for 8 minutes, or until crisp and golden brown.
5. Use kitchen tongs to gently transfer the rolls to a wire rack. Cool for at least 5 minutes or up to 30 minutes before serving.

Dark Chokolate Cookies

Servings: 4
Cooking Time: 50 Minutes
Ingredients:
- 1/3 cup brown sugar
- 2 tbsp butter, softened

- 1 egg yolk
- 2/3 cup flour
- 5 tbsp peanut butter
- ¼ tsp baking soda
- 1 tsp dark rum
- ½ cup dark chocolate chips

Directions:
1. Preheat air fryer to 310°F (155°C). Beat butter and brown sugar in a bowl until fluffy. Stir in the egg yolk. Add flour, 3 tbsp of peanut butter, baking soda, and rum until well mixed. Spread the batter into a parchment-lined baking pan. Bake in the air fryer until the cooking is lightly brown and just set, 7-10 minutes. Remove from the fryer and let cool for 10 minutes.
2. After, remove the cookie from the pan and the parchment paper and cool on the wire rack. When cooled, combine the chips with the remaining peanut butter in a heatproof cup. Place in the air fryer and Bake until melted, 2 minutes. Remove and stir. Spread on the cooled cookies and serve.

Mango-chocolate Custard

Servings: 4
Cooking Time: 40 Minutes
Ingredients:
- 4 egg yolks
- 2 tbsp granulated sugar
- 1/8 tsp almond extract
- 1 ½ cups half-and-half
- 3/4 cup chocolate chips
- 1 mango, pureed
- 1 mango, chopped
- 1 tsp fresh mint, chopped

Directions:
1. Beat the egg yolks, sugar, and almond extract in a bowl. Set aside. Place half-and-half in a saucepan over low heat and bring it to a low simmer. Whisk a spoonful of heated half-and-half into egg mixture, then slowly whisk egg mixture into saucepan. Stir in chocolate chips and mango purée for 10 minutes until chocolate melts. Divide between 4 ramekins.
2. Preheat air fryer at 350ºF. Place ramekins in the frying basket and Bake for 6-8 minutes. Let cool onto a cooling rack for 15 minutes, then let chill covered in the fridge for at least 2 hours or up to 2 days. Serve with chopped mangoes and mint on top.

Vanilla Butter Cake

Servings: 6
Cooking Time: 20-24 Minutes
Ingredients:
- ¾ cup plus 1 tablespoon All-purpose flour
- 1 teaspoon Baking powder
- ¼ teaspoon Table salt
- 8 tablespoons (½ cup/1 stick) Butter, at room temperature
- ½ cup Granulated white sugar
- 2 Large egg(s)
- 2 tablespoons Whole or low-fat milk (not fat-free)
- ¾ teaspoon Vanilla extract
- Baking spray (see here)

Directions:
1. Preheat the air fryer to 325°F (160°C) (or 330°F (165°C), if that's the closest setting).
2. Mix the flour, baking powder, and salt in a small bowl until well combined.
3. Using an electric hand mixer at medium speed, beat the butter and sugar in a medium bowl until creamy and smooth, about 3 minutes, occasionally scraping down the inside of the bowl.
4. Beat in the egg or eggs, as well as the white or a yolk as necessary. Beat in the milk and vanilla until smooth. Turn off the beaters and add the flour mixture. Beat at low speed until thick and smooth.
5. Use the baking spray to generously coat the inside of a 6-inch round cake pan for a small batch, a 7-inch round cake pan for a medium batch, or an 8-inch round cake pan for a large batch. Scrape and spread the batter into the pan, smoothing the batter out to an even layer.
6. Set the pan in the basket and air-fry undisturbed for 20 minutes for a 6-inch layer, 22 minutes for a 7-inch layer, or 24 minutes for an 8-inch layer, or until a toothpick or cake tester inserted into the center of the cake comes out clean. Start checking it at the 15-minute mark to know where you are.
7. Use hot pads or silicone baking mitts to transfer the cake pan to a wire rack. Cool for 5 minutes. To unmold, set a cutting board over the baking pan and invert both the board and the pan. Lift the still-warm pan off the cake layer. Set the wire rack on top of the cake layer and invert all of it with the cutting board so that the cake layer is now right side up on the wire rack. Remove the cutting board and continue cooling the cake for at least 10 minutes or to room temperature, about 30 minutes, before slicing into wedges.

Choco-granola Bars With Cranberries

Servings: 6
Cooking Time: 20 Minutes
Ingredients:
- 2 tbsp dark chocolate chunks
- 2 cups quick oats
- 2 tbsp dried cranberries
- 3 tbsp shredded coconut
- ½ cup maple syrup
- 1 tsp ground cinnamon
- ⅛ tsp salt
- 2 tbsp smooth peanut butter

Directions:
1. Preheat air fryer to 360°F (180°C). Stir together all the ingredients in a bowl until well combined. Press the oat mixture into a parchment-lined baking pan in a single layer. Put the pan into the frying basket and Bake for 15 minutes. Remove the pan from the fryer, and lift the granola cake out of the pan using the edges of the parchment paper. Leave to cool for 5 minutes. Serve sliced and enjoy!.

Peanut Butter Cup Doughnut Holes

Servings: 24
Cooking Time: 4 Minutes
Ingredients:
- 1½ cups bread flour
- 1 teaspoon active dry yeast
- 1 tablespoon sugar
- ¼ teaspoon salt

- ½ cup warm milk
- ½ teaspoon vanilla extract
- 2 egg yolks
- 2 tablespoons melted butter
- 24 miniature peanut butter cups, plus a few more for garnish
- vegetable oil, in a spray bottle
- Doughnut Topping
- 1 cup chocolate chips
- 2 tablespoons milk

Directions:
1. Combine the flour, yeast, sugar and salt in a bowl. Add the milk, vanilla, egg yolks and butter. Mix well until the dough starts to come together. Transfer the dough to a floured surface and knead by hand for 2 minutes. Shape the dough into a ball and transfer it to a large oiled bowl. Cover the bowl with a towel and let the dough rise in a warm place for 1 to 1½ hours, until the dough has doubled in size.
2. When the dough has risen, punch it down and roll it into a 24-inch long log. Cut the dough into 24 pieces. Push a peanut butter cup into the center of each piece of dough, pinch the dough shut and roll it into a ball. Place the dough balls on a cookie sheet and let them rise in a warm place for 30 minutes.
3. Preheat the air fryer to 400°F (205°C).
4. Spray or brush the dough balls lightly with vegetable oil. Air-fry eight at a time, at 400°F (205°C) for 4 minutes, turning them over halfway through the cooking process.
5. While the doughnuts are air frying, prepare the topping. Place the chocolate chips and milk in a microwave safe bowl. Microwave on high for 1 minute. Stir and microwave for an additional 30 seconds if necessary to get all the chips to melt. Stir until the chips are melted and smooth.
6. Dip the top half of the doughnut holes into the melted chocolate. Place them on a rack to set up for just a few minutes and watch them disappear.

Blueberry Cheesecake Tartlets
Servings: 9
Cooking Time: 6 Minutes
Ingredients:
- 8 ounces cream cheese, softened
- ¼ cup sugar
- 1 egg
- ½ teaspoon vanilla extract
- zest of 2 lemons, divided
- 9 mini graham cracker tartlet shells*
- 2 cups blueberries
- ½ teaspoon ground cinnamon
- juice of ½ lemon
- ¼ cup apricot preserves

Directions:
1. Preheat the air fryer to 330°F (165°C).
2. Combine the cream cheese, sugar, egg, vanilla and the zest of one lemon in a medium bowl and blend until smooth by hand or with an electric hand mixer. Pour the cream cheese mixture into the tartlet shells.
3. Air-fry 3 tartlets at a time at 330°F (165°C) for 6 minutes, rotating them in the air fryer basket halfway through the cooking time.
4. Combine the blueberries, cinnamon, zest of one lemon and juice of half a lemon in a bowl. Melt the apricot preserves in the microwave or over low heat in a saucepan. Pour the apricot preserves over the blueberries and gently toss to coat.
5. Allow the cheesecakes to cool completely and then top each one with some of the blueberry mixture. Garnish the tartlets with a little sugared lemon peel and refrigerate until you are ready to serve.

Mixed Berry Hand Pies
Servings: 4
Cooking Time: 15 Minutes
Ingredients:
- ¾ cup sugar
- ½ teaspoon ground cinnamon
- 1 tablespoon cornstarch
- 1 cup blueberries
- 1 cup blackberries
- 1 cup raspberries, divided
- 1 teaspoon water
- 1 package refrigerated pie dough (or your own homemade pie dough)
- 1 egg, beaten

Directions:
1. Combine the sugar, cinnamon, and cornstarch in a small saucepan. Add the blueberries, blackberries, and ½ cup of the raspberries. Toss the berries gently to coat them evenly. Add the teaspoon of water to the saucepan and turn the stovetop on to medium-high heat, stirring occasionally. Once the berries break down, release their juice and start to simmer (about 5 minutes), simmer for another couple of minutes and then transfer the mixture to a bowl, stir in the remaining ½ cup of raspberries and let it cool.
2. Preheat the air fryer to 370°F (185°C).
3. Cut the pie dough into four 5-inch circles and four 6-inch circles. Spread the 6-inch circles on a flat surface. Divide the berry filling between all four circles. Brush the perimeter of the dough circles with a little water. Place the 5-inch circles on top of the filling and press the perimeter of the dough circles together to seal. Roll the edges of the bottom circle up over the top circle to make a crust around the filling. Press a fork around the crust to make decorative indentations and to seal the crust shut. Brush the pies with egg wash and sprinkle a little sugar on top. Poke a small hole in the center of each pie with a paring knife to vent the dough.
5. Air-fry two pies at a time. Brush or spray the air fryer basket with oil and place the pies into the basket. Air-fry for 9 minutes. Turn the pies over and air-fry for another 6 minutes. Serve warm or at room temperature.

Vegan Brownie Bites
Servings: 10
Cooking Time: 8 Minutes
Ingredients:
- ⅔ cup walnuts
- ⅓ cup all-purpose flour
- ¼ cup dark cocoa powder
- ⅓ cup cane sugar
- ¼ teaspoon salt
- 2 tablespoons vegetable oil
- 1 teaspoon pure vanilla extract
- 1 tablespoon almond milk

- 1 tablespoon powdered sugar

Directions:
1. Preheat the air fryer to 350°F (175°C).
2. To a blender or food processor fitted with a metal blade, add the walnuts, flour, cocoa powder, sugar, and salt. Pulse until smooth, about 30 seconds. Add in the oil, vanilla, and milk and pulse until a dough is formed.
3. Remove the dough and place in a bowl. Form into 10 equal-size bites.
4. Liberally spray the metal trivet in the air fryer basket with olive oil mist. Place the brownie bites into the basket and cook for 8 minutes, or until the outer edges begin to slightly crack.
5. Remove the basket from the air fryer and let cool. Sprinkle the brownie bites with powdered sugar and serve.

Coconut Crusted Bananas With Pineapple Sauce

Servings: 4
Cooking Time: 5 Minutes
Ingredients:
- Pineapple Sauce
- 1½ cups puréed fresh pineapple
- 2 tablespoons sugar
- juice of 1 lemon
- ¼ teaspoon ground cinnamon
- 3 firm bananas
- ¼ cup sweetened condensed milk
- 1¼ cups shredded coconut
- ⅓ cup crushed graham crackers (crumbs)*
- vegetable or canola oil, in a spray bottle
- vanilla frozen yogurt or ice cream

Directions:
1. Make the pineapple sauce by combining the pineapple, sugar, lemon juice and cinnamon in a saucepan. Simmer the mixture on the stovetop for 20 minutes, and then set it aside.
2. Slice the bananas diagonally into ½-inch thick slices and place them in a bowl. Pour the sweetened condensed milk into the bowl and toss the bananas gently to coat. Combine the coconut and graham cracker crumbs together in a shallow dish. Remove the banana slices from the condensed milk and let any excess milk drip off. Dip the banana slices in the coconut and crumb mixture to coat both sides. Spray the coated slices with oil.
3. Preheat the air fryer to 400°F (205°C).
4. Grease the bottom of the air fryer basket with a little oil. Air-fry the bananas in batches at 400°F (205°C) for 5 minutes, turning them over halfway through the cooking time. Air-fry until the bananas are golden brown on both sides.
5. Serve warm over vanilla frozen yogurt with some of the pineapple sauce spooned over top.

Fried Banana S'mores

Servings: 4
Cooking Time: 6 Minutes
Ingredients:
- 4 bananas
- 3 tablespoons mini semi-sweet chocolate chips
- 3 tablespoons mini peanut butter chips
- 3 tablespoons mini marshmallows
- 3 tablespoons graham cracker cereal

Directions:
1. Preheat the air fryer to 400°F (205°C).
2. Slice into the un-peeled bananas lengthwise along the inside of the curve, but do not slice through the bottom of the peel. Open the banana slightly to form a pocket.
3. Fill each pocket with chocolate chips, peanut butter chips and marshmallows. Poke the graham cracker cereal into the filling.
4. Place the bananas in the air fryer basket, resting them on the side of the basket and each other to keep them upright with the filling facing up. Air-fry for 6 minutes, or until the bananas are soft to the touch, the peels have blackened and the chocolate and marshmallows have melted and toasted.
5. Let them cool for a couple of minutes and then simply serve with a spoon to scoop out the filling.

Strawberry Donuts

Servings: 4
Cooking Time: 55 Minutes
Ingredients:
- ¾ cup Greek yogurt
- 2 tbsp maple syrup
- 1 tbsp vanilla extract
- 2 tsp active dry yeast
- 1½ cups all-purpose flour
- 3 tbsp milk
- ½ cup strawberry jam

Directions:
1. Preheat air fryer to 350°F (175°C). Whisk the Greek yogurt, maple syrup, vanilla extract, and yeast until well combined. Then toss in flour until you get a sticky dough. Let rest covered for 10 minutes. Flour a parchment paper on a flat surface, lay the dough, sprinkle with some flour, and flatten to ½-inch thick with a rolling pin.
2. Using a 3-inch cookie cutter, cut the donuts. Repeat the process until no dough is left. Place the donuts in the basket and let rise for 15-20 minutes. Spread some milk on top of each donut and Air Fry for 4 minutes. Turn the donuts, spread more milk, and Air Fry for 4 more minutes until golden brown. Let cool for 15 minutes. Using a knife, cut the donuts 3/4 lengthwise, brush 1 tbsp of strawberry jam on each and close them. Serve.

Fudgy Brownie Cake

Servings: 6
Cooking Time: 25-35 Minutes
Ingredients:
- 6½ tablespoons All-purpose flour
- ¼ cup plus 1 teaspoon Unsweetened cocoa powder
- ½ teaspoon Baking powder
- ¼ teaspoon Table salt
- 6½ tablespoons Butter, at room temperature
- 9½ tablespoons Granulated white sugar
- 1 egg plus 1 large egg white Large egg(s)
- ¾ teaspoon Vanilla extract
- Baking spray (see here)

Directions:
1. Preheat the air fryer to 325°F (160°C) (or 330°F (165°C), if that's the closest setting).
2. Mix the flour, cocoa powder, baking powder, and salt in a small bowl until well combined.

Tower Air Fryer Cookbook

3. Using an electric hand mixer at medium speed, beat the butter and sugar in a medium bowl until creamy and smooth, about 3 minutes, occasionally scraping down the inside of the bowl.
4. Beat in the egg(s) and the white or yolk (as necessary), as well as the vanilla, until smooth. Turn off the beaters and add the flour mixture. Beat at low speed until thick and smooth.
5. Use the baking spray to generously coat the inside of a 6-inch round cake pan for a small batch, a 7-inch round cake pan for a medium batch, or an 8-inch round cake pan for a large batch. Scrape and spread the batter into the pan, smoothing the batter out to an even layer.
6. Set the pan in the basket and air-fry for 25 minutes for a 6-inch layer, 30 minutes for a 7-inch layer, or 35 minutes for an 8-inch layer, or until the cake is set but soft to the touch. Start checking it at the 20-minute mark to know where you are.
7. Use hot pads or silicone baking mitts to transfer the cake pan to a wire rack. Cool for at least 1 hour or up to 4 hours. Using a nonstick-safe knife, slice the cake into wedges right in the pan and lift them out one by one.

Dark Chocolate Peanut Butter S'mores

Servings: 4
Cooking Time: 6 Minutes
Ingredients:
- 4 graham cracker sheets
- 4 marshmallows
- 4 teaspoons chunky peanut butter
- 4 ounces dark chocolate
- ½ teaspoon ground cinnamon

Directions:
1. Preheat the air fryer to 390°F (200°C). Break the graham crackers in half so you have 8 pieces.
2. Place 4 pieces of graham cracker on the bottom of the air fryer. Top each with one of the marshmallows and bake for 6 or 7 minutes, or until the marshmallows have a golden brown center.
3. While cooking, slather each of the remaining graham crackers with 1 teaspoon peanut butter.
4. When baking completes, carefully remove each of the graham crackers, add 1 ounce of dark chocolate on top of the marshmallow, and lightly sprinkle with cinnamon. Top with the remaining peanut butter graham cracker to make the sandwich. Serve immediately.

German Streusel-stuffed Baked Apples

Servings: 4
Cooking Time: 40 Minutes
Ingredients:
- 2 large apples
- 3 tbsp flour
- 3 tbsp light brown sugar
- ⅛ tsp ground cinnamon
- 1 tsp vanilla extract
- 1 tsp chopped pecans
- 2 tbsp cold butter
- 2 tbsp salted caramel sauce

Directions:
1. Cut the apples in half through the stem and scoop out the core and seeds. Mix flour, brown sugar, vanilla, pecans and cinnamon in a bowl. Cut in the butter with a fork until it turns into crumbs. Top each apple half with 2 ½ tbsp of the crumble mixture.
2. Preheat air fryer to 325°F (160°C). Put the apple halves in the greased frying basket. Cook until soft in the center and the crumble is golden, about 25-30 minutes. Serve warm topped with caramel sauce.

Fried Oreos

Servings: 12
Cooking Time: 6 Minutes Per Batch
Ingredients:
- oil for misting or nonstick spray
- 1 cup complete pancake and waffle mix
- 1 teaspoon vanilla extract
- ½ cup water, plus 2 tablespoons
- 12 Oreos or other chocolate sandwich cookies
- 1 tablespoon confectioners' sugar

Directions:
1. Spray baking pan with oil or nonstick spray and place in basket.
2. Preheat air fryer to 390°F (200°C).
3. In a medium bowl, mix together the pancake mix, vanilla, and water.
4. Dip 4 cookies in batter and place in baking pan.
5. Cook for 6 minutes, until browned.
6. Repeat steps 4 and 5 for the remaining cookies.
7. Sift sugar over warm cookies.

Fast Brownies

Servings: 4
Cooking Time: 25 Minutes
Ingredients:
- ½ cup flour
- 2 tbsp cocoa
- 1/3 cup granulated sugar
- ¼ tsp baking soda
- 3 tbsp butter, melted
- 1 egg
- ¼ tsp salt
- ½ cup chocolate chips
- ¼ cup chopped hazelnuts
- 1 tbsp powdered sugar
- 1 tsp vanilla extract

Directions:
1. Preheat air fryer at 350ºF. Combine all ingredients, except chocolate chips, hazelnuts, and powdered sugar, in a bowl. Fold in chocolate chips and pecans. Press mixture into a greased cake pan. Place cake pan in the frying basket and Bake for 12 minutes. Let cool for 10 minutes before slicing into 9 brownies. Scatter with powdered sugar and serve.

Wild Blueberry Sweet Empanadas

Servings: 12
Cooking Time: 8 Minutes
Ingredients:
- 2 cups frozen wild blueberries
- 5 tablespoons chia seeds
- ¼ cup honey
- 1 tablespoon lemon or lime juice
- ¼ cup water

- 1½ cups all-purpose flour
- 1 cup whole-wheat flour
- ½ teaspoon salt
- 1 tablespoon sugar
- ½ cup cold unsalted butter
- 1 egg
- ½ cup plus 2 tablespoons milk, divided
- 1 cup powdered sugar
- 1 teaspoon vanilla extract

Directions:
1. To make the wild blueberry chia jam, place the blueberries, chia seeds, honey, lemon or lime juice, and water into a blender and pulse for 2 minutes. Pour the chia jam into a glass jar or bowl and cover. Store in the refrigerator at least 4 to 8 hours or until the jam is thickened.
2. In a food processor, place the all-purpose flour, whole-wheat flour, salt, sugar, and butter and process for 2 minutes, scraping down the sides of the food processor every 30 seconds. Add in the egg and blend for 30 seconds. Using the pulse button, add in ½ cup of the milk 1 tablespoon at a time or until the dough is moist enough to handle and be rolled into a ball. Let the dough rest at room temperature for 30 minutes.
3. On a floured surface, cut the dough in half; then form a ball and cut each ball into 6 equal pieces, totaling 12 equal pieces. Work with one piece at a time, and cover the remaining dough with a towel. Roll out the dough into a 6-inch round, much like a tortilla, with ¼ inch thickness. Place 4 tablespoons of filling in the center of round, fold over to form a half-circle. Using a fork, crimp the edges together and pierce the top with a fork for air holes. Repeat with the remaining dough and filling.
4. Preheat the air fryer to 350°F (175°C).
5. Working in batches, place 3 to 4 empanadas in the air fryer basket and spray with cooking spray. Cook for 8 minutes. Repeat in batches, as needed. Allow the sweet empanadas to cool for 15 minutes. Meanwhile, in a small bowl, whisk together the powdered sugar, the remaining 2 tablespoons of milk, and the vanilla extract. Then drizzle the glaze over the surface and serve.

Pecan-oat Filled Apples
Servings: 4
Cooking Time: 20 Minutes
Ingredients:
- 2 cored Granny Smith apples, halved
- ¼ cup rolled oats
- 2 tbsp honey
- ½ tsp ground cinnamon
- ½ tsp ground ginger
- 2 tbsp chopped pecans
- A pinch of salt
- 1 tbsp olive oil

Directions:
1. Preheat air fryer to 380°F (195°C). Combine together the oats, honey, cinnamon, ginger, pecans, salt, and olive oil in a bowl. Scoop a quarter of the oat mixture onto the top of each half apple. Put the apples in the frying basket and Roast for 12-15 minutes until the apples are fork-tender.

Healthy Chickpea Cookies
Servings: 6
Cooking Time: 25 Minutes
Ingredients:
- 1 cup canned chickpeas
- 2 tsp vanilla extract
- 1 tsp lemon juice
- 1/3 cup date paste
- 2 tbsp butter, melted
- 1/3 cup flour
- ½ tsp baking powder
- ¼ cup dark chocolate chips

Directions:
1. Preheat air fryer to 320°F (160°C). Line the basket with parchment paper. In a blender, blitz chickpeas, vanilla extract, and lemon juice until smooth. Remove it to a bowl. Stir in date paste and butter until well combined. Then mix in flour, baking powder, chocolate chips. Make 2-tablespoon balls out of the mixture. Place the balls onto the paper, flatten them into a cookie shape. Bake for 13 minutes until golden brown. Let cool slightly. Serve.

Sultana & Walnut Stuffed Apples
Servings: 4
Cooking Time: 30 Minutes
Ingredients:
- 4 apples, cored and halved
- 2 tbsp lemon juice
- ¼ cup sultana raisins
- 3 tbsp chopped walnuts
- 3 tbsp dried cranberries
- 2 tbsp packed brown sugar
- 1/3 cup apple cider
- 1 tbsp cinnamon

Directions:
1. Preheat air fryer to 350°F (175°C). Spritz the apples with lemon juice and put them in a baking pan. Combine the raisins, cinnamon, walnuts, cranberries, and brown sugar, then spoon ¼ of the mix into the apples. Drizzle the apple cider around the apples, Bake for 13-18 minutes until softened. Serve warm.

Coconut-custard Pie
Servings: 4
Cooking Time: 20 Minutes
Ingredients:
- 1 cup milk
- ¼ cup plus 2 tablespoons sugar
- ¼ cup biscuit baking mix
- 1 teaspoon vanilla
- 2 eggs
- 2 tablespoons melted butter
- cooking spray
- ½ cup shredded, sweetened coconut

Directions:
1. Place all ingredients except coconut in a medium bowl.
2. Using a hand mixer, beat on high speed for 3 minutes.
3. Let sit for 5 minutes.
4. Preheat air fryer to 330°F (165°C).
5. Spray a 6-inch round or 6 x 6-inch square baking pan with cooking spray and place pan in air fryer basket.
6. Pour filling into pan and sprinkle coconut over top.
7. Cook pie at 330°F (165°C) for 20 minutes or until center sets.

Recipes Index

"fried" Pickles With Homemade Ranch 95

A

Almond-crusted Fish 61
Almond-roasted Pears 99
American Biscuits 12
Apple Cornbread Stuffed Pork Loin With Apple Gravy 73
Apple French Toast Sandwich 12
Apple Fritters 12
Aromatic Ahi Tuna Steaks 61
Asian Five-spice Wings 90
Asian Sweet Chili Chicken 48
Asparagus & Cherry Tomato Roast 20
Avocado Fries 89
Avocado Toasts With Poached Eggs 11

B

Bacon & Chicken Flatbread 47
Bacon Wrapped Filets Mignons 70
Bacon, Broccoli And Swiss Cheese Bread Pudding 16
Bacon-wrapped Asparagus 24
Bagels With Avocado & Tomatoes 16
Baharat Lamb Kebab With Mint Sauce 74
Balsamic Beet Chips 25
Balsamic Caprese Hasselback 32
Baltimore Crab Cakes 61
Barbecue-style Beef Cube Steak 79
Barbecue-style London Broil 69
Basic Chicken Breasts(2) 53
Basic Corn On The Cob 24
Basil Crab Cakes With Fresh Salad 60
Beef & Sauerkraut Spring Rolls 68
Beef Fajitas 68
Beef Meatballs With Herbs 78
Beer Battered Onion Rings 89
Beet Chips 92
Best-ever Roast Beef Sandwiches 84
Black Bean Stuffed Potato Boats 32
Black Bean Veggie Burgers 83
Black Cod With Grapes, Fennel, Pecans And Kale 64
Blossom Bbq Pork Chops 70
Blueberry Cheesecake Tartlets 102
Breakfast Chicken Sausages With Apples 17
Breakfast Frittata 12
Brie And Cranberry Burgers 79
Broccoli Au Gratin 23
Broccoli Cheddar Stuffed Potatoes 33
Broccoli Tots 24
Buffalo Chicken Wings 92
Buttered Brussels Sprouts 21
Buttered Chicken Thighs 53
Buttery Chicken Legs 48
Buttery Lobster Tails 65

C

Cajun Chicken Kebabs 46
Cajun Pork Loin Chops 80
Cajun-seasoned Shrimp 55
Calf's Liver 75
Cal-mex Turkey Patties 49
Cantonese Chicken Drumsticks 44
Caprese-style Sandwiches 38
Caribbean Skewers 62
Carrot Chips 90
Carrots & Parsnips With Tahini Sauce 24
Cauliflower "tater" Tots 89
Charred Cauliflower Tacos 35
Cheddar Bean Taquitos 32
Cheeseburger Sliders With Pickle Sauce 68
Cheesecake Wontons 99
Cheesy Green Wonton Triangles 93
Cheesy Mushroom-stuffed Pork Loins 70
Cheesy Tuna Tower 60
Cheesy Zucchini Chips 93
Chicano Rice Bowls 40
Chicken & Rice Sautée 53
Chicken Adobo 44
Chicken Burgers With Blue Cheese Sauce 52
Chicken Cordon Bleu Patties 52
Chicken Cutlets With Broccoli Rabe And Roasted Peppers 47
Chicken Flautas 43
Chicken Fried Steak With Gravy 49
Chicken Gyros 86
Chicken Parmesan 52
Chicken Parmigiana 50
Chicken Pasta Pie 45
Chicken Salad With Sunny Citrus Dressing 19
Chicken Saltimbocca Sandwiches 86
Chicken Schnitzel Dogs 46
Chicken Shawarma Bites 89
Chicken Strips 50
Chicken Tikka 45
Chicken Wellington 48
Chili Blackened Shrimp 56
Choco-granola Bars With Cranberries 101
Cinnamon Apple Crisps 96
Cinnamon Pear Cheesecake 99
Cinnamon Roasted Pumpkin 29
Cinnamon Rolls With Cream Cheese Glaze 14
Cinnamon Sugar Banana Rolls 100
Citrus Pork Lettuce Wraps 77
City "chicken" 68
Classic Crab Cakes 56
Coconut Cream Roll-ups 100
Coconut Crusted Bananas With Pineapple Sauce 103
Coconut Jerk Shrimp 59
Coconut-custard Pie 105
Corn Au Gratin 23
Corn Dog Muffins 95
Country Gravy 14
Cowboy Rib Eye Steak 72
Crab Rangoon Dip With Wonton Chips 95
Crab Stuffed Salmon Roast 55

Crabby Fries 92
Cream Cheese Deviled Eggs 17
Creamy Horseradish Roast Beef 78
Creole Chicken Drumettes 44
Crispy Apple Fries With Caramel Sauce 32
Crispy Avocados With Pico De Gallo 40
Crispy Chicken Cakes 13
Crispy Fried Onion Chicken Breasts 47
Crispy Noodle Salad 21
Crispy Pork Medallions With Radicchio
And Endive Salad 76
Crispy Samosa Rolls 12
Crunchy And Buttery Cod With Ritz® Cracker Crust 55
Crunchy Chicken Strips 53
Crunchy Flounder Gratin 64
Crunchy Pickle Chips 90
Crunchy Roasted Potatoes 19
Curried Cauliflower With Cashews And Yogurt 20
Curried Cauliflower 40
Curried Fruit 23

D

Dark Chocolate Peanut Butter S'mores 104
Dark Chokolate Cookies 100
Dauphinoise (potatoes Au Gratin) 26
Dijon Roasted Purple Potatoes 22
Dijon Shrimp Cakes 55
Dijon Thyme Burgers 86

E

Easy Corn Dog Cupcakes 14
Easy Scallops With Lemon Butter 64
Easy Turkey Meatballs 45
Easy-peasy Beef Sliders 68
Easy-peasy Shrimp 62
Effortless Mac `n´ Cheese 39
Extra Crispy Country-style Pork Riblets 79

F

Fake Shepherd's Pie 38
Family Fish Nuggets With Tartar Sauce 63
Fancy Chicken Piccata 51
Fast Brownies 104
Fish Cakes 62
Fish Nuggets With Broccoli Dip 57
Fish Piccata With Crispy Potatoes 59
Flank Steak With Caramelized Onions 16
Florentine Stuffed Tomatoes 23
Fluffy Vegetable Strata 16
Friday Night Cheeseburgers 74
Fried Apple Wedges 93
Fried Banana S'mores 103
Fried Eggplant Slices 21
Fried Oreos 104
Fried Oysters 63
Fried Potatoes With Bell Peppers 36
Fried Scallops 65
Fried Spam 71
Fry Bread 11
Fudgy Brownie Cake 103
Fusion Tender Flank Steak 72

G

Garam Masala Cauliflower Pakoras 94
Garlic Wings 91
Garlicky Brussels Sprouts 22
German Streusel-stuffed Baked Apples 104
Glazed Chicken Thighs 43
Goat Cheese Stuffed Turkey Roulade 45
Golden Fried Tofu 41
Gorgonzola Stuffed Mushrooms 26
Granola Three Ways 97
Greek Pita Pockets 73
Greek Street Tacos 91
Greek-style Pork Stuffed Jalapeño Poppers 80
Green Egg Quiche 15
Grilled Cheese Sandwich Deluxe 96

H

Ham & Cheese Sandwiches 13
Harissa Chicken Wings 44
Hazelnut Chicken Salad With Strawberries 46
Healthy Berry Crumble 100
Healthy Chickpea Cookies 105
Healthy Living Mushroom Enchiladas 35
Herby Roasted Cherry Tomatoes 22
Holliday Lobster Salad 58
Home Fries 20
Home-style Fish Sticks 57
Home-style Pumpkin Pie Pudding 99
Honey Mesquite Pork Chops 80
Honey Pear Chips 39
Honey Pecan Shrimp 60
Honey-roasted Parsnips 24
Horseradish Crusted Salmon 65

I

Indian Chicken Tandoori 48
Inside Out Cheeseburgers 87
Inside-out Cheeseburgers 83
Intense Buffalo Chicken Wings 49
Irresistible Cheesy Chicken Sticks 50
Italian Herb Stuffed Chicken 46
Italian Roasted Chicken Thighs 43
Italian Stuffed Bell Peppers 37
Italian-style Fried Cauliflower 34

K

Korean-style Fried Calamari 56

L

Lamb Burger With Feta And Olives 72
Lamb Burgers 83
Lamb Koftas Meatballs 70
Lazy Mexican Meat Pizza 69
Lentil Burritos With Cilantro Chutney 31
Lovely Mac`n´cheese 20

M

Maewoon Chicken Legs 51
Mango-chocolate Custard 101
Maple-peach And Apple Oatmeal 12
Mashed Potato Tots 27

Tower Air Fryer Cookbook

Meatball Subs	78
Meatless Kimchi Bowls	36
Mediterranean Cod Croquettes	59
Mediterranean Salmon Burgers	63
Mediterranean Sea Scallops	62
Mexican Cheeseburgers	84
Mexican Turkey Meatloaves	50
Mexican Twice Air-fried Sweet Potatoes	34
Mini Bacon Egg Quiches	15
Mini Meatloaves With Pancetta	80
Mini Pita Breads	11
Mixed Berry Hand Pies	102
Mongolian Beef	75
Morning Chicken Frittata Cups	13
Mushroom & Quinoa-stuffed Pork Loins	80
Mushroom & Turkey Bread Pizza	44
Mushroom Lasagna	38
Mushrooms, Sautéed	22
Mustard-crusted Rib-eye	75

N

Nordic Salmon Quiche	14
Nutty Banana Bread	99
Nutty Shrimp With Amaretto Glaze	66

O

Okra	27
Orange Rolls	15
Oregano Cheese Rolls	92

P

Panko-breaded Cod Fillets	59
Paprika Onion Blossom	90
Parmesan Crackers	94
Parmesan Garlic Fries	27
Parmesan Garlic Naan	13
Parmesan Pizza Nuggets	91
Parsley Egg Scramble With Cottage Cheese	16
Peachy Chicken Chunks With Cherries	53
Peanut Butter Cup Doughnut Holes	101
Pecan-oat Filled Apples	105
Peppered Steak Bites	71
Perfect Burgers	86
Perfect Strip Steaks	75
Pine Nut Eggplant Dip	39
Pinto Bean Casserole	39
Pinto Taquitos	33
Pizza Eggplant Rounds	36
Pizza Portobello Mushrooms	33
Polenta Fries With Chili-lime Mayo	96
Popcorn Crawfish	58
Pork Cutlets With Almond-lemon Crust	78
Pork Cutlets With Aloha Salsa	81
Pork Kabobs With Pineapple	74
Pork Loin	71
Pork Schnitzel With Dill Sauce	76
Pork Tenderloin Salad	28
Pork Tenderloin With Apples & Celery	69
Potato-wrapped Salmon Fillets	61
Provence French Fries	26

Q

Quick Chicken For Filling	43
Quick Shrimp Scampi	58
Quinoa Green Pizza	35

R

Reuben Sandwiches	85
Rice & Bean Burritos	32
Rich Clam Spread	94
Roast Sweet Potatoes With Parmesan	27
Roasted Brussels Sprouts With Bacon	24
Roasted Garlic	26
Roasted Peppers With Balsamic Vinegar And Basil	27
Roman Artichokes	29
Rosemary Potato Salad	21

S

Salmon Burgers	85
Salmon Croquettes	58
Salmon Puttanesca En Papillotte With Zucchini	60
Salt And Pepper Baked Potatoes	29
Salty German-style Shrimp Pancakes	65
Saucy Shrimp	57
Sausage And Pepper Heros	85
Sausage-cheese Calzone	69
Savory Brussels Sprouts	26
Seafood Egg Rolls	90
Seared Scallops In Beurre Blanc	63
Sesame Orange Tofu With Snow Peas	31
Shakshuka-style Pepper Cups	15
Shrimp Patties	57
Sicilian-style Vegetarian Pizza	40
Simple Peppered Carrot Chips	22
Simple Roasted Sweet Potatoes	19
Simple Zucchini Ribbons	23
Sirloin Steak Flatbread	72
Smashed Fried Baby Potatoes	28
Smoked Avocado Wedges	28
Smooth Walnut-banana Loaf	13
Southern Okra Chips	28
Southern-style Chicken Legs	46
Spiced Fruit Skewers	99
Spiced Pumpkin Wedges	22
Spiced Roasted Acorn Squash	21
Spicy Bean Patties	40
Spicy Bean Stuffed Potatoes	19
Spicy Hoisin Bbq Pork Chops	81
Spicy Honey Mustard Chicken	53
Spicy Sesame Tempeh Slaw With Peanut Dressing	34
Spicy Sweet Potato Tater-tots	94
Spicy Vegetable And Tofu Shake Fry	37
Spinach & Brie Frittata	31
Spinach And Cheese Calzone	36
Spinach And Feta Stuffed Chicken Breasts	51
Spring Chicken Salad	50
Spring Veggie Empanadas	31
Sriracha Salmon Melt Sandwiches	56
Sriracha Short Ribs	78
Strawberry Bread	11
Strawberry Donuts	103
Stuffed Avocados	26
Stuffed Onions	25
Stuffed Shrimp Wrapped In Bacon	56

Sultana & Walnut Stuffed Apples ... 105
Super-simple Herby Turkey ... 44
Sweet & Spicy Swordfish Kebabs ... 64
Sweet Plantain Chips ... 93
Sweet Potato Curly Fries ... 23
Sweet Potato–crusted Pork Rib Chops ... 70
Sweet Potato–wrapped Shrimp ... 63

T

Taco Pie With Meatballs ... 71
Tacos Norteños ... 77
Tacos ... 41
T-bone Steak With Roasted Tomato, Corn And Asparagus Salsa ... 74
Tender Steak With Salsa Verde ... 74
Teriyaki Chicken Legs ... 49
Teriyaki Tofu With Spicy Mayo ... 25
Tex-mex Fish Tacos ... 65
Thai Peanut Veggie Burgers ... 37
Thai-style Pork Sliders ... 83
The Best Oysters Rockefeller ... 62
Tomato & Squash Stuffed Mushrooms ... 33
Tortilla Crusted Chicken Breast ... 43
Tuna Nuggets In Hoisin Sauce ... 55
Turkey Scotch Eggs ... 52
Turkish Mutabal (eggplant Dip) ... 29
Tuscan Chimichangas ... 71

V

Vanilla Butter Cake ... 101
Vegan Brownie Bites ... 102
Vegan Buddha Bowls(2) ... 32
Vegan French Toast ... 39
Vegetable Couscous ... 38
Veggie Burgers ... 39
Veggie-stuffed Bell Peppers ... 35
Venison Backstrap ... 77

W

Warm Spinach Dip With Pita Chips ... 96
Wasabi-coated Pork Loin Chops ... 76
White Bean Veggie Burgers ... 84
Wild Blueberry Sweet Empanadas ... 104
Wrapped Smokies In Bacon ... 92

Y

Yellow Squash ... 19
Yukon Gold Potato Purée ... 25
Yummy Maple-mustard Chicken Kabobs ... 49

Z

Za'atar Garbanzo Beans ... 92
Zucchini Chips ... 91

Printed in Great Britain
by Amazon